# *Crescendo*

# *Crescendo*

## THE STORY OF A MUSICAL GENIUS WHO FOREVER CHANGED A SOUTHERN TOWN

ALLEN CHENEY

WITH JULIE CANTRELL

W Publishing Group

An Imprint of Thomas Nelson

Published in Nashville, Tennessee, by W Publishing Group, an imprint of Thomas Nelson.

The author is represented by Alive Literary Agency, 7680 Goddard Street, Suite 200, Colorado Springs, Colorado 80920, www.aliveliterary.com.

Thomas Nelson titles may be purchased in bulk for educational, business, fund-raising, or sales promotional use. For information, please e-mail SpecialMarkets@ThomasNelson.com.



ISBN 978-0-7852-1760-2 (eBook)

**Library of Congress Cataloging-in-Publication Data**

Names: Cheney, Allen, author. | Cantrell, Julie, 1973- author.
Title: Crescendo : the story of a musical genius who forever changed a southern town / Allen Cheney with Julie Cantrell.
Description: Nashville, Tennessee : W Publishing Group, [2019] |
Identifiers: LCCN 2018061568 (print) | LCCN 2019012666 (ebook) | ISBN 9780785217602 (Ebook) | ISBN 9780785217404 (softcover)
Subjects: LCSH: Allen, Fred, 1935—Fiction. | Musicians—Fiction. | Music teachers—Fiction. | GSAFD: Biographical fiction.
Classification: LCC PS3603.H4557 (ebook) | LCC PS3603.H4557 C74 2019 (print) | DDC 813/.6—dc23
LC record available at https://lccn.loc.gov/2018061568

*Printed in the United States of America*

19 20 21 22 23 24 PC/LSCH 10 9 8 7 6 5 4 3 2

*This book is dedicated to the beautiful, unique, and vibrant community of Thomasville, Georgia. Thank you for embracing the magic of music and empowering generations of youth to truly shine.*

# *Preface*

It has been said that we are lucky if we can find one person who restores our hope when all is lost. One who sees something of worth in us, even when we fail to see it in ourselves, or one who helps push us to be better than we thought we could be. For thousands of students who grew up in the quaint southern town of Thomasville, Georgia, that one person was a music teacher by the name of Fred Allen, a man born poor and hungry in the shadows of a cotton mill.

Fred's life could easily have become just another tale of broken spirits and the blues, never to be freed from the clutches of poverty. Thankfully that has not been his story at all. In fact, Fred's legacy is one of show tunes and stardom, resiliency and faith. This is a story of mercy and melody and, above all else, love—plus a miracle or two thrown in for good measure.

Of course, that doesn't mean his triumph came easy. Nothing worthwhile ever does.

In a world where success is measured by fame and fortune, Fred's story matters more than ever. He teaches us the value of a meaningful life, a life of purpose. A life well lived. And he leaves each of us asking, How can I best use this time I've been given? How can I make it count?

As I share the story of Fred Allen, I write not to tell you *who* he is but to examine *why* he is and to learn all we can from this musical prodigy, a man who overcame absolute brokenness to become one of the most influential music mentors ever known.

*CRESCENDO*

(cre·scen·do / krə-'shen-dō)

*noun:*

a gradual increase in loudness in a piece of music

*adverb and adjective:*

increase in loudness or intensity

# *One*

In 1935, as the sweltering summer heat oppressed the downtrodden mill village in LaGrange, Georgia, a young man lay dying. Muffled sobs fell from the corner house on Thornton Street, where curious children eavesdropped outside the open bedroom window. When the shift whistle blew, men and women began to filter out of Dunson Mills. Soaked in sweat and cotton drift, they followed the worn paths, passing neighbors heading in to take their turn at the looms.

Fred Freeman had not been all that different from the others whose lives revolved around the whistle. Poor. Tired. Broken by life's hardships. Aside from his innate ability to shake a song from a piano or guitar, he had spent his days in one of two places: working the looms or drinking away his frustrations.

The Freeman-Allen home was also the same as every other house in the village, painted white like the cotton that dotted the land in rows. With three bedrooms each, these houses were simple in form but solid in construction, and because they were provided rent-free in exchange for work at the mill, the dwellings lured plenty of workers despite the low wages.

With the Great Depression bearing down across the nation, many houses overflowed with outsiders desperate for work. This is how the Freeman-Allen home came to be filled with generations of extended relatives as well as absolute strangers willing to pay for a corner cot as they chased day-pay jobs from town to town.

With some Cherokee blood and little education, Fred Freeman's life had already been both harsh and hurtful despite being barely two brief decades in measure. But now the young man gasped his final breaths in that back bedroom of his family's crowded home. And as the aunts and uncles circled round him, there was nothing anyone could do but let him go.

*Taken too soon by the Lord.* That's what his loved ones said as they pulled the sheet over his pallid face and prayed for him to find peace in the hereafter. They weren't a churchgoing bunch, but they knew the decent thing to do was to pray in times such as these.

As the spirit was leaving Fred Freeman, his sister, Velma Freeman Allen, cried out. Hers was a howl not only of grief but also of surprise as a sudden gush of water fell from her womb. Just as her mother, Peg Freeman, had warned, the stress of her brother's death seemed to have induced an early labor. In the swirling chaos, Velma moved away from her brother's deathbed and into her own tiny bedroom, preparing her body to embrace the blessing of birth. Clenching her fists through contractions, she called out, "Go! Fetch Mayhayley!"

Mayhayley Lancaster was not only a friend to Peg Freeman, she was also a teacher, an activist, and, perhaps most interestingly, an *oracle* whose gifts were revered both far and wide, even by those most skeptical. While well respected in her Christian church, she was known to run the numbers and tell fortunes, cast spells and speak with spirits. But to women like Velma, who labored through home births in the south Georgia summer, Mayhayley was known above all else as a midwife. A life-giver. A godsend.

By the time Mayhayley arrived, Velma was writhing in pain, shrieking and sweating as female relatives scrambled to comfort her.

"This labor ain't nothing like my first!" Velma screamed, a statement Mayhayley validated by announcing, "The baby is stuck!"

Quite experienced in matters of birth, the midwife solicited the women to help calm the mother, but despite steady reassurances, Velma seemed unable to bear the searing contractions, struggling to keep her breathing steady between waves of nausea and escalating spikes of pain.

Also, there was blood. Too much blood.

Mere hours after the death of Velma's brother, two more lives were now in peril as her body quaked and a baby boy was born blue. While Mayhayley's primary focus was on saving Velma, the wizened oracle took one look at the chalky shroud across the newborn's head and smiled. "A *caulbearer*," she said, proudly lifting the child into the air to examine the thin, milky membrane that draped his face.

Velma cried from the bed, eager to see her son, but the many women blocked her view, warning he had been born "behind the veil" and would likely not make it through the night.

"Cursed!" hissed a cousin, pushing the child away.

"Nonsense," Mayhayley argued. With tender hands she pulled the film from the baby's face and willed his color to change from a sickly gray to healthy pink. Then, with her one good eye, she gave him a close examination. "You're a special one, aren't you?" She turned her missing eye toward the door, tilting the marble-filled socket away for a better view. "Yes, yes. I can already see."

Mayhayley brought the baby to the bedside. "You've got one more reason to be strong now, Velma. This boy needs his mother."

Too frail to hold her son, Velma was growing weaker by the minute, even as the women cooled her with damp cloths and worked to stop the bleeding. With his mother teetering between life and death, the crying baby was set aside while the midwife's attention went to saving Velma.

Hours passed between the prayers. Slowly, the health of both mother and son began to improve, and before the stroke of midnight, Mayhayley was finally able to press the infant to his mother's breast. "He's not like other children," the soothsayer warned. "He's been touched."

Velma's eyes grew wide as she caressed her son's soft skin. She had long heard talk of caulbearers born with psychic powers, special souls connected to both the living and the dead. She stared at her infant child with a fear-filled love. Emotions flowed as the realization of all that had happened in the last twenty-four hours finally began to sink in. The sting of her brother's death. The dangerous and painful delivery. And now this child, this beautiful boy born cloaked in mystery.

The baby's eyes, blue as cobalt, already seemed to carry a sensitivity that Velma had only seen in one other man. "He's got my brother's eyes," she said, her voice hoarse from the battlefield of birth. "We should name him Fred. In his honor."

"He's got more than just his eyes," Mayhayley replied with a knowing nod.

Velma was too exhausted to ask for explanation. Instead, she cradled her son against her chest and fell into a deep sleep, the weight of grief still heavy upon her.

# *Two*

After surviving such a traumatic entry into this world, the baby carried his late uncle's name and soon became known to all as Fred Allen. Though his years had been short, Uncle Fred Freeman had developed quite a reputation for his musical talents, playing several instruments even though he had never taken a single lesson. So when the younger Fred showed an interest in song, the family wasn't surprised to see him follow in the footsteps of his namesake.

Despite their poverty, the Allens had acquired an old upright piano, and while it couldn't hold much of a tune, Velma could hammer out a few familiar hymns and folk songs. In his earliest days, Fred would sit in Velma's lap and toy with the keys as she played, her fingers bearing calluses from working double shifts in the weaving room.

Like many toddlers, Fred began tapping a few simple rhythms on the ivories, but his talents quickly proved to be anything but typical. By the tender age of three he was already performing entire songs on the piano by heart. Having been warned at her son's birth that he had been "touched," Velma was alarmed by this unusual behavior—so much so that she tried to keep Fred's talents a secret, even from her husband, Grady, a hard worker known to numb his many frustrations by making it to the bottom of a bottle.

Because Fred not only shared his uncle's talents but also his blue eyes and strong jawline, Velma feared that Mayhayley may have been correct in her claims: "Sometimes, when a child is born so near in time and place to another person's death, the spirits can intersect. Seems to me," the midwife had warned, "your son is carrying his uncle's spirit. An old soul. Sent back here to do some very important work."

Mayhayley's psychic abilities were accepted by nearly everyone across both Troup and Coweta Counties, including the community's most devout churchgoers who were known to consult the soothsayer. She was well liked, a woman of "good Christian standing." Even the sheriff was not above seeking her guidance on difficult cases. So Velma—already a superstitious soul—had taken Mayhayley's warning to heart and was determined to protect her son from any curse that might have cut her brother's life too short.

Despite wanting to guard Fred from danger, rotating shifts often kept Velma and Grady working more than sixteen hours each day. Even when they were home, they were usually far too exhausted to interact with their young son. So the piano became Fred's closest companion, and while other children tuned their ears to the sounds of bedtime stories and playground chants, music became Fred's native tongue.

One day Fred's little three-year-old legs dangled from the piano bench as he began to tap the keys. When the insurance collector made his way to their screen door seeking payment, the man was stunned to find such a young child playing "The Old Rugged Cross" without any flaws, not a note missed by the pint-size preschooler.

"How'd he do that?" The man stepped inside uninvited, his eyes wide as the screen door slammed behind him.

All color drained from Velma's face, and she protectively pulled her son away from the ivories. Young Fred stretched for the keys again, despite his mother's resistance. She nudged him toward the porch, trying to shoo the collector back outside too.

But the man wanted more. Beads of sweat pearled atop his brow as the heat of summer beat down on the family's humble home. He bent low toward Fred, stared at the boy's small hands, then looked him in the eye. "Think you can you play 'Amazing Grace'?" The collector began to hum the familiar tune.

Fred barely reached to his mother's waist. He lifted his face to her and smiled.

"Go on outside now, Fred." Velma's voice was tight, and her words came fast, so he did as he was told.

The relentless collector moved toward the piano and held out a shiny nickel, no small sum during those times. "I want to hear him play 'Amazing Grace.'"

Outside, the shift whistle blew. Velma took a long look at that nickel. Then she looked to the keys. Looked out to her young son now chasing cotton fly as it drifted like snow through the village. "I'll play it for you." She hit the opening notes, letting her own meek voice carry the words through the small space.

The man pulled another nickel from his pocket while Fred's mother crooned. Then he placed both coins atop the piano, creating an echo through the cavernous chamber of strings.

Velma stopped singing, but her fingers kept striking the chords, softer now, slower.

"It's real money, ma'am. Real money." He eyed the family's shabby quarters, the broken windowpane, the two missing piano keys. Outside, a gang of mill children crowded the tiny yards. Most had already spent the morning picking cotton or cleaning looms, their chatter a constant reminder of hungry mouths to feed.

The work-weary woman stilled her hands. Then she turned back toward the door and called, "Fred?"

The man stood eager at the old upright. His mind seemed to be spinning while the young boy clambered barefoot back into the house. Velma tapped her lap, and Fred climbed up to greet the keys again.

"He wants to hear you play 'Amazin' Grace.'" This time, Velma's voice was steady, without emotion. She hit the first few notes. Then Fred moved his fingers under hers, and she yielded the lead to her son.

Fred didn't have to look at his hands. He played the song by ear while Velma kept her focus on the insurance collector, his brows lifting, his grin spreading wide. When Fred finished, the man jingled more coins in his pocket, and Velma tensed, grinding her teeth. The collector leaned closer. "'By and By.' You know that one?"

Velma's hands began to shake, but she paired middle C with F and played the first verse all the way through. Then Fred took over just in time for the second. By the time he circled back around to strike middle C and F again, one of the few chords his tiny fingers could reach, the collector was nearly moved to tears, a reaction that surprised both mother and son.

"That one gets me every time. Every time." The man had a way of repeating himself, a trick that likely came in useful when demanding payments from his long-suffering clientele. "Your boy has a gift. You know that, ma'am? A real gift."

Velma stood and smoothed her cotton housedress, its hemline worn and frayed. She led the collector to the door, hoping he had forgotten the original purpose of his visit, and even more so that he would soon forget her son's "gift."

Fred noticed his mother's jaw clench when she said, "Have a good day, sir." She had barely ushered the man off the porch when young Fred began yet another hymn. From the kitchen, Mrs. Allen whispered a worried prayer as her son's small voice lifted above the sound of the strings:

I sing because I'm happy,
I sing because I'm free.[1]

# *Three*

While some boarders in the Allen house paid a small rental fee, many of the extended relatives were unable to contribute financially due to lack of steady work. Most had costly drinking habits too, so the money never seemed enough, even when Fred's sister, Novis, eight years his elder, dropped out of school to take her own double shifts at the mill. When the adults *were* home, they were usually inebriated or asleep. This lack of supervision was not only frightening for such a young boy, it was quite dangerous. Gangs of unsupervised adolescents roamed the village, as did a number of shady adults. The situation was of great concern to Fred's grandfather, Noah Freeman, a man of Cherokee descent whose extensive knowledge about natural resources had landed him a job teaching botany at nearby Carrollton A&M.

Noah and his wife, Peg, both valued education and had tried to give ample opportunity to their four children, but the crashed economy had taken a heavy toll on the already-impoverished state of Georgia. That, in addition to the cultural prejudices against anyone with Native American blood, had given Velma and her siblings few options and left them with even less than their hardworking parents had managed to acquire. Like many in that situation, Velma had married young, and her husband, mill worker Grady Allen, a Scots-Irish southerner, brought a toxic mix of dysfunction into the Freeman family.

When the poor economy resulted in Noah's job loss, he moved into Velma and Grady's mill village home hoping to help care for his young grandson, Fred. His wife, Peg, had also lost her job at the normal school—a two-year program designed to educate teachers—and had since moved in with an older, ailing relative who needed her care. Times were tough, and people had to learn to make ends meet, even if that meant married couples separating for a while.

Despite the Freemans' education, the Allens did not have the kind of home where bookshelves lined the walls. In fact, the old family Bible was the only book to be found. But Noah had managed to acquire a ragged set of encyclopedias for the Allen household before leaving his college position, so he set out to educate his young grandson with the tools he had at hand.

During these times, Noah would sit on the small porch with Fred at his side and read aloud from the leather-bound volumes. At four pounds each, the gold-embossed books were a bit too heavy for the preschooler to manage, but he was given the task of turning the flimsy pages as the cross-generational duo aimed to read all the way from A to "Zymotic Diseases," with forty million words in between.

When Noah and Fred weren't reading about some obscure medical experiment or mapping a continent far away, they could be found in the family's humble yard, where Noah taught Fred the deeper lessons he knew by heart. While LaGrange was notorious for its cotton mills, it also had garnered tremendous praise for its flower gardens. So much so that the owners of the mill would hold gardening contests, and the locals would compete for cash prizes. The mill also provided free seeds, encouraging those in the village to take pride in landscaping their small lots.

Noah made the most of this opportunity, teaching his young grandson everything he knew. But unlike others who only grew flowers and a vegetable or two, Noah's knowledge was far more extensive than root-shoot-fruit. Still carrying on his family traditions, he could not only identify the plants that grew wild around LaGrange, he also knew the medicinal uses of each. He quickly developed a reputation as a healer, and many mill workers who could not afford to see a proper doctor turned to Noah for less expensive remedies.

It was not unusual for Fred to help his grandfather gather roots for locals who wanted to boost their immune function. Noah taught Fred the power of the mullein leaf and often brewed an infusion when Fred showed the slightest sign of a cough. If neighbors complained of sinus trouble, the two would make a tincture using goldenrod, yarrow, or nettles, but their favorite all-around preventative was elderberry syrup, which they sold by the jar. While supplying natural remedies helped supplement the family's income, it was never enough to keep bellies full.

One day a client listened to Noah lament about the lack of job opportunities for a man his age. Fred eavesdropped as his grandfather complained. "As bad as it is in the mills, at least those men get paid to work."

"True," the woman said, her southern twang thick on her tongue. Her long hair held a bright pink bloom, visible to little Fred when she bent to inhale the fragrance of the summer roses.

When she moved toward the poppy patch, she brushed her palms over the vibrant flowers and said, "Seems to me you got all the money you'd ever need right here in your own backyard." She plucked a poppy from the plot. "Times like these, everybody and his brother be itchin' for more." The woman looked Noah in the eye. "Name your price, ol' man."

Fred's grandfather laughed away the absurd suggestion and turned his attention to the setting sun. "I don't roll in the mud by choice. No matter how hot the day might feel."

"Choice?" The woman looked around at the crowded mill houses. She eyed young Fred, barefoot, with too little meat on his bones. She examined the old man's threadbare collar and the hole worn through his straw cap. "Seems to me, you ain't got much *choice* at all." Then she lifted the hem of her skirt to reveal a secret pocket. "Trick Mayhayley taught me," she said with a grin. "Extra-wide seams. Nobody never suspects a thing."

From the hem, she pulled a fold of cash and placed two bills in Noah's hand. "Gimme all you can get. And start plantin' more. We'll run through this in no time flat."

The old man looked at his hand as if there might be a new lesson written there just for him. Then his tired eyes lifted to his garden, to the woman standing there before him and the grandson left to his care. But then he looked away from her, and to the boy it seemed Noah was trying to take in the whole world all at once.

After that long, uneasy silence, the old man slid the cash into his faded pocket. "I'll sell you the bulbs. What you do with them is your business."

"I don't have time for all that. I'll be back next Tuesday. For the *opium*." She stressed the last word to make clear her intentions. Fred reached to hold his grandfather's hand as the woman walked away.

The next morning, just after sunrise, young Fred helped his grandfather clip the poppy bulbs, then watched as Noah knifed each of them with the sharp blade of his razor. Throughout the week, drops of thick, white gum oozed from the slash marks. With extra care, the old man then scraped the sticky gum into small glass containers, warning young Fred not to touch this strange new medicine.

As promised, the woman returned on Tuesday. "That's as far as I'll go," Noah said, handing the client a sack of vials, each filled with milky opium gum.

"Far as I'm concerned, you're just sellin' me remedies." The woman winked, tucking the bottles into the hem of her skirt. When she walked away, the glass jangled like tiny bells announcing the beginning of something. Or the end.

---

As business increased, Fred learned to save the tiny black poppy seeds to keep the crop in full rotation. But word began to spread that the old man in the mill village was a local supplier for the opium dens. Fred and his grandfather were together on the porch, reading encyclopedias, when the sheriff pulled in front of the family's stoop. Noah was a man who had long refused to take Fred to see the westerns at the picture show, insisting he couldn't stomach the vicious cowboys slaughtering Indians and the corruption that was too frequently celebrated by gunslingers with a shiny badge on-screen. Now the sheriff's own badge shone in the sun as Noah rose to greet the law enforcer.

The sheriff gave Fred's grandfather a long once-over. "That your garden out there?" He leaned around the corner of the porch to inspect the well-tended display of blooms that now stretched into the neighbors' plots on both sides.

"Yes, sir," Noah answered. "And this is my grandson, Fred. I'm the one who takes care of him." He smiled at the young boy, hoping to tap a soft spot in the sheriff's heart.

But the sheriff didn't acknowledge Fred. Instead, he moved toward the garden, eyeing a large patch of stalks where poppies had just been clipped. "Word is, folks come to you for what ails 'em."

Noah nodded.

"You reckon you got anything for pain? I've been fighting this toothache for days." The sheriff drew his hand to his cheek, wincing.

Noah was suspicious, but he welcomed the sheriff to have a seat on the porch while he went inside to brew a cup of willow bark tea. He was tying the small bag of bark chips when the lawman made his way inside, uninvited. As the tea steeped, the sheriff took a look around the family's home, studying the rows of mason jars and various herbal tinctures. Sure enough, he spotted the vials of opium gum. "Forget about that tea," the sheriff said, pulling a pair of handcuffs from his hip and telling Noah, "Come with me."

Once the cuffs were snapped shut around Noah's wrists, young Fred began to cry. He chased after his grandfather, yelling, "Papa! Don't take my Papa!"

The elder Freeman folded himself into the back seat of the patrol car without resistance. Then he looked his young grandson in the eye and said, "Whatever you do, Fred . . . don't ever get yourself backed into a corner. Sometimes, there's no way out."

Fred chased the cop's car down Thornton Street as fast as his little legs would take him. But no matter how loud he yelled or how fast he ran, the sheriff did not stop. And before he knew it, the man he loved most in the world was gone.

# *Four*

With Noah in jail for selling opium and a steady flow of boarders still streaming through the house, the safest hours of Fred's childhood were those spent at the Dunson School. A small building for kindergarten through sixth grade, it was run by a strict but fair disciplinarian by the name of Mrs. Mary Duncan. The school hours passed quickly, so each afternoon Fred was left to survive in a world becoming more dangerous by the day.

Soon it was time for the kindergarten graduation ceremony, an annual event in which mill families were invited to celebrate their child's milestone progression into first grade. It was one of the few days when parents were able to leave their hardscrabble lives and attend something special with their children. Like the other kids, Fred was excited to show off his classroom, and as the minutes ticked closer to the ceremony, his anxiety grew. He could hardly wait for Grady and Velma to see his drawing of an elephant. He had sketched it to match the image he'd seen in Noah's encyclopedia, carefully drafting the oversize ears and curled trunk. His teacher had tacked it on the wall behind her desk where she displayed only the "best work."

But sadly, as other parents arrived from the mill to take their places beside their children, Fred sat alone, watching the door with eager eyes. Mrs. Duncan stood protectively close to Fred—it had been no secret that Fred was facing increasing neglect at home, and the principal had made a frequent habit of sneaking him extra fruit portions or dropping a clean pair of socks in his bag. While there was no telling why Velma and Grady didn't show up that day, the possible reasons were endless. Drugs, alcohol, domestic violence, exhaustion, forgetfulness. Or maybe just apathy. Whatever the reason, Fred sat alone.

Mrs. Duncan had been friends with Peg Freeman since their days studying together at the normal school, so as Fred began biting his lip and tugging nervously at his shoelaces, she leaned close over the shy young boy and whispered, "Fred, your grandmother told me you're pretty good on the piano. Would you like to play us a song?"

Fred was five years old at the time, and he had been strictly warned by Velma never to "show off" his gift. Still convinced her son had been "cursed" by his untimely birth, she greatly feared word getting out that he was carrying his uncle's spirit. What would the neighbors do if they learned of this ill-fated child? As for Grady, well, he hadn't given the issue any attention at all, insisting only that Fred "not play that thing" while he was trying to sleep, but he had never been able to quell Velma's fears, which seemed to be growing by the day. Sensing Fred's reluctance, Mrs. Duncan gently reassured her timid student that it would be okay, and that "it sure would make everyone happy" to hear him play a song. Then she smiled and looked him in the eye. "You can do it, Fred. I believe in you."

With that gentle encouragement, Fred let the principal lead him to the piano. Then she placed her hand on his shoulder, helping the nervous young boy summon his courage. He sat on the bench, closed his eyes, and began to play. Mrs. Duncan probably expected him to perform a simple childhood tune like "Twinkle, Twinkle Little Star." Instead, without a sheet of music, Fred performed a near-flawless rendition of a classical piece that left the audience in awe.

Mrs. Duncan, a musician in her own right, shook her head, astounded. "That's Chopin! Polonaise no. 2."

All those present watched in stunned silence. No one could believe what this timid young boy had done. His legs were too short to reach the damper pedal, his fingers too small to stretch the full octaves. But he had nailed the melody, stirring some to gasp as they listened to his smooth tones and emotional delivery.

The principal's breathy voice revealed her shock when she asked, "Where did you learn to play such a song?"

Fred pointed to his heart and smiled.

The crowd erupted in applause, and Fred beamed.

Even if they didn't quite know what to call a child with such rare abilities, the parents now circled the boy, asking him to play another. Sensing Fred's apprehension, Mrs. Duncan stepped up to offer shelter. "Thank you, Fred," she said, guiding him back to his seat. "That was a wonderful treat for all of us. You do indeed have a *very special* gift."

For the first time in his life, Fred's talents were being celebrated instead of silenced. But on the way back to his chair, he overheard one of the men snicker, "Won't do him no good in the mills."

---

After the ceremony word quickly spread about Fred's mysterious gifts. Velma began to fear the worst—not only that the mill people would shun them but that perhaps the fates had been tempted and now her son would die an early death, exactly like his namesake, Fred Freeman. Exactly as Mayhayley had warned. This anxiety seemed to progressively overtake her, and she became even more restrictive, refusing to allow Fred to ride a bicycle or roam freely with the other children in the village. Like many people, Velma feared what she could not understand, and her son's genius clearly terrified her.

Perhaps these superstitious fears got the best of Fred's father too, or maybe the uneducated couple simply didn't know what to do with their son's unusual talents, or maybe they were too broken and insecure to elevate their child beyond their own low level of living. Or maybe Grady simply grew tired of hearing Velma go on about it all. Whatever the reason might have been, not long after his stunning performance at the kindergarten graduation, Fred was playing the piano at home when Grady stormed into the room and slammed the keys. "Enough!"

Grady was a kindhearted and gentle man when sober, but like many men in the village, the bottle made him prone to fits of rage. Most evenings, Fred would lay low while his mother kept a detached and silent gaze. By then she had learned to do anything to keep the peace, and there was little left of her spirit as she became an almost absent, voiceless member of the family.

But that day, as Grady ranted across the house, Velma not only did nothing to defend her young son, she fueled the fire by saying, "It just ain't right for him to be able to make music like that, Grady. He ain't even heard them songs. How on earth could he know how to play 'em? People've been talkin'. They say it's *magic*."

Grady stumbled toward Fred, spewing his thoughts through a drunken slur. "Lots better things to do in life than *magic*."

Velma pulled Fred, crying, from the piano. Then, together, the couple rolled the heavy instrument into a back corner of their bedroom. Once they had it in its new position, Grady closed the door and locked it behind him, leaving Fred with one final warning. "Stay out of that room if you know what's good for you!"

# *Five*

With his piano now trapped behind lock and key, Fred was starved for attention and affection. Life in the village was changing by the day, and he was more vulnerable than ever in the hours outside of school.

The Great Depression soon gave way to the surge of jobs needed to support the war. This opened more shifts as Dunson Mills grew to become the largest cotton plant in Georgia. The mill owners had long tried to create a sense of community in the village, constructing the school, playgrounds, and even a swimming pool for local families. They also dedicated an old building to be used as a recreation center, hosting dances into the early morning hours. Soldiers from nearby Fort Benning, who were home on leave, frequently found their way to the village in search of "a big time."

While traveling boarders were landing secure jobs now and no longer desperate to rent a cot by the day, a new situation was brewing in the Allen home, one that proved even more confusing and dangerous for young Fred. Many extended relatives continued to share the home, even if for short stays, and a string of random men seemed to drop by frequently for what they called "visits." Most were drunk, loud, or threatening. And the circle of women, well, Fred suspected not all of them were really his "aunts" as he was now expected to call them. He did his best to steer clear, but as Fred's aunts welcomed soldiers into the Allen home at night, they were not discreet, and the behaviors that began taking place around Fred exposed him to a world far too dark for any young boy to see.

If Velma was opposed to the new situation, she was apparently too beaten down by that point to object. Far outnumbered and outplayed, she submitted, quietly, and Fred was left to fend for himself. It was during those dark, lonely nights that Fred first began to journal, scrapping together whatever notebooks he could salvage and turning to writing as a tool to survive the ongoing neglect, even as a young boy.

Through those elementary school years, it wasn't just the soldiers who frequented Fred's home for pleasure, it was also the local baseball players. This motley crew of mill worker–athletes were hailed as heroes of the day, and while some lived up to that stellar role, the behavior of a few players proved worse than the soldiers'. One was a man who had married into the family, Fred's uncle Dirk. With the team based in LaGrange, he and his more corrupt cohorts would make their rounds through the village, frequenting the Allen home.

During that time, Fred began to waste away. While food had always been a luxury throughout his neglectful childhood, it had now become something Fred could barely swallow. He was sinking into a dark depression by only eight years of age, isolating himself as the adults around him lost control.

No one seemed to notice as this innocent young boy slowly came undone. If they noticed, they certainly didn't seem to care—not until a woman named Eleanor was released from prison.

Rumor had it Eleanor had served time for attempting to murder a man—or maybe she *had* murdered a man, depending on who you asked. Her rough reputation preceded her arrival in the village, women claiming she had been a prostitute and quite possibly still earned money by turning the occasional trick. The one thing on which everyone could agree was that Eleanor was not one to mock. So when she showed up to live at the Allen home after marrying Fred's uncle Ed, the young boy struggled to make sense of the situation.

Eleanor was not a big woman. Fairly slight in build, she stood barely five foot six. Homemade henna dye stained her hair the color of tea, and her face "wasn't much to look at," according to her mean-spirited husband, a man whom Fred had never seen sober or kind a day in his life. Unlike the other women who tended to do whatever the men told them to do, Eleanor had spunk, and through the eyes of a young boy, her crass comebacks could be frightening. But she also seemed to take a liking to Fred, keeping careful watch over him even when he tried to shy away.

One night, while a few members of the baseball team were at the house, eight-year-old Fred slipped through the kitchen, careful to dodge the half-dressed couples who filled the home. Bottles lay scattered across the path to his room, and no one bothered to quiet down so Fred could rest. His stomach empty and his head throbbing, the boy had just nodded off when he was awakened by his bedroom door opening and closing quietly. Fred kept his eyes shut tight, pretending to sleep as the sound of drunken footsteps drew closer.

Just as the covers began to pull from Fred's small frame, the door opened again, slamming against the wall. Fred squeezed his eyes even tighter, fearing the worst. But this time Fred heard the bold voice of Aunt Eleanor. "Get the hell away from that boy right now if you know what's good for you."

A man laughed, tauntingly, as if he had no fear of the woman in the room. Fred opened his eyes to see Uncle Dirk glaring at Eleanor.

"You must not know about me." Her words came out with force and anger but also with a clarity that made Fred's uncle pay attention.

"Well, you must not know about *me*," Dirk mocked, standing far taller and stronger in stature than Eleanor and smirking to prove he was not afraid.

Instead of cowering, as others always seemed to do in the shadow of the star athlete, Fred's aunt stepped closer. "Let me make myself clear, boy. I just got out of the pen for trying to kill a man. This time, I'll make damn sure it counts."

Fred sat up in bed, half thinking this was all a dream. Sure enough, Aunt Eleanor was standing right there in his bedroom. She was holding a baseball bat, confronting his uncle as if she could hardly wait to take a swing.

"I ever see you as much as *look* at that boy again, I'll show you what this bat was really made for." She swung the weapon against the wooden floor, hard, missing Dirk's bare feet by less than an inch and causing Fred to flinch. "Now get the hell out of here. And take those monsters with you."

Uncle Dirk backed away in silence, his hands in the air. Just as he moved out of the room, Eleanor took another swing, harder this time, bashing the bat against the doorframe and splintering the trim. She followed Dirk through the house, smashing whatever was in her way and threatening the players as they scrambled to find their belongings and head for the hills. From the porch she yelled behind them, "Y'all ever step foot on this property again, I'll dig your graves myself!"

With that one act of defiance, Aunt Eleanor likely saved Fred's life. He had become so broken, so lost in the long-term isolation and neglect, that he had retreated deep within himself, no longer seeing the world as a safe space. Too much fear had damaged his spirit, and he no longer felt anchored by his own bones. Instead, he floated numbly amid the fray and tried only to survive.

---

A few nights after the incident, Eleanor found her young nephew sitting on the roof of the family's backyard shed, his eyes focused on the star-filled sky as if he wanted to be anywhere but here. Eleanor made her way toward the shed, glass of water in hand. "Thirsty?"

Fred shook his head, which was more than he would have done if the question had come from anyone else. Still, his reluctance did not deter her. She handed him the glass and said, "From the looks of it, you could use a home-cooked supper. Something to stick to your bones. How about you come give me a hand in the kitchen?"

Eleanor leaned against the shed and followed Fred's gaze to the new moon, its faint glow illuminating the small white homes that dotted the mill village. In the distance, the roofline of a much larger home anchored the vast stretch of stars, its pitched roof reaching far into the sky from its superior hilltop position, as if only the lucky few had access to the heavens.

"You're safe with me," she insisted. "I'm with you, Fred. Promise."

The young boy lifted his brows, suspicious. The only person who had ever really taken time to bond with him was his Papa. And even though Noah was no longer in jail, he hadn't returned—a blow that still carried a deep sting. But Aunt Eleanor had already proven she was on Fred's side. She may have been a little odd, maybe even scary, but she had shown she had heart.

Allowing Aunt Eleanor to lead him, Fred followed her into the family's kitchen. There they worked together late into the night, boiling a pot of potatoes and another of green beans. To Fred's surprise, Eleanor not only taught him how to mash the potatoes, adding just enough milk, butter, and salt to suit his taste, she also sat with him at the table and talked to him while they ate together.

Day after day Aunt Eleanor fed Fred and treated him like he was worthy of her kindness. She listened when he spoke, and he slowly began to come back to life. She also made sure, at every turn, that her young nephew knew he wasn't going to have to stand on his own in the world.

Their partnership lasted long enough for Fred to catch his breath and regain solid footing. Then the day came for his aunt to move on, leaving her abusive husband behind. She pulled Fred aside and left him with some final advice: "You gotta find a way to get out of this place, Fred. And don't you never let nobody break you. You were born for so much more than this."

---

While other kids still believed in Santa Claus and the Easter Bunny, Fred had to become what some would consider street-smart, honing his instincts as he navigated the many dangers of the world. If he wasn't an "old soul" at birth, as Mayhayley had proclaimed him to be, then he certainly had become one during his early elementary years, a time that should have been safe and carefree.

Operating in survival mode not only at home but also at school, the frail little boy had begun to dress in layers, covering his body in long sleeves and pants even on the hottest of days. He would barely touch his food, even though his weight was slight, and he carried dark circles under his sunken eyes. Eleanor was no longer there to guide him at home, but at school, the wise principal, Mrs. Duncan, realized something was wrong.

Fred had always been a student with high marks, excelling with academic ease on account of his advanced intellectual ability. But recently his grades had dropped, and he no longer completed his assignments. He had withdrawn from his peers and appeared sullen even during his favorite subjects. Having observed these changes taking place, Mrs. Duncan pulled the boy aside. "Fred," she whispered, "is there anything you want to tell me?"

He shrugged and shook his head, a conflicting response that drew even more alarm from the dedicated educator.

"I'm concerned, Fred. You don't seem yourself lately. What's happened?"

Again, no answer came. Instead, Fred kept his head down, his eyes lowered.

Mrs. Duncan had the reputation for being stern and, like many in those days, had been known to use physical discipline. While Fred had never been the kind to cause trouble, he now worried she was about to hit him as so many other adults had done. But rather than pull out her paddle or the rubber bike tube she'd been rumored to use when punishing children, the principal kept her voice soft and said, "I want to help you, Fred. Tell me, how can I help you?"

Fred slowly lifted his chin and dared to look Mrs. Duncan in the eye. It was the best he could do, and he hoped she would understand the unspoken message: *Yes. Help me, please.*

"Follow me," she said, leading him to the school piano. She pulled the wooden bench from its proper place and patted its worn center spot, nudging Fred to take a seat. She sensed the boy was too worn down to care anymore, even about music. He stared at the keys as if they held every ache, every fear. Every awful, horrible, terrible thing this world had shown him in such a short time.

Mrs. Duncan sat beside the fragile boy. She began playing a slow, comfortable rendition of "Over the Rainbow," a song that seemed to reach him. Fred did not sing or play even as Mrs. Duncan lifted her voice, but something in the young student seemed to shift as the music filled the empty space around them. It felt as if maybe he was exhaling for the first time in years, slowly releasing all he had been holding inside, all that had been pulling him downward.

"You know," Mrs. Duncan said, as she continued to play, "I've noticed you haven't learned your multiplication tables yet."

Fred stared blankly and offered no response.

"And I've also noticed that you can do anything you put your mind to," Mrs. Duncan continued. "Isn't that right, Fred?"

He turned toward the window. Outside, his peers played ball and jumped ropes. They laughed and ran and cheered, seemingly without a care in the world, as if they had no idea of the dangers he knew firsthand, the real-life monsters who prowled.

Mrs. Duncan continued playing, softly, now without singing the words. Above the sound of the notes, she said, "Fred, you are giving me no choice but to fail you. And if I fail you, you'll have to repeat third grade. I know you don't want to watch all your friends advance without you. That wouldn't be fair to you, now, would it?"

Fred shook his head. He certainly did not want to be a failure. He just didn't know how to care anymore, not about something as trivial as math facts. But if there was one thing he did care about, it was that he did not want to disappoint Mrs. Duncan, one of the few adults who had always made a point of believing in him, even when he didn't believe in himself.

"Tell you what I'm going to do," the principal said. "I'm going to give you another chance. You go home tonight, and you learn all those multiplication facts."

"All of them?" Fred asked, his voice weak with worry. He had long been considered an exceptional student, but learning all of his tables in one night seemed impossible.

"That's right. All of them. And then you come back tomorrow and you pass this exam. If you can do that, I'll replace your failing grade. But you have to earn it. You understand?"

"Yes, ma'am." He pulled away, feeling defeated.

The music stopped. "Fred?"

Mrs. Duncan moved closer, leaning an elbow on the piano's keys to face her fragile student. Placing her other hand on his shoulder, she offered the same gift of kindness he had received back in kindergarten when his parents had failed to attend his graduation ceremony. "I believe in you," she declared, not a hint of doubt in her tone. Her eyes held steady, waiting for the young boy to meet her gaze. "You have something wonderful inside you. Something I've never seen in anyone else. You can do this, Fred. And you will."

That night, Fred crawled into bed with his math facts and a full dose of self-confidence courtesy of Mrs. Duncan. He studied long and hard, memorizing all the multiplication patterns from zero through twelve.

When he returned to class the following day, Mrs. Duncan was eager to see the results of her challenge. Sure enough, her young student had mastered every row of his multiplication tables in only one night and earned a passing grade, much to his own relief.

"I never doubted you for a second," Mrs. Duncan said. She smiled and drew a big star on the math chart under Fred's name. Then she gave him a hug and said, "Don't ever sell yourself short again, Fred. You deserve a good life. Now go make that happen."

# *Six*

With a stronger spirit and a discerning eye, Fred began to rise again, focusing on finding better company than what was available in his family home. Over the next few years, he built healthy relationships with other children while testing his own frighteningly powerful intellectual capacities. Something began to shine through, a sense of self-belief, a confidence Fred had never felt before. But another force kept Fred engaged at school through those tumultuous years. Music! In such a positive and supportive environment, Fred was encouraged to explore his gifts freely, something that had never been possible inside his own home.

Through the rest of elementary school, Fred immersed himself in both academics and music under the direction of Mrs. Duncan. By the time he entered middle school, his parents had purchased some property about ten miles outside of LaGrange. Longing to try his hand at livestock, Grady moved the entire family away from the Dunson Mill Village, out to the rural Troup County community known as Hillcrest, where he began raising cows, chickens, and pigs.

A modest wooden structure, the home held a slanted porch and a tin roof that leaked when the rains came, but with this new address came a new school, one that served the whole town of LaGrange rather than exclusively teaching the mill families. The Allens continued working at the mill, and with only one old car between them, Fred struggled to find rides into town for after-school functions and community events. He was able to ride the school bus back and forth each day to LaGrange, but in order to take part in extracurricular activities, he frequently had to stay overnight with friends living in town.

It was about this time that his family began attending Shoal Creek Baptist Church. Until then his mother had sung hymns at home and the family Bible lay on the shelf, but Fred hadn't been exposed to any structured spiritual formation. The rural congregation welcomed the Allen family and gave Fred his first deep exposure to the Christian faith. Still, Fred had little interest in God. He had learned the hard way that if any higher power existed, then it wasn't interested in a family like his. No, the boy resolved to himself, he wasn't at church for the sermon. He was there for the music. And like others in the community, the tight-knit congregation quickly recognized Fred's extraordinary talents, asking him to play piano during their Sunday services.

Eager to spend as much time creating music as possible, Fred agreed. And with the preacher convincing Grady and Velma that this special ability was no curse but, rather, God's calling, they had little choice but to yield to their son's ever-growing determination. The church not only delivered an opportunity for the middle schooler to enhance his talents and share his gifts, Sunday services also proved to be one of the few activities his family experienced together.

Until this point, Fred's world had revolved around the mill. He had lived among the working-class families, attended the village school, and had no exposure beyond that little corner of the world. He had even spent his summers working the looms. But now he was attending a new school, one that boasted an award-winning choral group. At the recommendation of the school's music teacher, Mrs. Dudley, Fred auditioned and was selected to join this elite group of singers. This gave him a wonderful new opportunity to travel and perform across the region, opening his eyes to a much bigger world than he had ever known. More determined than ever to explore his talents, and with the blessing of church and school, there was no longer anything his parents could do to stop him.

The choral group consisted of four female and four male singers, each from families far wealthier than Fred's. Some children from Fred's place in life might have been too intimidated to join such an exclusive group, especially when his parents did nothing to encourage it, but Fred was smart enough to realize that *we are the company we keep*. He also proved a quick study, elevating himself by learning to fit in with the people who brought out the best in him, bonding with classmates he most admired.

One afternoon at choral rehearsal, the group was preparing for their first competition, and Fred's nerves spiked as he checked his hair in the mirror. The other boys had swept theirs to the side in one clean part, their sideburns tight around the ears. Fred had long relied on his father for haircuts, which sometimes meant a sober swipe of the blade in an even line, but most of those weekend clips had come with whiskey breath and the sting of a crooked hand. Fred's red-faced reflection revealed his shame. From the side of his eye, he watched as the popular Rick Lewis smoothed his own dark locks with a bit of pomade. Fred wet his hand beneath the faucet and mimicked Rick's moves, substituting water for gel. Rick straightened his collar in the mirror and gave his smile a quick check for approval. When he turned to leave the restroom, Fred shadowed, straightening his own collar and checking his smile too. Then he left the restroom, walking with a confident stride, exactly as Rick had done.

Throughout those years Fred kept his family's poverty a closely guarded secret from his schoolmates. While some of his teachers likely knew the truth about his impoverished homelife, he had learned to dress and behave above his means. Even the chorus friends he spent so much time with seemed never to suspect a thing—until one Sunday, when Fred, now a freshman in high school, was forced to face his greatest fear.

Fred had become a well-respected member of the choral group, and the eight singers had stuck together through the years, with Rick Lewis now one of his closest companions. That day the four male singers had been scheduled to rehearse at the First Methodist Church in LaGrange, but Fred couldn't find a ride into town. The church organist, Lucy Nixon, arrived to meet the boys, only to realize Fred was absent—along with the sheet music he had taken home with him. While she wasn't sure exactly where the Allen family lived, everyone knew that Fred sometimes struggled to find a ride into town and that he lived on the outskirts of Troup County. With the start time drawing near, Mrs. Nixon eyed the three teen singers and said, "Hop in the car, boys. Let's go get Fred."

Mrs. Nixon was from one of the wealthiest clans in town—the Lanier family who owned Westpoint Manufacturing—but she was known to be a good-natured soul who never focused on the materialistic priorities that many in her social circle seemed to care about most. Without any sign of frustration, she piled the teens into her car and rushed out to the Hillcrest community, stopping along the way to ask for directions to the Allen home.

Meanwhile, irritated by his failed efforts to convince one of his many relatives to drive him to the church, Fred had retreated to his bedroom in defeat. He lay on his bed, rehearsing songs in his head, when a knock sounded at the front door. He didn't bother leaving his room. The only visitors they ever received were either debt collectors, sheriff's deputies, or people there for reasons he would rather not know. But when the knock came again, followed by a loud shout for "Fred!" he could ignore it no longer.

Sick of living in a house of "no-counts," as some in town had called them, Fred made his way to the wide-open door, where, much to his horror, the ever-posh Mrs. Nixon stood waiting. She smiled as if the absurd situation was nothing out of the ordinary. This is how upper-crust socialites always behaved, he thought. They kept their cool and never showed emotions, at least not that Fred had ever seen, but he'd not yet learned to master such self-control. While Mrs. Nixon may have remained calm and collected, Fred's pulse raced with fear, a feeling that only intensified when a pack of scrawny dogs drew his attention to the dirt lane. The mutts had surrounded Mrs. Nixon's Cadillac and barked at Fred's three best friends who waved from the back seat.

Fred quickly looked away, fighting a rush of nausea as his heart throbbed with a speed that made his head spin. *This can't be happening!* he thought to himself. *They shouldn't be here!* Fred had spent years trying to be one of the guys, determined to be respected like Rick Lewis, the upper-class leader of their clique. He had been careful to never let anyone know the secret of his deprivation, but now his truth had been revealed.

To make matters worse, Mrs. Nixon stood mere inches from Fred's drunken uncle Ed, her high heels balanced near his muddy boots as he lay passed out in a heap across the rickety porch planks. In addition to the barking dogs, the weed-filled yard held countless chickens, all scrapping about for any bit of protein they could find between the scattering of bottles. Inside, the scene was even worse, with a house full of folks who had been broken by life. Some had spent time in jail. Others were shackled by addiction and poverty. Some were hard workers, but all had known their fair share of suffering and all had found the Allen home to be a place where they could numb their pain any way they chose, guilt-free. If there was any common link among them, it was defeat. Lack of education and opportunity seemed to have left them feeling powerless, inadequate, worthless, and now, as some gathered around the table smoking cheap cigarettes and playing a dirty hand of poker, they shared the kind of crude laughter found in the deepest pits of hopelessness and despair. Fred's dysfunctional life lay in clear view for Mrs. Nixon, and there was nothing he could do to hide it anymore.

Showing consistent class, Mrs. Nixon smiled politely and kept her voice steady when she said, "I've come for the music."

"Wait here." Fred quickly closed the door behind him, sickened by the heartbreaking realization that his friends now knew the truth he had kept hidden for so long. He rushed through the house, stepping over a few men too drunk to stand despite the daylight hour. As he grabbed the sheet music, Uncle Dirk plucked the papers from Fred's hands. "Well, lookie here," he taunted, his voice cruel and cold.

Fred was still a young teen, but he was learning to stand his ground. "Give it to me."

With his bloodshot stare, Dirk gave the musical notations a long glare, then eyed Fred's clean appearance and church-ready trousers, his nice brown leather shoes. "You think you're better than us, don't you, boy?" The crowd stirred, laughing as Dirk passed the papers around the room for each to see. "The world don't work like that, kid. Ev'ry man got his place. You best stick to it."

As the clock ticked, Fred's sister, also broken by the heavy gravitational pull of dysfunction, watched this cruel interaction. Fred never expected she would intervene, but he hadn't noticed the tension in her neck, the draw of her tightened lips. Like his mother, she had learned early in life to keep her head down, stay silent, and never do anything to anger the men.

But much to Fred's surprise, Novis moved toward the unruly crew and grabbed the music, handing it back to Fred. "Don't pay them no mind," she whispered, straightening her brother's collar and offering him a kind smile.

It was a stark moment of defiance for his meek sister, one that led to an equally rare moment of family affection as Fred hugged her close and tight. He knew Novis stood little chance of ever finding her own way to freedom, especially now that she was working in the mill as a high school dropout and following the same sad steps of their broken mother. With a quiet thank-you, Fred accepted her gift and rushed back to the organist, music in hand, more determined than ever to break free of the shiftless souls who filled his abusive home.

But when he saw Mrs. Nixon's pleasant smile, the heavy noose of shame closed on any pulse of courage that had begun to rise. "Aren't you riding with us to rehearsal?" she asked, accepting the sheet music as if she had not noticed the chaos swirling around her.

Fred was too humiliated to look her in the eye, too horrified to wave to his friends—much less get into the car with them. How could he possibly endure that long stretch of highway between this disgraceful world he inhabited and the more respectable one he longed to call his own?

"We can't sing without you, Fred. You're first tenor," Mrs. Nixon said, yet to acknowledge the drunken uncle splayed near her feet.

Her young singer stared at the collapsed heap of a man and kept quiet.

"All right then. Truth be told, you probably already know the music better than any of us anyway." Mrs. Nixon smiled again. "But promise you'll still show up Sunday to sing."

Fred kept his head low and his voice even lower. "I'll try." Then he closed the door without any additional explanation. He watched from the hazy kitchen window until the Cadillac pulled out of sight and the chickens stopped their clucking.

Moments later, Grady and Velma arrived home from the mill, parking their battered Ford under the same tree where Mrs. Nixon's expensive car had just claimed space. The dust had already settled back down on the long dirt lane when Novis realized her brother hadn't joined the others. "Don't you have practice?"

Fred nodded, unable to conceal his disappointment. Behind him, the raucous crew of poker players laughed and coughed, trading nickels for cards as if they weren't a bunch of losers.

"You gotta sing," Novis said matter-of-factly, grabbing the keys to the family's car.

"I doubt they want me there after seeing *this*." Fred's voice was heavy with despair.

His sister stepped closer. He wished he hadn't said it because he knew he wasn't the only one who carried the weight of this shame.

"Let's go," she said, nudging her brother out to the faded Ford. When he hesitated at the passenger door, she gave him a long look and added, "Fred, you're the only one of us who's got any hope of breaking outta here. And I love you too much to let you quit now."

Fifteen minutes later, when Novis finally pulled the car to a stop in front of the First United Methodist Church in LaGrange, she followed Fred's gaze toward the towering steeple. They sat together, staring up at the tall, white beacon—its peak a shingled spire above the town. Their faces were blank, their eyes hollow, as if the pinnacle represented nothing holy at all, only more proof of God's unequal mercies. Then Novis turned toward her only sibling and said, "Go show 'em what you're made of, Fred. And whatever you do, promise me you won't end up like the rest of us."

After a final nudge from Novis, Fred ran into the sanctuary without a minute to spare. Avoiding any communication with his friends, he made it through rehearsal while his sister waited outside in the dented car, the only one in the lot with a missing fender. And when the session ended, he departed just as quickly, preventing anyone from mentioning to him what they'd seen at the Allen home.

That night Fred tossed for hours, earning not a wink of sleep. When the sun rose the following day, he was not only exhausted; he was also terrified to return to school. Now that his friends knew the truth about his family, would they taunt him? Cut him out of their peer group? Refuse to be associated with someone so low-class?

While slaves and sharecroppers were a thing of the past, LaGrange was only a half step removed from its Old South roots, and the small circle of elite families still held the inherited wealth and, thus, the power. Fred had been accepted by these upper-class students because he had developed street-smart survival skills. He had learned to fit in with the right crowd, not in an effort to con anyone but rather to elevate himself beyond his hard life of suffering. He'd done it to break free of the generational cycles of anger, addiction, and abuse that loomed, always ready to claim him as their rightful heir.

But now his mask had been removed, and there was no chance of hiding anymore.

He also knew enough to know that talk spread quickly in a town the size of LaGrange. So as he arrived at school the next day, Fred prepared himself for ridicule and rejection. He was certain he would be called either white trash or a half-breed mutt and that he'd be stuck with such labels for the rest of his schooling.

Instead, just as Fred had learned from his Cherokee grandfather, Mrs. Duncan, and Aunt Eleanor, sometimes people can surprise you. Rather than distancing themselves from Fred as he'd feared, his friends carried on as if nothing at all had changed. They treated him exactly as they had always treated him, as if he were their equal, as if he deserved their friendship and respect, as if it did not matter one bit how much money his parents earned or how many drunk uncles lay passed out on his porch.

Fred learned a valuable lesson from his friends that day. He learned that while there were people in this world who wanted to break him down, take what they could get, use him and abuse him, there were others who truly wanted to lift him up, care for him, and support him—even when he felt he had nothing at all to offer in return. At an age when many teens experience brutal rejection, bullying, and fear, Fred found people who would help him find his way out of the turmoil once and for all.

That afternoon, when it was time to head home again, Rick Lewis proved this to be emphatically true as he walked beside Fred out of the music room. "You still like cobbler?" he asked.

Fred shrugged, which of course meant, *Yes, I like cobbler. Who doesn't?*

"Mom said she'd have plenty."

---

The Lewis home was one of the largest in LaGrange, the kind of house that had been given an official name: Highpoint. The design boasted angular, slate rooflines with rows of oversize awnings and arches yielding both a welcoming and impressive atmosphere for anyone who entered. Perched in the midst of a luxuriously landscaped six-acre spread, the 1920s estate looked more like it belonged in the posh hill country of Europe than on Broad Street, where the expansive Tudor abutted the edge of the LaGrange College campus.

Fred had already spent many a night there when he couldn't find a ride into town for school events and performances, but this time

Mrs. Lewis welcomed her son's friend with an especially thoughtful offer.

"I made your favorite, Fred." She led the boys into the kitchen for a warm scoop of peach cobbler. Fred was always eager to taste anything better than the canned tomatoes and fruit pudding he had relied on for many a meal in the Allen home. But Mrs. Lewis not only fed the boys a predinner treat, she gave her son's friend an even bigger surprise.

"Fred, I know it's difficult for you to make it back into town sometimes. So I figured we might as well go ahead and set you up with your own bedroom," she said. "Let's consider this your standing invitation."

The teen kept focused on his cobbler, not sure of what to say or where to look. Finally his eyes met Rick's, then Mrs. Lewis's, and he took a big bite and smiled. "This is good," he said. Then he added, "Thank you." It was all he could think to say.

From that day on the Lewis family went out of its way to make Fred feel right at home, even granting him full access to their grand piano. From his second-story bedroom window, there wasn't a single hint that a poor side of town existed at all. Now, instead of viewing scrawny hens and flea-ridden dogs, drunken uncles and broken-spirited women, Fred had a pristine view of the college campus. Just beyond his windowpanes a thick magnolia stood like a wizened warrior guarding him from his past, its oversize white flowers a timeless promise that beauty remained in the world.

At times, when the storms swooped in, winds shook the more fragile dogwoods and cherry blossoms, but his magnolia barely stirred. Instead, its large pointed leaves stayed stiff, saluting the sky as if they knew the sun would return. And when it did, as it always did, the light would sparkle from their waxy surfaces, an ever-present symbol that he, too, could weather any storm.

# *Seven*

Life in the Lewis house introduced Fred to an entirely different world. No longer worried about finding food, avoiding inebriated house guests, or hiding his musical talents from his superstitious clan, he was finally free to explore the creative arts to his heart's content while being immersed in a model of a healthy family relationship. With true stability and support for the first time in his life, doors began to open.

Like others in the LaGrange community, Fred's middle school and high school music teacher, Mrs. Dudley, had taken him under her wing from the time he'd first entered her sixth-grade classroom. But now that his basic needs were being met, she began to challenge Fred to take his talents to the next level. He'd tested well above his grade level in all subjects, and his intellect had become a fascination for his teachers, if not a frustration for those less secure. But despite his many gifts in both academics and music, Mrs. Dudley began to suspect Fred might not actually know how to read music. Because he had always been able to play even complex classical pieces by ear, he'd never had to rely on sight-reading. He simply heard the song once or twice and then used the sheet music as a visual guide while trusting his natural talents to get him through each performance.

In 1949, Fred was nearing the end of his freshman year in high school when Mrs. Dudley placed some sheet music on the piano and looked Fred in the eye. "Play this," she said, tapping the first measure as a starting point. The title and credits had been concealed, no lyrics were included as clues, and Mrs. Dudley did not offer to perform it first as an example. This left Fred with nothing but the musical notation. He was certainly able to distinguish the treble clef from the bass. He understood how to read the signatures. And he could make a fair attempt at the melody, simply due to his natural ability to process the world through music. But a full sight-reading proved difficult, and Mrs. Dudley had called his bluff.

As he struggled through the classical piece, his teacher curled her lips and leaned against the piano. "You can't read music, can you?"

Fred kept quiet, too ashamed to admit he'd made it this far without learning the basics.

"Don't worry," Mrs. Dudley reassured him. "This is quite common for people who can play by ear. You haven't had to rely on reading notes like the rest of us. But let me ask you something."

His eyes shifted, expecting a reprimand. Would she remove him from the choral group? Pull him from out-of-town competitions?

Mrs. Dudley moved toward her desk and asked firmly, "Do you want a career in music?"

Fred was silent again. No one had ever asked what he planned to do with his life, even though many close to him had encouraged him to find his way out. In a small town like LaGrange, there weren't many options. Those who came from money were on track to enroll in expensive private colleges. Then they would launch into adulthood with a hefty trust fund, a home, a vehicle, and usually a business or two already in their name. Those who came from mill-working families would be fortunate to make it through high school. And even then their paths usually led them to the mill or the military, neither of which appealed to Fred.

"There are many ways to build a career in the musical arts, Fred. Every church has a choir director. Every commercial needs a jingle. Most schools have a music teacher," Mrs. Dudley said, smiling. "Entertainers exist in every town on one level or another. Think about it. You can't turn on the radio without hearing a song. You've spent many years focusing on music, and you're so creative, Fred. I'm assuming you want some sort of career in the arts. Am I correct?"

Again, Fred sat quiet on the bench. He certainly had never imagined his life without music. But he'd never really given much thought to how that was going to look after high school.

Mrs. Dudley pulled her theory binder from her desk and opened it to the introductory section. "Well, at least know this. If you do want a career in music, you'll be doing yourself a big favor if you learn to read the notes."

By holding firm and not letting Fred take the easy way out, Mrs. Dudley became another woman who saved him. Just like Mrs. Duncan, who whispered, "I believe in you," Aunt Eleanor, who protected Fred from danger, and Mrs. Lewis, who gave him a safe place to call home, Mrs. Dudley gave Fred the time and attention he needed to develop solid sight-reading skills and to learn the basics of music theory. She cared enough to not only recognize both his strengths and weaknesses but to prepare him for what might come next in his life.

What did come next was an introduction to a highly acclaimed voice instructor at LaGrange College—Madame Elizabeth Gilbert. Madame, as she preferred to be addressed, was in her seventies by the time Fred auditioned for her, but she was lively and spirited and young at heart, and when she welcomed the nervous teen into her college studio with an operatic greeting, he could tell at once that she had much to teach him. The only problem was, Madame was not only highly selective in choosing her private students, she was also very expensive.

Even if she did agree to tutor this high school freshman, how was he supposed to pay her?

"Mrs. Dudley tells me you've got quite a voice," Madame said. Fred could only blink. He still wasn't sure he had any special abilities to speak of. He only knew he loved music and he wanted to learn all he could about it.

The instructor walked from the door and placed a well-worn stack of sheet music on the piano. Fred had never seen anyone carry herself with such presence, and he wondered if maybe she had led a privileged life in some foreign country before landing here in LaGrange. "She's got you playing for the Episcopals too, I hear?"

Trying to feign confidence, Fred kept his spine straight, his chin up, determined to make a strong impression despite the anxious twitch in his gut. "She asks me to help her sometimes at the Episcopal church," he answered, "but I've actually been playing since sixth grade over at Shoal Creek Baptist."

"You're in high school and you've already worked as a pianist for two churches?"

Fred nodded. "Organ too."

Madame smiled. "That takes commitment. Shows you've got a real work ethic. And Mary tells me you accompany too?"

"Yes, ma'am. I'll play for whoever asks me."

"Well, that's no small talent," Madame said kindly. "There are many who can sing. Many who can play. But not many good accompanists. Even I have trouble finding one for my students."

Fred exhaled. Mrs. Dudley had insisted he was talented enough to at least meet Madame, but when he first entered the college studio, he'd suddenly felt too young, too inept to be there. Now the instructor's kindness eased his fears.

"Would you like me to play while you sing?" Fred asked. "Anything."

"Oh, I like your style," Madame said with a laugh. "How about 'There Is a Time'? Familiar with that one?" Surprisingly, she began to sing the jaunty bluegrass number and Fred jumped in by the second stanza, matching her step for step on the keys.

Fred kept careful watch over the joyful instructor, noticing the slight upturn of her lips as she sang, the warm glint in her eyes as he played the jovial tune. He sensed she was pleased, and he gave his all, keeping his fingers light and the tempo upbeat as the lyrics delivered hope: "*The path is new, the world is free.*"[1]

When the song came to its end, Fred held his hands on the keys as the sound faded from the strings. He knew he could play well enough to make people happy, but he was not convinced a woman of Madame's esteem would have any interest. Her choice of song seemed to suggest she doubted he had any classical abilities. Surely she was simply doing her friend a favor and entertaining herself with the teen's performance.

"All right. Now, how about you sing for me," Madame said. "Let me see what we're working with here."

Fred politely agreed, taking a look at the familiar sheet music as he kept his seat on the bench of the concert grand. He had never played such a high-quality instrument. Shoal Creek Baptist had a hollow-sounding upright. The school owned a banged-up spinet. The Episcopalians had a baby grand, but it was tinny in the upper octaves. As his fingers rested lightly on the slick ivory keys, he could hardly wait to play another song on this shiny Steinway.

"You want to play while you sing?" Madame asked, a tinge of surprise in her tone. It was rare to find a student who chose to sing and play at the same time, especially those focused on higher levels of vocal performance.

He held his breath, hoping she'd allow it.

Madame waved her hand over the keyboard, a graceful gesture suggesting he go right ahead.

With that, Fred delivered a beautiful rendition of "I Heard a Forest Praying." He had been rehearsing the song for weeks with Mrs. Dudley, and he struck every note with deep emotion. As the final chord faded, Fred exhaled. He'd nailed it!

"Well, Fred. I'll be honest," Madame said. "I'm quite impressed. And I'm not easily impressed." She smiled. "I'm sure Mary told you I don't have any openings in my schedule right now, but . . . I do have an idea."

Fred held his breath.

"I am in dire need of an accompanist for my students. Perhaps you could help in exchange for private lessons? Fair enough?"

Once again, fate had delivered an unexpected opportunity, and Fred was eager to accept the challenge. He thanked her kindly, and with that, Madame set a schedule, hiring this high school teen to accompany college students during their private voice lessons. It was an ideal opportunity for him to grow on many levels, one that proved to be the beginning of Fred's budding career.

# *Eight*

With access to Madame's instruction, Fred began to dream of a career in music. He was barely a sophomore in high school when—thanks to his uncanny work ethic and the many connections music had already made for him—Fred stopped by the local radio station, WTRP FM, to pitch an idea. Within minutes, he had signed on to launch his very own show in partnership with one of Madame's students, a talented Miss Georgia beauty queen who had relied on Fred's accompaniment for her public events. Soon this dynamic duo was on air each evening at five o'clock, producing *Songs for You*. Together they would sing everything from classical opera pieces to old standards, with catchy show tunes and hymns in between—anything people wanted to hear. The show offered fresh variety along with a comfortable conversation and quickly became a prime-time hit.

Soon listeners began prodding Fred to audition for the Horace Heidt Youth Opportunity Program, a televised talent competition quite similar to modern shows such as *American Idol* or *The Voice*. Each week several acts would perform, and viewers would vote for a winner, many of whom were catapulted into successful entertainment careers after the victory. With encouragement from teachers, friends, and the greater LaGrange community, Fred entered the competition during tenth grade. And even though the auditions proved grueling, Fred made it to the championship stage.

Mrs. Dudley drove Fred more than an hour to Atlanta, where Horace Heidt's crew was busy setting up to film the final round of the competition. Palpable excitement filled the room, the stakes being so high. The winner would be guaranteed a regular spot on Freddie Miller's Atlanta-based *Stars of Tomorrow* show, a regional partner for the national talent competition. Fred's nerves were wound tight as he rubbed sweat from his palms.

At Mrs. Dudley's suggestion he had passed each level by performing Frankie Laine's chart-topping hit "I Believe." Now he resolved to cling to the meaning of those lyrics, relying on his fragile faith to ease his fears. In the silence of his mind, he surprised himself by offering a simple prayer: *Thy will be done.*

Then he took to the stage. The lights found him as he claimed the black piano bench and adjusted the heavy microphone. Cheers filled the room while he readied his hands, and once the roar lulled, he began to play. Those in attendance seemed to ride the notes with him, surfing the sound waves as his voice carried a powerful message to the crowd.

I believe for everyone that goes astray
Someone will come to show the way
I believe, I believe

I believe above the storm the smallest prayer
Will still be heard
I believe that someone in the great somewhere
Hears every word[1]

By the time the handsome sophomore hit the last note, the audience was already on its feet for a standing ovation. The cheers lasted so long, the announcer had to quiet the crowd.

Sure enough, Fred took home top honors, skyrocketing the teenager's popularity and garnering him a broader recognition for his innate talents. It also landed him that coveted spot on Freddie Miller's show. From that day forward, Fred would hitch a ride to Atlanta once a month so he could perform as a regular guest on the popular program. Television being a fairly new form of technology at the time, it was a big deal to be broadcast from WAGA studios right into America's living rooms, where families gathered for their evening entertainment.

As his status increased, doors continued to open, and Fred became more determined than ever to see where those opportunities might take him. Occasionally he would sit back and take a long look at all he was accomplishing at such a young age. If ever a shadow of doubt dared to sink him, he would return to the piano and sing the song that had launched his budding career, never stopping until he'd made it to the last line: "*Then I know why I believe.*"

# *Nine*

By his senior year it was time for Fred to consider his next steps. The LaGrange community had proven themselves time and again in the key people who refused to allow their local musical prodigy to fall through the cracks. But as college drew near, Fred's financial hardships could no longer be denied. As his well-off peers selected dorms and received new cars for graduation, he found himself with no way to afford higher education on his own.

Once again the generous people of LaGrange came through, granting Fred a full scholarship to study at LaGrange College, including a dorm room on campus. With his expenses covered, Fred gratefully enrolled at the small Christian institution, excited that it offered a strong focus on the performing arts.

While Fred had already garnered great regard statewide for his talents, it was about this time that he also began to be recognized for being a notable heldentenor. Fred knew enough about the history of music by now to know that, in opera circles, heldentenors were revered and quite rare, earning some of the most grueling roles. Known to have a darker, deeper vocal tone, especially within the mid- to low registers, they carried a weight that was key in nineteenth-century Wagnerian operas. The best heldentenors produced an almost hybrid sound, as Madame had explained, exhibiting a texture similar to that of a baritone but with a broader pitch range. This was the vocal quality Fred had learned to create, and so by college, he was already being compared to legendary opera greats such as Bernd Aldenhoff and Ernst Kraus.

Of course, his voice was not his only talent. Accompanying was Fred's true joy. Sympathetic to other vocalists, he was known to adapt the music to suit their skills, breathing along with them as they sang. As a vocal performer, he understood what a singer needed from the piano, and he delivered.

In 1952, just before the official start of his first semester, Fred strolled through the oak-draped quad with his friend Johnny York, talking and laughing beside the colorful perennial blooms. Suddenly Fred came to a cold stop. His focus was set on a dark-haired beauty crossing campus, her light-blue dress catching the breeze, her smile seeming brighter than the sun.

When Johnny noticed Fred's abrupt shift, he grinned and said, "That's Winnie Langley from Columbus."

Fred had no words. His entire body warmed.

"Come on," Johnny said. "I'll introduce you."

Fred shook his head. "She's far out of my league."

"Oh, come on." Johnny patted his friend's shoulder for a firm show of support. "Voted Most Popular. Don't tell me you've already forgotten high school."

Winnie passed the young men as she headed for the women's dormitory. Johnny said "Hi," and she gave him a demure smile. Then he raced to open the door for her.

"Thank you," Winnie said shyly.

She glanced at Fred.

Fred looked away.

Once she was out of sight, Fred finally exhaled. Johnny returned to his friend's side and said, "If you don't ask her out, I will."

The following day, as Fred was walking into the Fine Arts Building for work with Madame, he glanced up toward Winnie's dormitory. The oldest on campus, it claimed the highest elevation and boasted stellar views from its top floor. As he searched each window, his heart throbbed, anxious to get another sight of the beautiful young woman in the blue dress. Then he found her, perched on the ledge of her open window with her floral skirt billowing in the breeze, and his heart filled with excitement. Their eyes connected, and Fred hurried away, embarrassed. He glanced back just long enough to see Winnie's sweet smile, her eyes still following him through the azaleas.

The following day Fred could hardly wait to pass the dorm again. He'd dreamed about Winnie that night, and he was hoping to find her at the window once more. This time he would make a point to offer a friendly wave, maybe even shout hello.

As he looked again to Winnie's room, there stood the girl he could not get out of his mind. Their eyes met, longer this time. Heat rushed to his face as he waved and smiled. She laughed kindly and returned the gesture.

With classes starting the following week, Madame called a glee club meeting, hoping to get rehearsals off to a strong start. As fate would have it, Fred and Winnie each had signed up. It turned out Winnie was not only considered to be one of the most sought-after young women on campus because of her striking beauty and charming personality, she was also a respected vocalist in her own right, already garnering praise for her exceptional skills as an operatic soprano. With Fred's luck in full gear, Madame asked Fred to accompany Winnie. He jumped at the chance, taking his seat on the bench while trying not to let his nerves show.

He had certainly accompanied many attractive young women, but as Winnie leaned in to ask him to play "Summertime," he became dizzy.

By her first note Winnie captivated Fred with her lyric coloratura soprano, a voice capable of the highest ranges and smoothest transitions. Here stood this beautiful coed with a Scarlett O'Hara waistline, eyes that drew him in like magnets, and a smile that lit up the entire room. Plus, she could sing like an angel!

Winnie delivered the lyrics with emotion, singing about high cotton as only a true southern girl could do. But when she sang this verse, his whole heart was sunk:

> One of these mornings you're gonna rise up singing
> And you'll spread your wings and you'll take to the sky.[1]

The lyrics spun around Fred, and he couldn't stop staring at her as he played. Then Winnie turned his way and their eyes met, just as they had from her dorm window, and in that instant, she skipped the entire next part of the verse.

Fred handled it like a champ, skipping along with her, keeping right in step at the keys. None of the glee club students seemed to suspect a thing, and if Madame caught the faux pas, she didn't acknowledge it.

After the meeting, Winnie waited for Fred in the hallway.

"How on earth did you do that?" she asked, moving to his side as he left Madame's studio.

"Do what?" he managed to say. Fred was determined to play it cool despite the swell of anxiety he felt in Winnie's company.

"You know." She smiled. "How'd you make it look like I didn't make a mistake? I skipped half a verse, and no one even noticed."

Fred shrugged, the way Johnny York would have done, grateful she couldn't see his palms sweating. "That's my job. To make the singer look good."

Winnie's brow raised. "Even if they sing off-key or drop a lyric?"

"Especially then," Fred said, humble as ever.

Her brilliant smile persisting, Winnie shook her head in disbelief. "I think I'd better keep you in my pocket, Fred Allen."

Fred nodded, feigning confidence. "Yes. You do that."

# *Ten*

Fred was enamored of Winnie but still convinced that she was too good for him. He focused on his music and simply sighed when his friend Johnny York soon began dating her. It made sense. Johnny was *Mr. Everything*—charming, good-looking, smart, athletic, talented, *and* charismatic. Plus, Johnny had the one thing Fred didn't: the wealth and upper-middle class lineage that a girl like Winnie Langley deserved.

Still, as promised, Winnie kept the talented accompanist in her pocket and did her best to always perform with Fred at her side. Fred was more than eager to be in her company any chance he could get—even if she was dating his best friend. His schedule remained packed tight, but he always went out of his way to clear space for Winnie.

By that time one of the Baptist churches had begun paying Fred to serve as their official organist. Sometimes Winnie was paid to sing for the larger Methodist church in LaGrange, and Fred would slip away to accompany her on those Sundays she needed him. But one weekend Winnie received an invitation to sing at her family's hometown church an hour away, and she was eager for Fred to join her.

"I don't want to sing without you, Fred. Mother and Daddy said you're welcome to stay at our house. We'll head down Friday in time for dinner with the family. Then, Saturday, I'll show you all around

Columbus. You'll love it. Of course, we'll swing by the church for a quick rehearsal, and we'll perform for Sunday morning services before heading back here."

Winnie always had a plan. What she did not expect was Fred's furrowed brow when she made the suggestion. "Why worry? They'll love you."

And so, despite his insecurities, Friday afternoon Winnie and Fred shared the one-hour trek with fellow friends, laughing together in the back seat all the way to Columbus. As the car turned down a pristine lane, a heavy lump rose in Fred's throat. The Langleys' neighborhood looked like something from a television show, with a beautiful bower of oaks draped over the shady streets. Each lawn was meticulously maintained, floral wreaths decked every door, and large front porches welcomed visitors. The scene represented everything Fred could have ever wanted—safety, security, family, community. Home.

Their friends had barely pulled out of the driveway before Winnie's parents came rushing out with warm hugs. "Fred Allen, it's so nice to finally meet you," Mrs. Langley said, insisting he call her Nell. Winnie's teenage brother, Bill, gave Fred a firm handshake and grabbed the luggage. Mr. Jim Langley made a strong impression too, living up to the family history Winnie had shared during the hour car ride from LaGrange. He had grown up in Camp Hill, Alabama, a very small town of only two or three hundred residents. Unlike Fred's parents, Jim's had been determined to nurture his creative talents. At the young age of thirteen, they sent him by train all the way to Detroit, Michigan, where he enrolled in the art school of his dreams. He returned with the skills to land a job as a commercial artist, a career that from the looks of it seemed to be serving him well, more proof that Mrs. Dudley was right. Maybe there really was a way to make a living in the arts.

As Winnie led Fred into the living room for appetizers, Jim turned on the radio, low in volume, just enough to fill the background with lighthearted melodies. Fred paid close attention to Jim's behavior, noticing the way he gave his wife a playful wink when she set a tray of deviled eggs on the coffee table and announced, "Help yourselves."

Fred followed Winnie's lead, waiting for her to sit before finding his place on the comfortable sofa. The upholstery was modern, a vibrant display of the family's artistic nature. The Langleys were proving to be exactly as Winnie had described—joyful and supportive.

"We're all eager for Sunday," Jim began. "Your extraordinary talent is all we've been hearing about, Fred. How Winnie's never met anyone so gifted."

"Now, Jim. You'll embarrass him," Nell said, passing Fred a small china plate and a monogrammed ivory napkin, its cotton folds ironed perfectly, suggesting that even though they were a forward-thinking family, they still valued southern traditions.

Fred added one of the halved eggs to his plate although he was far too nervous to eat. In the background the radio played a song about a poor boy trying to make it big. Fred swallowed hard and eyed the others. *Had anyone else caught the lyrics?* He reached for the fruit, trying to pretend he was someone else.

"Tell us about yourself," Jim said. "You grew up in LaGrange?"

"Yes, sir," Fred answered. The last thing he wanted to talk about was his background, especially with a man like Jim Langley, a man whose family owned both a funeral home and a furniture store back in Camp Hill, where his father also served as county commissioner.

"What do your parents do there?" Jim asked. It was a friendly question, a sincere effort to launch neutral conversation, but Fred felt sweat beading across his hairline. What would they think if he told them his family worked at the mill?

"Oh, you know. I . . . I don't see them much now that I'm in college," Fred stuttered and tried to change the subject. "Y'all should have heard Winnie in the last glee club performance. She sang a rendition of '*Quando me'n vo*' that had the whole room excited."

Jim got the hint, and the discussion shifted to Winnie's dreams of stardom and her family's belief in her. Then he leaned in and asked, "You're friends with Johnny York, aren't you, Fred? Tell us everything we need to know about this fella."

"Daddy," Winnie protested and adjusted her skirt as Fred tried not to trace her fingers with his stare. "You'll meet Johnny soon. He's wonderful. Isn't he, Fred?"

"Sure," Fred said. "He's a stand-up guy."

Conversation began to circle the living room with an easy flow, moving through every topic imaginable, from the news of Elizabeth becoming queen of England to current hit songs on the radio to Winnie's brother Bill's hopes of one day playing college baseball. There was nothing they didn't discuss, and Fred found their self-effacing humor a comfort, especially the way they teased one another, delivering playful jabs with wholehearted love and affection.

"You do realize, Winnie's a princess," joked Bill. "Quintessential southern belle."

Winnie simply smiled and said, "I see absolutely nothing wrong with that."

It seemed laughter was par for the course here in the Langley home. Even when tackling serious topics, Winnie's father had a sharp wit, and his jokes kept the family's spirits light.

"But don't let her fool you," Nell said. "Winnie comes from tough stock, Fred. She ever tell you about my family, the Newtons?"

Fred lifted his brows and turned toward Winnie, curious. "No, ma'am."

"Well, I grew up on an Arkansas homestead," Nell continued. "No running water, no electricity. Did all the work ourselves. Made our own lye soap. Washed clothes in buckets. Cooked on a woodstove. Milked cows. Gathered eggs. Churned butter. You name it, we did it. And I made sure Winnie had those same experiences by sending her by train for extended stays each summer."

Fred couldn't hide his surprise. "Can't really imagine you milking cows," he teased.

"It's all true," Winnie confessed. "My grandparents insisted we learn as much as we could. College education was a must, but so were practical life skills."

"They stem from Sir Isaac Newton," Jim said. "Smartest people I've ever known."

If Fred hadn't already been impressed by Winnie's family, he certainly was now. He was also in awe of the sweet relationship he witnessed between Winnie's parents. They didn't behave like the adults he'd been around. In fact, the Langleys acted as if they were truly in love. As they sat close together, Jim would pat his wife's knee or drape his arm around her with a natural affection. She'd lean her head down against her husband's shoulder or rub his back with gentle approval. They were, especially, nothing like his own parents, who'd never shown a spark of genuine interest in one another, much less a moment of romance in all his life.

The Langleys seemed at ease, authentic, balanced. A true professional, Jim had developed a strong reputation painting Coca-Cola murals by hand all across the United States. But Nell was equally respected in her job as an office manager for a local internist named Dr. Dillard. Fred could hardly imagine how it would have felt growing up in a family like this one: to spend evenings sharing stories, laughing together around a home-cooked dinner.

As they moved into the dining room, the entire family helped serve pot roast, salad, and snap beans, plus warm bread pudding for dessert. "Nell makes the most delicious dinners," Jim said. "I try to do my part, but she's the one with the culinary talents."

When Fred later asked how she'd cooked the bread pudding, she grinned and said, "Family secret," crediting her grandmother for the heirloom recipe. The entire scene was playing out like one of the episodes of his favorite television show, *Mama*, a popular program with a beautiful, young actress named Rosemary Rice narrating sentimental stories about her happy fictional family. Not only had the serial served as a regular escape through Fred's high school years, he still enjoyed watching it every Friday night. It was the closest thing he had found to the kind of homelife he'd always craved. One that served up affection, attention, approval, security. *Love.*

After helping Winnie wash the dishes, Fred suggested they take a walk around the neighborhood. It was already dark, but Winnie graciously accepted the invitation and led Fred on a leisurely stroll as early autumn leaves fell around them. "What do you think?" she asked, eager for Fred's take.

"I think you don't know how lucky you are," Fred admitted, walking on the street side of the sidewalk, the way any gentleman would do.

"They're great, aren't they?" Winnie beamed.

"They do seem very happy together," Fred said, resisting the urge to take her hand. In that moment he wanted nothing more than to marry Winnie and become part of the Langley family. He stepped away instead, trying his best to keep from kissing her right there beneath the moon.

Above them the stars shone across a milky sky. Night frogs sang in the distance, and porch lights shone yellow across the line of well-manicured lawns. The last of the season's fireflies dotted the trees as

Winnie shouted, "Did you see that? A shooting star! Make a wish! Quick!"

Fred watched as she closed her eyes, completely lost in the wonder of such simple things. Winnie opened her eyes to see Fred staring at her. She blushed and said, "Tomorrow, I want you to meet the Lands. They're like family to me, and they'll just eat you up. They love music as much as we do." With that, they made their way back to the Langley home.

The next day Winnie toured Fred around Columbus as promised. They ran through a quick rehearsal at her family church, and then the couple joined the Lands for dinner. After an enjoyable conversation and dinner, Fred charmed them all by playing their piano like a pro as the others gathered around the keys. They each named their requests, failing to find a song to stump Fred, until Winnie slid next to him on the bench and said, "How about 'Lucky in Love'? From *Good News*. I've been wanting to try it as a duet for the glee club."

As his fingers struck the familiar notes, Winnie was alight.

Lucky in love, lucky in love
What else matters if you're lucky in love[1]

Fred could not have looked down at the keys even if he'd wanted. He was absolutely captivated by Winnie's flawless voice and her eyes, aglow.

The song had barely ended when Mrs. Evelyn Land pulled Winnie to the kitchen. While filling the sink with sudsy water, she gave Winnie a knowing grin.

"What?" Winnie tightened her jaw, perplexed.

Evelyn laughed. "Honey, you're absolutely head over heels in love with that boy. And he's in love with you too."

"Oh, that's ridiculous," Winnie argued. "Fred's just a friend. Nothing more."

"Argue all you want," Evelyn insisted. "Anyone can see the two of you were made for one another. And when you *do* finally realize what I already know to be true, then he's going to ask you to marry him. And that means it won't be too far in the future when you welcome a baby of your own."

"Goodness gracious! What on earth was in your cocktail?" Winnie, flustered, grabbed the scrub brush and took her anxious energy out on the dishes.

"All I'm saying is, don't forget . . . I want to be the baby's godmother."

Laughter swelled between the two women, and nothing more was said about the handsome music man.

On Sunday morning Winnie performed her solo while Fred accompanied her on the piano. The wonderful acoustics in the historic church made Winnie's beautiful voice sound even more glorious. Morning light poured in through the stained-glass windows, and the familiar lyrics carried out across the pews while candle flames flickered in response. As she held the final note of "His Eye Is on the Sparrow," Fred imagined walking the aisle with her, beneath this very steeple. And Winnie, well, Winnie couldn't help but look at her gifted accompanist and hear the echo of Evelyn's words: "You're . . . in love with that boy. And he's in love with you too."

# *Eleven*

With school in full swing, life was busier than ever. Fred was not only working, taking private voice lessons, tackling a full course load at college, and performing every chance he could get, he also was running the *Songs for You* radio show with the striking beauty queen whose wedding date was drawing near. With his cohost needing more time off the air, Fred frequently invited his best friend and soloist, Johnny York, to join as a substitute. When Johnny wasn't available, he began asking Winnie to manage the second microphone.

When Winnie joined the show, everything changed. Fred felt it the minute the "On Air" sign lit the back wall of the studio, and Winnie's face shone even brighter with the glow of excitement. It seemed she had been born for the spotlight. She was energetic and passionate, playfully taking the lead as a natural conversationalist between songs. When it came time to read the listener requests, she'd add personal stories about the many people she knew around the region. "Oh, here's a note from my dear friend Helen. You all know Helen, don't you? She's got the most beautiful blonde hair and the kindest heart." Then she'd go on to charm her way through every request, as if the listeners were right there with them, shooting the breeze.

By the end of the show, the phones were ringing with callers suggesting

Winnie come back the following night. They adored the new guest host. Like Fred, the audience was hooked.

Just before the end of their freshmen year of college, Miss Georgia resigned, leaving an opening for a permanent new costar. Fred didn't bother interviewing anyone else. He'd already decided that Winnie was the perfect fit. The chemistry between the hosts was apparent, even over the airwaves, so when Fred asked Winnie to become his official new partner, she excitedly said yes. The next day, they signed a contract, uniting to produce the show.

Because they were both freshmen studying toward a degree in the performing arts, Fred and Winnie shared most of their classes together. They also sang regionally as a duo on many occasions, and now they were joined in producing *Songs for You*. Rain, shine, sleet, or snow, the duo shared the six-block walk together back and forth to WTRP five days a week, a routine both performers enjoyed even as Fred fought against his every desire to take Winnie's hand along the way.

Soon the two were not only rehearsing and producing their daily show, they were also sharing meals at the dining hall, studying for exams, and booking additional weekend gigs both near and far. Even when they weren't together, Fred wrote Winnie endearing letters, daring to address them "Dear Partner," a gesture Winnie found to be both kind and respectful, if not a tad romantic.

Still, their partnership remained platonic even after Johnny York moved with his family out of state, ending his courtship with Winnie. Despite Winnie's new single status, Fred and Winnie were reluctant to explore a romance because neither wanted to risk losing such an ideal musical coupling. Both had aspirations to become professional performers, so Fred showed nothing but patience as Winnie continued to introduce him as "friend" or claimed she loved him "like a brother."

It wasn't until the end of their sophomore year when he finally made his move.

By then Fred and Winnie had become part of a popular vocal ensemble at LaGrange. They traveled frequently with the other vocalists, who had all become close friends. That evening two of the singers, Julia and Oz, were heading to the drive-in "picture show."

"Why don't you and Winnie tag along with us?" Oz suggested.

Fred gave it some thought. He and Winnie had shared many moments with these mutual friends, and this could be just another casual outing. But two couples going to a drive-in movie theater could also be considered a double date. *Would an invitation like this cross the line for Winnie?* Fred wondered. *Would she be offended?*

"Don't wimp out," Julia nudged. "Everybody knows you two will end up together eventually."

A powerful chemistry was definitely brewing between Fred and Winnie, and in the last year their devotion to one another had become stronger by the day. Maybe Oz and Julia were right. Perhaps it was time to test the waters. So that evening, Fred gave it his best shot and invited Winnie to join him, Oz, and Julia for a late-night movie. Much to his surprise, she agreed, and the foursome ventured off in Oz's car to the drive-in.

Oz proved to be a pro at double dating, parking near the back of the crowded lot. The big screen glowed with a hazy light, drawing the buzz of fireflies as a symphony of night sounds swelled around them. The slim moon made the night even darker than usual. Maybe it was the shadowy sky. Maybe it was the back-row privacy. Or maybe it was time. The stars had finally aligned for this dynamic duo. When Fred slid closer, his hip pressing against hers, Winnie didn't pull away. And when Fred reached for Winnie's hand, she let him take it.

Later that evening, after Oz and Julia had gone their separate way,

Fred walked Winnie to her dorm. They lingered beneath the moss-draped oaks, stretching the minutes that remained before curfew. With the magic of the movies still in the air, just before Winnie had to race inside for nightly sign-ins, she playfully broke into song right there in the quadrangle: "*Summertime, and the livin' is easy.*"[1]

As she was singing and spinning beside the wisteria-covered trellises, Fred found himself drawn into a trance. This was the very spot where he had stood when he first laid eyes on her nearly two years earlier. He remembered the moment clearly—she had walked by in her blue dress, and just moments before entering her dorm, she had turned back to offer Fred a subtle smile. His heart had raced that day when Johnny York said her name. And it had raced again the first time he heard her sing these lyrics, when fate had brought them together during Madame's glee club meeting. Now, Fred knew one thing for sure—he wanted to share the rest of his life with this girl.

Just as she twirled around to face him, Fred mustered all his courage and pulled her close against him. "Winnie Langley, I want to kiss you."

"Then what are you waiting for, Fred Allen?"

# *Twelve*

While Fred had spent many weekends getting to know Winnie's family back in Columbus, she hadn't yet met Fred's. By the end of their sophomore year in college, Winnie insisted they take the next step. She sat beside him on the piano bench and said, matter-of-factly, "It's time I meet your family."

Fred's stomach sank. He had kept her curiosity at bay for nearly two years, but now he had run out of excuses. It was time to put Winnie's love to the test.

While Fred lived in a dormitory just off campus, the Allens had remained in the country home where they'd moved when he'd started middle school. Fred still didn't own a car, but earlier that year Winnie had been gifted her uncle's old Model A Ford. It was a vintage car that set Winnie apart from her peers, especially if it dared to rain while they were out and about. The hole in the roof would then require the passenger to open an umbrella, a favorite sight for locals who admired the way lighthearted Winnie always handled storms in stride. But the antique ride certainly wasn't reliable enough to make the evening drive out to the Hillcrest community. She didn't even bother asking her father for permission, knowing Mr. Langley would never have allowed her to drive those rural roads after dark.

Without Winnie's car, Fred had to find another solution. His sister, Novis, had still been giving him the occasional lift when needed, but that day Fred insisted she let him borrow the old Ford. Novis agreed, delivering it to him on campus before hitching a ride home with a friend.

Now Fred gripped the wheel tightly in both hands while driving Winnie toward the outskirts of LaGrange. As cotton fields and cow pastures replaced the college buildings, Fred's nerves were beginning to get the best of him. Winnie had spent enough time with Fred to know his quirks. She could always tell when his anxiety was on the rise. He'd grind his teeth or tune out, even as she was telling him about new operatic songs she wanted to master.

"Fred?" Winnie asked, noticing his white-knuckled grip on the steering wheel and pearls of sweat around his hairline. "There's nothing that could stop me from loving you. You know that, don't you?"

He gritted his teeth. Winnie had no idea what she was about to walk in to, he thought. Her family was educated and cultured. They shared enriching conversations around the dinner table, played games by the fireplace. They laughed and sang and had fun together, never afraid to show their uncensored vulnerabilities. The arts were celebrated in her house, not cursed. Even religion meant something real to the Langleys, not just a Sunday sermon after too many Saturday drinks.

Winnie had never seen Fred more worried, and as the miles tugged them toward his family's home, she had to encourage him to keep driving, her trademark optimism propelling him on through his fears. But when they arrived at the dilapidated structure, Fred observed Winnie carefully, expecting the worst. How many childhood days had he spent trying to leave this place? How many ways had he learned to act, trying to prove he was no different from his friends?

Holding his breath, Fred opened the door for Winnie and escorted her to the house. Even along such a short walk, he noticed many flaws.

The battered wood panels that lacked paint. The slanted porch that had held many a passed-out partier over the years. The knee-high grass that begged to be maintained. But instead of showing judgment or criticism, Winnie kept calm and revealed nothing. Much like the way Mrs. Lucy Nixon had remained pleasantly unrattled the day she had shown up unannounced to fetch the sheet music, Winnie behaved as if she were being welcomed into any other household. As if she had visited many homes just as worn down as this one.

Unlike the Langleys, who had rushed out to greet Fred and Winnie with affectionate hugs, no one issued forth from the Allen home to offer any kind of welcome. Fred tried to bite back his bitter shame. He knew there was nothing more he could do. If he stood any chance at all with Winnie, she would have to be able to accept his impoverished roots. If not, then he would have no choice but to let her walk away and find a *better man*.

Fred led Winnie up the rickety steps to the family's front door. The entrance held nothing decorative. Instead, there were cobwebs, muddy boots, and a litter of scraggly kittens mewling in hunger for their mother—a feral feline nowhere to be found. Fred knocked as if it wasn't his own family home, and then, embarrassed, laughed about it. "Never know what you might find in there. Better to give them fair warning."

With impeccable manners, Winnie followed Fred inside once his mother had opened the door. She greeted Velma with genuine affection, and as the couple made their way to Grady in the kitchen, Winnie was already bragging about her talented partner, filling Fred's parents in on all their son had managed to accomplish at the college and beyond.

The Allens didn't seem to know how to respond. Winnie was too polite to bring up controversial issues about politics or religion. She wasn't one to gossip. And the talk of college life seemed of little interest to Fred's parents, so she quickly ran out of things to discuss.

There were no romantic neighborhood streets to stroll, no family friends to meet, and no shared interests to explore. The air was suffocating to Fred, and he was just about to pull Winnie back to the car when Novis walked into the kitchen and said, "Nice to finally meet you, Winnie. All this time I keep seeing you when I give Fred a ride somewhere. And we all listen to that show y'all do together. Don't we, Mama?"

This came as a surprise to Fred. Never had the Allens mentioned the radio program, and his stomach settled a bit, having learned they actually cared enough to listen to *Songs for You*.

Novis and her husband, Charles, were living with the Allens while they saved for a home of their own. The family matriarch, Peg Freeman, had also moved back in with the Allens. She hadn't handled Noah's passing very well and had since declined into severe dementia. As they all gathered around the dinner table, the Allens slowly began to let their guard down. Then, without warning, Fred's uncle Dirk arrived and helped himself to a heaping bowl of dumplings. By that time, the ex-baseball player who had once been chased away by Aunt Eleanor had ironically become a sheriff's deputy. He'd built his own home next door and frequently showed up uninvited. Winnie's instinct told her something wasn't right about Dirk. She couldn't quite put her finger on it, but she certainly didn't trust him and was relieved when he gobbled down his food and left for his nightly patrol.

After a mostly quiet supper, Fred helped Velma transition Peg to bed. Winnie, not quite familiar enough to join such an intimate exchange, assisted by opening doors and withdrawing the bed linens, wondering how Velma would have managed to do this job on her own. Once Fred's grandmother was settled in the bedroom, his mother locked the door to secure the elderly woman for the night. "We find her wanderin' out in the woods sometimes," she explained to Winnie. "It's the only way I know to keep her safe once it gets dark."

Winnie's empathy shone through as she gave Mrs. Allen a gentle nod. With so many contrasts to the Langley lifestyle, Winnie had no way of knowing the conditions she now beheld as Fred's homelife had improved significantly since his younger years. His parents were older and wiser now, and having retired from the mill, they were no longer broken by the oppressive work conditions. The random boarders and military men were long gone, as were the "aunts" his uncle Ed had kept around through the earlier years. Velma had found work as a nursing assistant, and Grady had even kicked the bottle and taken work with a construction crew, helping to build churches around the region. Still, it was a world apart from Winnie's family life.

As the evening wound down, Fred was eager to get Winnie out of there before something went wrong. So far she had not bolted in disgust, and she seemed to be enjoying herself well enough. Fred was feeling more certain than ever that she was the girl for him. But as soon as the young couple bid the Allens farewell, Fred's uncle Ed came stumbling down the hill from Dirk's house. He was too drunk to walk straight, and the stench of stale booze found Winnie and Fred on the porch long before Ed reached them.

"Let's go," Fred said sternly. He held Winnie's hand and hurried her to the car.

"Wait up, wait up, now, Fred!" Ed hollered with a slur.

Fred gave him a side-eye warning and closed Winnie's passenger door. He was not going to let this man ruin this for him. Not on his life.

Ed swaggered closer and then lunged at the passenger window, crashing his hands hard against the glass and causing Winnie to jump with a startle. "Boo!" he said, laughing obnoxiously. "What you so scared of, little girl?"

"Leave her alone." Fred pulled his uncle from the window, holding him with an aggressive stare, refusing to fold.

"What you gonna do about it? Go run and tell your music teacher? Cry to your uppity friends? We all know you're ashamed." Then he turned to Winnie, who watched the full display from inside the car. "Oh, you thought he was something more than this, didn't you, little girl? You thought he was gonna buy you some shiny big diamond? Put you up in a house on a hill? Ha!"

This was all Fred could take. He drew his arm back and laid a powerful punch right into his uncle's drunken cheek. Winnie shrieked.

Fred didn't bother saying anything more. The sting of the hit would make his message clear. Instead, he hurried to the driver's seat and slammed the heavy steel door while cranking the worn engine. The muffler sputtered as Fred pulled away from his family home, leaving Ed bleeding in the moonlit lane, swallowing dust.

For the entire drive to campus, Fred said nothing. He brought Winnie back to her dorm and let her leave in silence, certain she would never want to see him again.

The next morning when he arrived for class, Winnie was waiting for him. "I wrote out our songs for today's show." She handed Fred a note card. Just as his wealthy friends had done back in high school, Winnie surprised him. Instead of judging him, she hadn't changed one bit after visiting the Allen home—not even after seeing him punch his uncle Ed.

Now Fred knew she really loved him, and he wanted nothing more than to marry her. However, the sad fact remained that Uncle Ed was right about one thing. An official engagement meant Fred would need to buy a ring. And buying a ring meant money.

Once again a community member came to the rescue. Mr. Rosser, a well-liked member of the Kiwanis Club, had watched Fred overcome many obstacles to make something of himself. One day, after Fred and Winnie had performed for a Kiwanis Club event, Mr. Rosser greeted Fred. "I see you're still dating that beautiful gal from Columbus."

"Yes, sir." Fred stood straight and proud.

"When the time comes to pop the question, swing by my jewelry store. I'll help you choose a stone."

One afternoon the couple stopped by, and the kind gentleman really did name a price Fred could afford. With Winnie's tasteful approval, they selected the diamond and struck a deal. Someday Fred would make the engagement official. Until then he would work to pay regular installments, determined to give Winnie a proper ring.

As they left the store, Fred wanted to drive straight to Uncle Ed and prove him wrong. He had been able to buy Winnie a diamond after all. And if he had anything to do with it, he would give her that house on a hill someday too.

# *Thirteen*

In the two years that Fred and Winnie had been studying at LaGrange, Madame had become especially fond of her star students. They had what she had learned to call the *It* factor—that indescribable star quality that set them apart from the others.

Madame had connected Fred with Atlanta's highly acclaimed vocal instructor Ralph Erolle, a tutorship that was proving especially beneficial in more ways than one. Understanding that Fred and Winnie were both hungry for more than what Georgia could offer, Madame and Ralph set out to find an opportunity that would push the ambitious vocalists to the next level.

They knew of a reputable program in upstate New York, a summer study that helped rising talents sharpen their skills in the performing arts. The vocal portion was geared around the Chautauqua Opera Company, an organization that was almost as renowned as the Metropolitan Opera and nearly as old. Each summer the company offered an eight-week intensive program for young singers, but the auditions were tough and acceptance was not guaranteed. Madame nevertheless encouraged them to apply, helping prepare their audition and gathering glowing recommendation letters.

All were excited when Fred and Winnie were admitted to the prestigious program. Once again, the community came through when a generous benefactor, Mr. Banks, sponsored the entire summer experience for both students.

With funding secured, Madame and her friend Ms. Beard drove the young performers north for the special opportunity. It was the summer of 1954, and Fred and Winnie rode in the back seat all the way to New York, stopping along the way to view famous landmarks, including Niagara Falls. There, the starry-eyed couple leaned out over the railing, hoping to feel the spray from the treacherous drop. The waters roared their thunderous song, and Fred's entire being responded to the power of nature's music. The experience was far removed from the small black-and-white image he had seen years ago in Noah's battered encyclopedias.

Perched at the top of the view, Fred took Winnie's hand, and together they stared out into the churning currents. "There's so much for us to learn," Fred said. "The world is bigger than we know, and I want to see it all. With you."

Winnie's heart raced as she thought, *Yes, this is the man for me.*

That afternoon, the foursome reached the historic lakeside community of Chautauqua, where bright white sailboats dotted the lake and stately homes added to the charm. With help from Madame and Ms. Beard, the two excited students moved their belongings into the summer quarters—Fred in the building for boys and Winnie in the one for girls.

Winnie introduced herself politely to a group of fellow residents, but they laughed at her southern accent and rolled their eyes when she asked where they were to meet for breakfast.

"Don't let them worry you," Madame said. "You've seen New York now, but how many of them have ever seen Georgia?" As usual, their wise mentor had known just what to say to boost Winnie's confidence.

That afternoon, Madame led the way to the grand amphitheater where many of the nation's most prestigious singers had performed. As they strolled together through the meticulously landscaped grounds, they noted the grandeur of the historic buildings, especially the unusual rooflines and cedar shingles. "I would have given anything for this experience when I was your age," Madame said. "Make the most of it. Promise me."

"We promise," Winnie said, enthusiastically. She certainly didn't want Madame to sense her nervousness.

For the next two months Fred and Winnie spent every waking hour together. They attended lectures by the nation's leading vocalists, studied opera under the world-renowned Julius Huehn, and attended top-bill performances at the legendary outdoor amphitheater, journaling every detail of the unique experience. It was their first time to hear such premier singers perform live, including one of their favorites, Eileen Farrell.

The other students all hailed from the north, and they didn't seem to know what to make of Fred and Winnie's genteel manners. They never welcomed the couple to their dining tables or invited them to gather with the group in the evenings. But Fred and Winnie had one another, and they made the most of the opportunity they'd been given.

On the weekends, they would travel. One Friday afternoon they rode a bus past the horses and buggies of Amish country, heading straight for the Big Apple, where the intensity of the noise and the flurry of lights proved more energizing than they had ever imagined. As they strolled beneath the marquee signs on Broadway, they didn't bother complaining that the tickets were too expensive for them to see an actual play. Instead they spied on the performers arriving for evening shows and sneaked through the back alleys to eavesdrop on post-rehearsal conversations.

The young couple took in as much as they possibly could. They explored Central Park all the way to Chinatown and covered as much of the city as time would allow. Wide-eyed and curious, they pointed out the countless contrasts from their world back home in Georgia. It was easy to focus only on the glamour, especially in the Upper East Side of Manhattan, where they spotted long limousines and European sports cars, decadent jewels and designer handbags that cost more than their entire semester's budget. They took no offense to less posh areas of the city, where honking car horns fought for attention and garbage cans crowded the sidewalks. Even there, Winnie was not deterred, telling Fred, "It's what I've always wanted. How could anyone not love a place like this? So much to do. So much to see!"

Together they walked for miles, exploring various blocks, fantasizing about owning a penthouse in the upscale districts. When they strolled past the old Metropolitan Opera House on Broadway and Thirty-ninth Street, Winnie's eyes ignited. Fred was equally inspired.

"It's nice, but I pictured something . . . fancier," Winnie admitted, standing on the sidewalk beneath the industrial awning that now paled in comparison to the elaborate architectural designs they'd been admiring.

"I don't know," Fred said. "Imagine coming here in the 1800s, when there were gaslights on the corners." He fanned his hand across the air, as if directing a play. "Picture the carriages. The men in long black tails."

"Ahhh, yes. I can see it," Winnie played along. "Or jump ahead, to streetcars. Ladies with long strands of pearls, wrists wrapped with diamonds. Full-length evening gowns and furs to drape them all."

They were both lost in the scene. Then Fred eyed the door. "Wanna look inside?"

He extended his arm as if a nineteenth-century escort, and Winnie hooked her hand inside the crook of his elbow with her chin tilted high and proud. Together they sneaked into the expansive lobby, pretending they were being welcomed in for a night of opulence. Winnie gasped as they headed up the grand staircase. With no one in sight, she exaggerated her walk, imitating Elizabeth Taylor's glamorous stride as if she owned the place.

The building's intimate interior made up for its bland first impression. Even Fred caught his breath when they entered the empty theater. Five levels of intricate balconies wrapped the room, rising straight up, with only twenty rows between the decadent lofts and the famous stage. The impact was significant, and when Fred folded into one of the upper center seats, he not only imagined himself as an audience member, he felt the heat of the stage lights on his face, heard the rounds of hearty applause, scanned the sea of captivated faces as he gave them what they needed most—a reminder that this was just the place to tap into deep emotions, to shake loose from all societal restraints, and to feel completely free again.

"How about we move to New York, Winnie? I mean, really do it." Fred held a serious tone and an equally thoughtful expression. "We'll head up here after graduation. Give it our best shot. What do we have to lose?"

Winnie beamed. She had always dreamed of a life on stage, and she could envision her aspirations coming true. But it wasn't just her own goals of stardom that had set her eyes on the future. He could have suggested they move to the Arctic and live in an igloo for all she cared. She would have followed Fred Allen anywhere. As long as they could be together, secure, safe . . . she would be happy.

Just as they were losing themselves in the magic of the moment, a guard shouted from behind them. "Hey! What are you two doing in here?"

Fred grabbed Winnie's hand, and they raced out the nearest exit, running full-speed down the grand staircase, as Winnie called out behind them, "Sorry, sir!"

That afternoon they rode the ferry out to the Statue of Liberty and ate a hot dog from a street cart. They even mastered the subway, heading to Coney Island where they rode the roller coaster at sunset. They sat close together as the ride twisted and turned, shaking them into a riot of laughter.

Fred and Winnie found themselves drawn especially to the bohemian vibe of Greenwich Village, where beatniks gathered to recite poetry in the coffee shops. Alleys held sketch artists and poets for hire. Music flowed from every stoop, the food was as exotic as the languages that fell from the tongues, and rules seemed not to apply to this restless group of free spirits.

They had never seen a place more embracing of artists, musicians, and actors. Around the corner, the wide-eyed couple passed a group of street performers singing "Two Lost Souls" from *Damn Yankees*. On a whim, Fred and Winnie jumped in and joined the impromptu performance, feeling absolutely free.

"We'll live here, in the Village," Fred said, as they danced in the street with perfect strangers. "We'll make friends from all around the world."

"Artistic friends. People who think like we do," Winnie chimed in.

"And we'll spend our lives creating," Fred added. "Music. Theater. Always creating something new."

"Yes!" Winnie cheered.

By Sunday they were still starry eyed. But before heading back to Chautauqua, Fred said there was one more place he wanted to see. An employee at the bus terminal pointed out the desired destination on a map, and together Fred and Winnie made the thirty-minute ride through the Upper West Side, out toward Riverside. There, on the corner of Broadway and 121st Street, Fred stood speechless as he gazed up at the oldest independent, nondenominational center of religious studies in America. Union Theological Seminary was constructed of sturdy brick and limestone, a Gothic Revival design that stretched for nearly two full blocks. Its intimidating spires rose high above the city streets, with a long path shadowed by the institution's trademark tower. It looked nothing like the modern skyscrapers they had seen all weekend and seemed more like something found in Europe from at least a century earlier.

Fred's awe was evident as he surveyed the historic campus. "This is it, Winnie. The School of Sacred Music. All those songs we've learned at LaGrange? Many were composed right there in those buildings. And you know what else is in there?"

Winnie shook her head, stumped.

"Some of the world's best organs. Madame told me they produce the purest tones she's ever heard."

Just then majestic bells rang out from back near the Hudson River, where another series of spires stretched toward the skies. "That must be Riverside." Fred was speaking faster, already heading toward the iconic church. "It's got a Möller organ too, one of the largest ever built."

"I bet they're about to start services." Winnie hurried beside Fred as the bells continued to toll. "Listen!"

Together the couple wove their way through the colossal entrance, noting the series of concentric arches in the doorway where sculpted figures formed majestic pillars of stone. Inside, the elaborate nave felt cavernous, with room for more than two thousand congregants, sturdy arches stretching high overhead. The pair threaded their way among fellow attendees to claim a spot on a back pew. Neither said a word throughout the entire service. As the organ hummed, its vibrating tones pulsed through the stones beneath their feet. Rich waves flowed through the pipes in layers, growing louder and louder as the choir added to the sacred sound, singing in perfect, powerful harmony that brought a hum to one's bones. Winnie caught a glimpse of light in the corner of Fred's eye. Sure enough, as the organ reached its powerful crescendo, a small tear pooled there, and Winnie sensed a shift in Fred's mood.

After the benediction Fred led Winnie through the emptying sanctuary. The service had lifted his spirit in the way only music could do. "What I would give to play an organ with that kind of sound to it. Or conduct a choir like that."

"Give it a few years," Winnie said with a smile. "Anything is possible."

---

By Monday morning Fred and Winnie were back in Chautauqua in time for their final week of lessons, and the following weekend they were stepping aboard a Trailways bus bound for Georgia.

Back at Hillcrest the Allen home provided a stark reminder of all the reasons Fred wanted to move to New York. Music had become an escape for Fred; creating, his refuge. The stage had not only given him a voice; it had long supplied a source of the much-wanted attention, approval, and affection he had lacked from his family.

For Winnie, though, music was simply a joyful expression of her talents. While they now shared a plan to chase their dreams, Winnie sang because she had been loved; Fred performed because he had been deprived of love.

When Fred and Winnie returned to school after their summer in New York, they were no longer two naive kids from Georgia working on random degrees. Now they knew where they were heading, and they were eager to finish their studies at LaGrange so they could move to the next phase. Together.

On August 16, 1954, Fred celebrated his nineteenth birthday. To mark the occasion, he and Winnie had planned a romantic outing to Pine Mountain, a forty-five-minute drive from LaGrange. It was a beautiful area made famous when Franklin D. Roosevelt, seeking relief from polio, had built a small vacation cottage nearby. It was in that little white house that FDR suffered a stroke in 1945 and died. But not quite a decade later, Fred and Winnie climbed to the top of that mountain to celebrate life.

After a picturesque hike and a lovingly prepared picnic, the couple drew close to one another as the sun sank low behind the trees. "Beautiful," Winnie said, staring out at the majestic sunset. "When we get really old, around sixty-five or so, we should come back here and hold hands and jump off the mountain together. Go out with a bang before we become irrelevant."

"You? Irrelevant?" Fred laughed. The sky shifted slowly, moving from pastel pinks to tones of orange, pale as summer melons. As the earth kept spinning, the light soon reflected the color of plums across the horizon. Finally cloaked in the safety of a night sky, Fred counted to ten in his head, trying to steel his nerves.

Inhaling deeply, he pulled the engagement ring from his pocket and placed it in Winnie's hand. He did not get down on one knee. He didn't even ask if she would marry him. Instead, he sat there close to Winnie and held his breath.

Without a word, Winnie slipped the ring onto her finger. Neither spoke as the stars began to fill the sky. Moonlight broke from behind a cloud, catching Winnie's glistening eyes. Then she leaned her head softly on his shoulder with gentle affection, and Fred knew her choice was true. She had chosen him.

# *Fourteen*

Fred and Winnie were married on April 8, 1956, the wedding ceremony taking place in the beautiful sanctuary of St. Paul Methodist Church in Columbus, where Winnie walked the aisle in a classic white ball gown, long-sleeved and layered with tulle and lace. Nearly four hundred guests were in attendance, including the many close friends who had stood by Fred since middle school, despite his family's poverty and trials.

Fred made a dapper groom, dressed to the nines in his black bow tie and white dinner jacket. The couple could not have been more stunning, both blessed with good looks to match their charming personalities and outstanding talents. Winnie, too, was surrounded by her closest friends as attendants, and as her minister led the ceremony, she allowed herself to take it all in.

Her parents hosted the wedding of her dreams, with flickering candles and fresh flowers, a towering cake and beautiful music. After the ceremony the president of LaGrange College gifted the newlyweds a week's honeymoon in his family's rural mountain cabin. It was a generous gesture, one that reminded Fred and Winnie yet again of the value of community.

The world was alive with possibilities for the newlyweds. Elvis released his debut album that year, Buddy Holly recorded his first session, and Fred was invited to join Mensa, an international society for people with exceptionally high IQs. The talented couple continued performing, studying, and dreaming of their star-filled future in New York.

By 1957, Fred had graduated with honors from LaGrange College, earning his bachelor of fine arts degree in music with a minor in German. Like many graduates in that era, Fred had no idea what to do next, but he continued dreaming of a bohemian life with Winnie in Greenwich Village, where he hoped they would spend their days creating music and sharing their talents with the world. If they worked hard, he believed they might even land a role on Broadway or with the Metropolitan Opera. Maybe he could even compose scores at the Union Theological Seminary School of Sacred Music or hone his craft with the professionals at Juilliard.

But as summer progressed, the couple remained in LaGrange. In addition to producing their radio show, Fred had continued working for local churches while accompanying various vocalists around the region. Winnie enjoyed her full-time job with the Troup County Chamber of Commerce while singing alongside Fred for public and church events. They were getting by as well as any young couples do, but they had yet to find their lucky break. One morning, Winnie joined Fred in the kitchen and said, "Honey, I want to move to New York as much as you do. But it's not happening right now. We've reached out to everyone we know there, and nothing has opened up. I think it's time we consider another option."

"What kind of option?" Fred asked, wrestling a copy of the *New York Times*. He had once again been circling employment ads.

"Well, right now, we just need to get settled," Winnie said. She had given this plenty of thought. "We could save some money. Gain some experience, and *then* give New York a try."

Fred's brow pinched. "I don't know. Shouldn't we just go ahead and move up there, give it our best shot? If it doesn't work, then we can settle for something else."

"How do we do that, Fred? I've been thinking this through, and I can't find a way to make it happen."

Silence brewed.

Fred folded the paper and put it off to the side. "Isn't that what we said we wanted to do? Rent a little place in the Village? See what comes?"

"So we move up there and do what? Wait tables? Stand in line for auditions with thousands of others hoping to get lucky? We might as well head to a casino. It's a gamble, Fred. And let's face it . . . we don't have that luxury."

Fred sat now, rolling the ink pen in his hand. "You're right that we have nothing to lose, so isn't that as good a reason as any to give it a try?"

Winnie eyed the paper. She'd spent her entire life dreaming of stardom, picturing herself on the silver screen or the stage. Madame and others had insisted she had what it takes to make it in New York or Hollywood, but now that it was time to take the big leap, she was struggling to find a viable path. "I just think it's better if we have a real plan, Fred. We need to keep making connections, take time to do some research. Build some savings. Then we'll be better prepared."

"You really want to stay here?" Fred's voice became tense, no longer able to conceal his disappointment.

"Not particularly," Winnie said, looking out the window of their humble apartment. "We both know there's not much work to be found here in LaGrange. But Columbus has three hundred thousand people, Fred. Mother and Daddy feel certain we can find good jobs there."

Fred hesitated. Columbus surely was a better option than LaGrange, but it wasn't what he had envisioned for their future. What had changed since he and Winnie had stood in awe in the cathedral or stared up longingly at Union and promised to return after graduation? "So you want to move to Columbus?"

"I don't know. I mean, it's not what I wanted either, honey. But . . ."

Winnie glanced at the framed photo on the entry table, remembering the four hundred well-loved guests who attended their wedding. "We do have family there. And so many friends."

"Maybe it doesn't have to be New York," Fred puzzled. "But I have to find a place where I can create music. I'm not myself if I don't have that outlet."

If Winnie noticed the hitch in his voice, she didn't say. And from that day forward, they set this new plan in motion. Winnie soon resigned from her job with the Troup County Chamber of Commerce, and after three and half years on air together, the couple ended their long-running program, *Songs for You*. Then they packed their belongings for the move to Columbus, one hour south of LaGrange.

With the connections they'd maintained, Fred and Winnie were given a warm homecoming. One particularly helpful friend was Nell Langley's boss, the internist, Dr. Dillard, who had gone out of his way to help the young couple get established. His son helped them find a rental duplex, and the doctor even offered Fred a chance to go to medical school. He, like everyone else, was impressed with Fred's intellect, and he was convinced the young man would make a fine physician. Fred, however, knew he was not cut out to be a doctor.

With medical school off the table, Dr. Dillard, who was also a member of the local school board, secured a job for Fred within the Muscogee County school system. It was a position that placed Fred in charge of music education for all the elementary schools in the district.

The afternoon it happened, Fred joined Winnie on the Langleys' front porch swing and told her the news. "Oh, honey. That's wonderful!" She threw her arms around him, filled with joy. "I knew things would work out for us here. I'm so relieved."

Fred didn't know what to say. It was a good job offer, but he was unable to silence the voice in his head. No matter how hard he tried to shake it, he kept hearing, *It's not Union Theological Seminary. It's not Broadway. It's not the Metropolitan Opera. It's not New York!*

Winnie leaned back. "What's the matter, honey? Aren't you excited?"

He gave it some thought before responding. "Grateful, of course. But excited?" He grew quiet again. He was young and creative and abundantly energetic. His mind had never really been challenged, and he still longed to head off for the Big Apple, where he hoped to *make it big.* "I've watched this happen to so many people, Winnie. They put their dreams on hold, and before they know it, it's too late."

"We're still young, Fred." Winnie gave her best smile. "Besides, you said it didn't have to be New York. Remember? You said as long as you get to create music, you could be happy. We both agreed to move here to Columbus. I thought this is what you wanted."

Fred shook his head. "Not exactly."

Winnie took his hand in hers and said softly, "Honey, I know this isn't everything we dreamed of. But it's a good start. In this position you'll not only have a career in music, you'll be helping children explore their own talents the way Madame and others have done for us."

With reluctance, Fred accepted the school position and began to shift from a student mind-set to that of a teacher. By the fall of 1957, he was earning a steady paycheck and decent benefits, so Dr. Dillard suggested the couple leave their rented duplex and purchase their first house. They found the perfect starter home, just a few miles from the Langleys, and with a loan from the ever-generous Dr. Dillard, they signed the purchase agreement.

Fred loved Winnie and relished seeing her so happy in her role as a homemaker. He also soon discovered how much he enjoyed teaching music to young students. As an educator, Fred proved successful. His classes provided a welcome and fun release from the more traditional courses the kids endured, and since he had been hired straight out of college, Fred could easily relate to the current trends and interests of the youth. Teaching was no easy gig though, and because Fred did nothing halfway, he poured immense passion into his role as their mentor. This often left him exhausted in ways he had never imagined, especially since he was also earning his master's degree at Auburn University at the same time.

Winnie noticed the way children responded to Fred. He had a natural gift of empathy, and his genuine spirit allowed him to connect deeply with people of all ages, adapting easily to various intellectual levels without ever making anyone feel less than him. He was charming and funny and talented and cool. The kids wanted not only to be around him, they wanted to *be* him.

This was especially evident one Saturday afternoon when Fred, who had barely been teaching a few months, gave his scrub bucket to two young neighbors eager to help the couple wash the family car. One of the kids accidentally sprayed the hose at Fred, only to have him race around the driveway, pretending to be upset.

Winnie chased after Fred, laughing. He let her catch him, wrapping her in his wet, soapy arms as she squealed. The children giggled as they covered the car in suds. Then Winnie said, to Fred, "You're going to be an incredible father."

Fred held her gaze as all sound seemed to disappear. "What did you say?"

"I said, you're going to be an incredible father. Our baby is going to love you to the moon and back."

"Baby?" His head spun dizzily.

"Baby," Winnie laughed. "Due in June."

The news slowly broke through to Fred, and he was overcome with pride. He gave his wife a kiss, right there in front of his red-faced students. Then he turned to them and announced, proudly, "We're having a baby. We're having a baby!"

The girls cheered, jumping up and down and showering the happy couple with the hose. The water trapped the dazzling sunlight, reflecting a rainbow of hues across the hood of the car. It may not have been stage lights or marquee signs, but to Winnie it was the most beautiful glow she'd ever seen. If ever there was magic in the world, this was it.

---

With news of the pregnancy Winnie focused all her efforts on creating a nursery, attending numerous showers, and preparing a welcoming nest for their child. By June 13, 1958, she had suffered an excruciatingly long and painful labor—endured solely by the never-ending flow of nitrous oxide—to shuttle their beloved baby into the world.

In the waiting room Fred joked with visitors who asked if he wanted a girl or a boy. "As long as the baby's not ugly, I'll be happy." His twist on the usual wish for a healthy child brought humorous relief to the nervous wait, but when he finally was allowed to see his new baby girl, he had a moment of panic. It seemed his lighthearted jokes had caused an ill-fated consequence. In the row of round-headed infants, his newborn's head had been distorted, stretched into a lopsided form with a sack of fluid swelling grotesquely beneath the scalp.

"What's wrong with her?" Fred asked the nurse in a panic.

"Nothing at all," she said with a smile, signaling an attendant to bring the baby out to meet the anxious father. "It's not unusual for the skull to shift under pressure, especially during a rough labor like Winnie's. This strong little girl of yours kept hitting the pelvic bone again and again for nearly two days. Plus, she's got a little bubble of fluid beneath the scalp, but that's nothing to worry about either. We call it caput. Very common."

Fred's worst fears surfaced as he took his baby from the attendant's arms. "Will she . . . will she be okay?"

"Absolutely," the nurse said and smiled. "Give it a little while. She'll be as perfect as can be."

Fred ran his palm across the baby's misshapen head. She carried a full cap of dark black hair, like her father, so long and thick that the nurse had pulled it back with a tiny pink bow. Now, as Fred held her, he no longer noticed the physical deformity at all. Even with the sac of fluid on her malformed skull, she was the most beautiful thing he had ever seen.

"She's already perfect," Fred said, moving to a chair as he fought tears. The baby's big blue eyes held his, and whether she could really focus on him or not, he felt truly seen. More than that, he felt loved. A love like nothing he had ever known. As he shifted her in his lap, she reached for his hand, wrapping her tiny finger around his and holding with a fierce grip as if to say, "I'm yours."

By the time they were allowed to enter Winnie's room, Fred had already developed a strong bond with his beautiful new baby girl. Together, the young parents named their darling daughter Allison Elizabeth in honor of their much-admired mentor, Madame Elizabeth Gilbert. As Winnie pulled her baby close, Fred stroked Allison's tiny hand. His gold wedding band was nearly as big as her fist, and his heart surged with protective adoration. As he gazed into the eyes of his child and his wife, he felt a powerful wave of gratitude. He leaned close, delivering gentle kisses to Winnie and Allison. Then he whispered, "You are the we of me."

---

With a family of three, Fred and Winnie were feeling happy and settled in Columbus, where Evelyn Land had become Allison's godmother and a loyal community surrounded the young family with love. They became involved in a large Methodist church near Fort Benning, where Fred played organ and served as choir director. His role in the schools continued to deliver the creative challenge he craved, and he became eager to build a more impactful music program for the kids of Columbus while also launching a television program to bring music education to a wider audience. When the newly constructed Richards Junior High School opened in 1961, Fred saw another golden opportunity. He took on the role of the school's choral director, creating a new choir for seventh and eighth grade girls.

Working directly with these adolescent singers proved to be a surprisingly ideal position for Fred. He was able to relate to their quirky personalities in a way many teachers failed to understand. And their talents blossomed. Soon the chorus began performing for school events and competitions. Then they started to receive invitations to sing at fairs and political rallies, ribbon cuttings and church revivals. They quickly developed a strong reputation for being the best in the state, and Fred continued to challenge the girls as they grew from grade to grade.

As it turned out, another perk to leading the choir was that Allison was growing up in the company of Fred's students, finding a real sisterhood. She often tagged along for the many practices and performances, and their father-daughter bond proved as tight as the connection Winnie and Allison shared.

People in LaGrange had always expressed such high expectations for Fred and seemed certain he would head off to the big city "to make something of himself." He certainly never imagined he'd be directing middle schoolers in Columbus. Yet the sounds he drew from them were heavenly, almost unnatural. He didn't talk down to the girls. Instead, he taught them using the same methods his college instructors had used, achieving a level of discipline inconceivable for such young students. As a result, the loyalty they offered him was devout. They truly loved Mr. Allen, and even better, he helped them learn to love themselves.

For most teachers this would be satisfying. But Fred was not like most teachers. His brain was always spinning, always searching for the next puzzle to solve. And so he began to wonder: If he could do this with a group of middle school girls, what could he do with a group of fully developed singers in New York? He had never forgotten the sound of that choir in Riverside, and he still longed to create music of that caliber.

One day in 1963, as the school year was in its final weeks, four-year-old Allison was playing in the living room while Winnie was carrying a box of baby clothes to the attic for storage. She had just reached the second rung from the top when Fred came crashing through the front door, shouting, "Winnie! Winnie!" The young mother, terrified by the sudden commotion, nearly lost her balance as she rushed back down the ladder, fearing the worst.

With her hair in a bandanna and sweating from the oppressive heat, Winnie ran toward Fred in a panic. "What? What's happened?!" She saw no blood, at least. "Are you okay? What's wrong?"

Fred held an oversize envelope in front of his wife and said, "I can't believe it. I've been accepted!"

Once Winnie caught her breath, she followed Fred into the kitchen, confused.

He was far too excited to sit down, and his sentences were flying faster than Winnie could process. "Union! I got into Union!" He lifted Winnie into such a big hug, her feet left the kitchen floor. Seeing the confusion on her face, he exclaimed, "Seminary! New York! I got into Union Seminary!"

"What do you mean you got in?" She laughed, nervously, squirming her way back to the ground. "When did you even apply?" As Fred told her the details, Winnie went pale. "You applied without telling me?"

Fred sighed, suddenly realizing Winnie had been blindsided. "Why would I have worried you with it? I never thought I'd actually be accepted." He couldn't stop smiling as he repeated, "Plus, I figured if I did get in, it would be a nice surprise."

"Surprise, indeed." Winnie forced a smile. "I . . . I don't know what to say."

Fred didn't seem to notice her hesitation. Instead he glided through the kitchen, overjoyed, repeating the good news as if he was still trying to accept it himself. "Can you believe it, Winnie? Union!" He waved the letter with enthusiastic celebration.

When Winnie didn't respond, Fred finally lowered his voice. "Aren't you excited for me?"

"Oh, goodness, yes. Of course I'm excited for you, honey. I'm so very, very proud of you! And happy. Yes, of course. I guess I'm just in shock. I mean . . . I didn't know you were even considering this." She read the letter again, sitting as she tried to process all it meant. "Fred, are you unhappy here? With our life?"

Fred stepped toward the window, where he spied the neighbors washing their dog on the front lawn. The scene reminded him of the day he had learned of Winnie's pregnancy. He looked at Allison, the physical evidence of years already passed since then. *Had he missed his chance to see what he could do with his talents?*

"Winnie, I love our life," Fred rushed to explain. "You and Allison . . . you're everything to me. And I'm proud of all we've accomplished here together. You've helped me build an incredible choir, not only at school but at church. But I want to see what more I can do out there. Union is the best music school in the country. It's not the kind of opportunity people walk away from."

Winnie stood, fighting tears. Around them were all the signs of a happy life. Allison's tiny clothes, folded neatly in the laundry basket. A magazine of party ideas for her upcoming fifth birthday. An herb-basted brisket in the oven, roasting for dinner. A burst of bloom from the outdoor flower gardens, tended lovingly in the early hours before the sun took hold. Sure, they had once dreamed of New York and stardom. But that was before they had Allison. Since then, they had built the perfect life right there in Columbus, and Winnie had never imagined it wasn't enough.

She looked at her husband, trying to understand his desire for more. "What does this mean for our family?"

Fred moved closer, wrapping her in his arms. "Well, I guess it means we're moving to New York." He kissed her forehead, gently, assuring her that he was with her and this was no solo gig.

Winnie lowered her voice. "We're so settled here, Fred. It's a lot to leave."

"It is," he agreed. "And we can always come back when we're ready."

"But what if you don't get a job here again? We were lucky to have all these pieces fall into place. It doesn't always happen that way. Not with a career in the arts."

Fred held Winnie's gaze and hoped his wife would understand. In the background "Because of You" played from the kitchen speakers, triggering a flood of memories from their college radio days.

"Dance with me?" Fred asked, swaying his wife to the music. Together, they moved slowly, singing along quietly to the song that had meant so much to them at LaGrange. As the final verse came to an end, Winnie looked up at her husband with a kind resolve.

Fred gazed into her eyes. "It isn't every day a man gets to dance with the love of his life."

Winnie softened her voice. "It isn't every day someone gets accepted into Union Seminary either."

Fred exhaled. "I know it's a lot to ask."

"It is," she admitted. "But what marriage doesn't involve some level of sacrifice? Besides, you would do the same for me."

As Allison ran to them, weaving between their legs with her adorable giggle, Winnie added one final thought. "I'll tell you what. I'm willing to give it a try. I'll leave my family, my friends. I'll take the risk for you, honey. Because I believe in you. And I love you more than words could ever say."

Fred lifted Allison between them, pulling them all together in a family hug. "I love you more, Winnie. I love you more."

"But Fred . . ."

"I should have known you'd strike a hard bargain," he teased, trying to lift any remaining worries. "What will it take? A pair of earrings? Frequent flights home to visit family? A flashy going-away party?"

Winnie wanted nothing of the sort. Instead, she looked at her daughter and, seeing ten years into the future, tried to picture Allison navigating adolescence so far from her extended family, her supportive and loving community—Winnie could not imagine how her own life might have been without such a strong foundation. She was also remembering the wild sights she had witnessed in Greenwich Village and the chaos of the crowded subway, the crime in the streets. What had once excited her now drew a mother's innate fear.

"Fred, we work with the girls in chorus. You see how fragile they are at that age. Rearing a teenage daughter is going to be difficult enough, even here in Columbus, but it could be downright dangerous in a place like New York."

"It *is* your nature to plan ahead," he said, laughing kindly.

"You knew that when you married me," Winnie said with a smile.

"I just want to give it a try," he countered. "See where music can take me. You knew that when you married *me*."

Another span of silence settled as Winnie shifted Allison to her hip.

"All right, honey. We'll do it. We'll follow you to New York, and we'll be your biggest fans. But please just promise we won't stay there forever. We'll move home before she turns thirteen. Deal?"

To Fred, this was a no-brainer. Without any worry about so many years in the future, he stole one more kiss from each of his girls and said, "Deal."

# *Fifteen*

In May 1963, the stars aligned to send this young family off to New York City. But first they would be spending the summer in Atlanta.

Fred had remained in touch with his Atlanta-based voice teacher, Ralph Erolle, a man who had introduced Fred to the city's famous Theater of the Stars. This prestigious program at Chastain Park was sponsored by Fox Theater and brought in some of the most acclaimed talents of the day. Ralph had encouraged Fred to audition, and after grueling rounds of competition with more than three hundred performers, Fred had been cast as one of only eight chorus singers to tackle the challenging productions.

Landing the coveted role proved to be both a tremendous honor and a major commitment. The entertainers were expected to perform eight shows a week and to master many of the latest musicals, performing acts from *Wildcat, Music Man,* and *Carousel* beneath the glow of the moon. The extra work would give the young family some much-needed money before heading off to New York for Fred's studies in the fall. Plus, it would give Fred the stage experience he had been missing, not to mention the reputable Actors' Equity card—proof he had officially become a professional.

As if that wasn't reason enough for Fred to be excited, a famed vocalist from New York City had been hired to direct Theater of the

Stars that summer. In his fifties by this time, Emile Renan was a renowned American stage director who had garnered countless accolades as an operatic bass-baritone. Well established with the New York City Opera, he frequently performed internationally.

Emile noticed Fred's uncommon talent while they worked together, and the elder vocalist complimented the young singer for his rich vocal tone and natural ear. The two soon began sharing regular lunch breaks at restaurants on Peachtree Street, where Emile mentored the promising performer. He was not a big man, but he was fit and affable, with a little mustache that was always perfectly groomed to frame his warm smile.

Being much older than the twenty-eight-year-old Fred, Emile was generous with his advice and encouraged the young performer to dream big. One night after a show, he walked with Fred through the broad outdoor amphitheater, chatting casually as they made their way beneath the haze of the fading lights. "You really do have it all. You know that?"

Fred stayed quiet, but deep down he wanted to smile. Not because he needed adoration but because he had always felt significant loss in his life from his own father's lack of understanding and encouragement. Here was Emile Renan stepping up to fill that void, telling Fred, *You have something special, and I value that in you.*

"I'm serious. You're a rare find, Fred. A true virtuoso. Tall, handsome, a talented singer and pianist. Dancer too. And don't tell me you don't see it. I mean, every night, you've got the audience in the palm of your hand!"

Fred, always humble, shrugged off the compliments and tried to shift the conversation back to his upcoming studies in New York.

But Emile was persistent. "It's true. A lot of people have one, maybe two star qualities. But you . . . you hit the jackpot." He put his arm around Fred with fatherly affection.

Emile had the charm and appeal of Clark Gable, with dark, pensive eyes and a penetrating stare that could shake even the strongest of souls. There was no easy way to ignore his incredible energy. He represented all Fred had ever wanted to be—smart, sophisticated, and successful—the absolute counter to the toxic male role models he had known from his own family. And now he was telling Fred that he could have it all too, if he wanted it. "Look me up when you get to New York. Let me connect you with the right people. Give you some lessons in my studio. See what happens."

The offer took Fred by surprise. By then he had learned that Emile was not only an opera powerhouse, he was an influential director and an esteemed voice teacher. This was not a man who had to *ask* people to take private lessons under him. This was a man with a waiting list too long to measure.

With Fred a bit thunderstruck, Emile wrapped up the conversation with another jovial laugh. Patting his protégé on the shoulder, he said, "Give me the chance, Fred. I'll turn you into the next Broadway sensation. Or, hell, Sinatra! The sky's the limit, son. Trust me."

As Fred made his way home that night, his head was in the clouds. It wasn't just a promising future in show business that had left him so dreamy eyed. It was the fact that Emile had called him "son."

# *Sixteen*

In September 1963, Fred, Winnie, and five-year-old Allison arrived in New York City just in time for the semester to begin. At that time The Juilliard School was located across the street from Union Theological Seminary, where Fred had been admitted to the prestigious School of Sacred Music, and Columbia University stood just down the street. With so many high-caliber institutions anchored in such close proximity, this district served as a thriving nucleus where intellectuals, theologians, and artists came together to study, worship, and create. In many ways, it was similar in spirit to Greenwich Village, but it carried a more affluent air to it, an elite professional blend of scholarship and faith that the rough-and-tumble Villagers seemed to be protesting against.

Not only had Fred been admitted to the School of Sacred Music, he had been given the rare opportunity to study at Union, Juilliard, and Columbia concurrently. The collaborative graduate program was offered to only the most elite students, and having been accepted, Fred was eager to face the challenge. As he headed off for his first day of class, he joked with Winnie, "What could be better than studying at Union, Juilliard, or Columbia? Studying at all three!" If he was nervous, he didn't let it show.

He was especially excited to study under one of the world's most preeminent organists, Dr. Claire Coci. It was the main reason he had wanted to attend Union, to learn from the best organ instructor he could find. Fred was a gifted pianist, accompanist, vocalist, and performer, but nothing had ever satisfied his creative needs quite like playing the organ. There was something about the multitasking required to maneuver the pedals and keys and stops all at once, mastering not only the melody but the pressures and pistons. Playing had felt as if he was controlling the breath of the instrument itself, and Fred had long dreamed of governing the dramatic inhales and exhales of an elaborate pipe organ.

When he entered Dr. Coci's studio, she was already dressed for an evening performance, greeting Fred in a navy gown that accentuated her petite figure. While older than her new student by a decade or two, she was an alluring woman who certainly knew how to hold a room. She wanted to know all about Fred's background, and when he confessed that he had never played an actual pipe organ, she seemed intrigued.

"But you were the organist for your church?"

He nodded. "Several churches in fact. Since sixth grade. Seems they could always find a pianist, but there weren't many people in town who knew the organ."

"Sounds a bit like my own story." Dr. Coci smiled.

As the conversation continued, the warmhearted instructor seemed smitten by Fred's down-home humility, saying, "I can tell you're the kind of man who enjoys an intellectual trial." By the end of their thirty-minute appointment, he had won her over.

As Dr. Coci escorted her new student to the door, she gathered her sheet music. "I've got a good feeling about this, Fred. I'm going to make a real organist out of you. Watch and see."

His first meeting with Hans Heinz at Juilliard went equally well.

Many considered Hans to be the premier tenor instructor at the famed music school, and as Fred began studying under Dr. Coci and Hans, as well as with top scholars at Columbia, some would have said it was all part of God's plan. Fred, however, could not have been as sure, as he was still searching for spiritual clarity.

As far as he was concerned, he had applied to the seminary not for theology but for music.

He had arrived in New York not by chance, but because he'd worked hard for it and dared to chase his dream.

He had been accepted to these three prestigious programs not because he had special connections or family money, but because he'd trained diligently for years, seeking out the best instructors and making the most of his time.

But the one piece he still could not explain was the fact that he'd been born with such unparalleled talents—both intellectual and musical—a truth he'd slowly learned to call his own. While he didn't believe in the superstitious fears that had plagued his own family, he couldn't help but wonder about the psychic midwife who pulled away his veil on the day of his birth. Throughout his childhood she had said he'd been sent to this world to do something important, that he had been given extraordinary gifts, and that God had a special plan for him. Now as he walked back through the courtyard at Union, he looked up at the familiar bell tower, and for the first time in his life, he wondered if one-eyed Mayhayley may have been right.

While Fred focused on his studies, Winnie once again created a loving home for the young family. Their assigned apartment was on the corner of Broadway and 121st Street, just across from the stately seminary. Behind that was the inspirational Riverside Church, where the couple had once sat in majestic wonder during a Sunday service. Its rhythmic bells chimed on the hour, giving song to the pretty park along the Hudson River. Because the church and seminary were a center of study for the world's leading ministers, lectors, and musicians, many families resided in facility housing, where a community of children offered friendship to Allison. With so many kids in residence, Riverside had opened a private kindergarten on the top floor and built a full playground for recreation.

Allison quickly adapted to her new school environment and was especially excited to discover that, from her classroom, she could see the big ships sailing in on the Hudson. Winnie walked her to school each morning, always taking time to count the boats with her young daughter. As the vessels plied their way up or down the river, Winnie never wondered where they had come from or where they were going. She simply enjoyed the view, feeling relieved to have found a way to keep her family knit tightly together in the midst of such a big city. And now her plans were falling into place. Winnie would be working right across the street, where Union's director of drama, Dr. Robert Seaver, had offered her a full-time position as his personal secretary—a role she was well prepared for, since she had taken shorthand, typing, and bookkeeping in high school.

The seminary had long been recognized as the nation's center for religious drama, and Dr. Seaver was well known for crafting many of the productions being performed in churches across the country. Winnie found him to be a talented man, fairly young but stern in his mannerisms. At the same time, he was flexible when Winnie needed time away from work to care for her young daughter, an essential perk given the fact that Allison had been struggling with sinus infections since the family's relocation.

Dr. Seaver also loved to work a stage. He'd earned a great deal of respect as a director, and Winnie took full advantage of this aspect of her job. She'd majored in drama at LaGrange College with a minor in voice, so working with the well-dressed eccentric afforded her the opportunity to learn the logistics of producing plays. It proved a wonderful outlet for her, both creatively and socially, as she collaborated with a steady stream of dynamic, creative people from all walks of life.

While Winnie stayed busy working and caring for Allison, the cross-academic program between Juilliard, Columbia, and Union demanded intense commitment from Fred. Another element adding an extra time crunch to the family schedule was the requirement that students serve as music director for a nearby church.

One afternoon Fred read the list of available positions to Winnie. While the idea of leading a choir excited him, the pressures of the schedule were mounting. "They're all in the suburbs," he said with a sigh. "The commute will take time. Time I don't have."

With her positive spirit, Winnie aimed to lift Fred's spirits. "You've always loved the process of building a choir, and you're good at it, honey. Just imagine working with a group that's already established and driven."

As it had done so many times before, her kindness brought relief. Indeed, by then Fred had taught musicians of all ages in many churches and classrooms. Most sang with passion and fervor, but many couldn't carry a tune or read a note when he first met them. It would be a nice change to work with a choir that, if Winnie was right, would consist of experienced vocalists with high expectations set by the interns from Union.

That week, Fred began to slog his way down the list. With each church visit, he became more disappointed by the poor-quality organs. He'd seen better in LaGrange, for heaven's sake. But just as he was about to surrender, he visited Bernardsville, New Jersey, a high-income community of equestrian retreats and weekend estates. After traveling an hour from the city by train, he took his time exploring the affluent boulevards where European-inspired architecture reminded him of Highpoint, the Lewis family residence he'd called home during high school.

Bernardsville's peaceful residential area felt far removed from the city's frenetic energy, a quality he believed Winnie would find appealing. With his expectations high, Fred made his way to the small stone chapel, a historic sanctuary that sat high on a hill and served as a well-loved landmark for the quaint downtown district. The church was a humble structure, one that reportedly had offered sacred space to settlers for at least a century.

Fred moved toward the arched entryway, pushed the latch, and gave his eyes time to adjust to the sudden change in light. Inside, he found a simple but beautiful sanctuary, a wooden space that originally had been built for a small congregation of about one hundred. But what caught his eye was the organ. It was small too, scaled to fit the modest space, but unlike many churches where the organ was kept tucked off to the side, this instrument had been placed lovingly at the back of the room, facing the choir. There was no official choir loft, just a series of folding chairs, but the organ's brass pipes flanked both sides of the apse, framing three tall stained-glass windows. Perhaps it was the way the sun filtered through the colored panes, illuminating all the iconic images, but as the window's cross glowed red above the pipes, all Fred could think was, *This is my church.*

The only problem with taking the part-time position at Bernardsville United Methodist was the commute. That first Sunday, Fred left his apartment at 3:00 a.m. in order to catch the subway out to the Hoboken terminal on the Hudson River Line. From there, he boarded the Erie Lackawanna Railway, scrolling a finger across the sign that read "Friendly Service Route" before claiming one of the vintage seats.

Suddenly it hit him: he was on a train headed to a church in one of the most affluent townships of New Jersey, an elite community where he'd been assigned to lead the choir as a student of both Union Theological Seminary and Juilliard—not to mention Columbia! He had been so busy managing his hectic schedule, trying to handle all the responsibilities of school and family while adjusting to this new academic life, he had not once taken time to let it all sink in. Now, as the train pulled him toward Bernardsville, he could see how far he had come from the impoverished Dunson Mill Village, from the lonely little boy who had been locked away from his cherished piano, from the sullen spirit who had been afraid his friends might learn the truth about his family's dark dysfunction. He had finally made it out of Georgia, out of the shadows of his own generational brokenness in LaGrange, and out from under the comfortable canopy of Winnie's family legacy in Columbus. He was finally making his own way.

Fred relaxed in his seat, feeling a strong sense of pride. Like the other early morning passengers, few in number as they were, he stayed quiet for the duration of the ride, taking in the view as the cars rattled away from the city and through more family-oriented communities. Slowly, skyscrapers were replaced with bigger and bigger lawns, not so unlike the neighborhoods he had known back home in Georgia.

The train would tirelessly deliver riders all the way to Bernardsville six days a week without fail, but on Sundays even the train celebrated a Sabbath, going only as far as Summit, which was still a thirty-minute drive from the church. Thankfully, a kind congregation member had arranged to meet Fred at the station.

As Fred stepped from the train, a tall and confident gentleman approached, offering a friendly handshake. "Glad to meet you, Fred." Then he broke into a cheerful smile. "Welcome to Jersey."

Fred couldn't help but notice the man's expensive Rolex and polished shoes. During the drive, Fred's host seemed kind and sincere, sharing the history of the church, the dwindling participation in the choir, and the need for revitalization. "I'm not the only one counting on you to whip us back into shape, Fred," he said. "We've got the talent, no doubt about that. Just need the right person to take the lead."

As Fred led the choir that first Sunday, he worked with a small group of vocalists, only a dozen members at most. But the congregation was welcoming and well trained, encouraging Fred with their shared vision to rejuvenate the music program.

As he'd hoped, Fred found the church members educated and diverse, cultured and engaged. They had high expectations and an even stronger work ethic. There was no doubt about it—this was the place for him. Now he only needed Winnie and Allison to find a place here too.

# Seventeen

It seemed Fred was off to a smooth start, leading the Bernardsville choir on Wednesdays and Sundays and making the most of his commute time by tackling academic assignments on the trains. While he had hardly a second to spare between school, church, and family obligations, he hadn't forgotten Emile Renan's invitation to look him up when he got to New York. Fred had no way of knowing if the opera star had been sincere in his offers to help him professionally, but there was only one way to find out. So one day he gave Emile a call. As the phone rang, he counted the coils on the cord, trying to calm his nerves.

"What a nice surprise, Fred. Wonderful to hear from you!" Emile's voice was kind and forthcoming, and he quickly extended an invitation for Fred to visit his exclusive Sutton Place apartment. Fred had heard of the upscale area where some of the city's most affluent residents held property. He'd even read about the enclave in J. D. Salinger's famous novel, *Catcher in the Rye*, and he'd sung about it in Rodgers and Hart's musical *On Your Toes.* But his cultural awareness did nothing to prepare him for the elegance he experienced when he was welcomed into Emile's luxurious world.

The building was only about nine stories tall, but everywhere Fred looked he found signs of excess and privilege. Two women gossiped beneath the awning. One wore a plush fur stole despite the early fall temperatures, and the valet soon announced the arrival of their driver, holding the door as the two women folded themselves into the back seat of a Rolls Royce.

Fred tried not to stare, but the opulence was mesmerizing, and as the doorman welcomed him into the decadent lobby, he envied the residents who called this place home. The polished marble floors ran beneath expansive crystal chandeliers countering their soft glow with an elaborate black-and-white design underfoot. Fresh floral centerpieces rose from antique urns, greeting visitors with the fragrant scents of autumn coneflowers and delicate tea olive blooms, a trigger that transported Fred right back to his grandfather's garden, where they would snip these same petals to make herbal teas.

Trying to shake his past and pretend he felt perfectly at ease, Fred found his way to the elevator, where he told the attendant he was there to see Emile. Fred squeezed into the cab and eavesdropped as a Realtor was trying to interest a couple in what she described as "one of the highly sought-after" units. "The original brownstones were constructed in the 1800s," she explained. "Kind of a rough area before the Vanderbilts and Morgans swept in and made it the place everyone wanted to be. Prices have been going up ever since. A surefire investment if ever there was one." The brass doors opened, and the trio exited the crowded cab. Fred sneaked a curious peek into the hall to see that the building was designed to hold only two large units on each floor. When the doors opened again, Fred stepped forth on the eighth floor.

He blinked nervously as Emile's wife, Doris, welcomed him with a kind smile. The gracious host led her young guest through the impressive foyer, directly into a section of the apartment where Emile housed his rehearsal studio. It had been rumored that some of the world's most admired singers frequently met here for practice, and as Fred entered, he wasn't disappointed. In rehearsal that day was the ever-popular

Eileen Farrell, the crossover superstar Fred and Winnie had heard perform in Chautauqua. She'd built a successful career as a gifted soprano and had recently become one of the most esteemed—albeit controversial—performers at the Metropolitan Opera.

"Eileen and I were just wrapping up here," Emile said, pointing Fred toward a plush green chair in the back of the studio while Doris left them to their work. "Take a seat there in the corner. You can watch and learn."

Fred wanted to pinch himself to make sure this was really happening. Emile turned to Eileen and said, "Mark my word. This kid is the next big thing. He's got it. I'm telling you. He's got *it*."

"You know what they say?" Eileen smiled at Fred. "When you've got it, you'd be wrong not to share it."

Fred could hardly believe his luck. Eileen had reached the pinnacle of opera performance by landing coveted roles with the Met, but here she was acting nothing like a diva. Instead, she was humorous and down to earth, tossing jokes as if she and Fred had been close friends for years. Never had he met a woman quite like her, and she defied all his preconceived stereotypes of stardom.

After a few more casual exchanges, Eileen adjusted her stance and began belting out the most impressively powerful soprano Fred had ever heard, mastering the voice of Leonora in Verdi's *La Forza del Destino* with an intensity that left his ears thrumming. As she sang the mournful Italian aria, her facial expressions revealed deep emotion as if she'd fully morphed into the grief-stricken Leonora, standing in the isolated cave, begging God to end her suffering.

*Pace, pace, mio Dio!*
*Cruda sventura*
*M'astringe, ahimè, a languir*[1]

Fred had studied this opera with Madame back at LaGrange, and the memory of its English translation returned with ease: "*Peace, peace, my God! Raw misfortune It pains me, alas, to languish.*" He closed his eyes and tilted his head back, letting Eileen's voice work its magic. The waves of sound rolled through him. Nothing in life ever moved him in the way he felt absorbed by music, and this was the best he'd ever heard. Fred still had chills when he opened his eyes, trying to imagine the impact such a passionate singer would have in a proper theater.

"Tell me you've ever heard a more emotional performance than that one," Emile said. "The vibrato! My heart's still pulsating!"

With a casual shrug, Eileen turned her stout shoulders toward Fred and said with a dimpled smile, "Don't let all this pomp and circumstance fool you. I'm a radio gal, Fred. My parents were vaudeville singers, for goodness' sakes."

Fred smiled, charmed by her humility.

"But look, if folks want to dress me up and pay me to sing, who am I to stop 'em?" Eileen rolled out a wholehearted laugh that made Fred feel as if he were in her family kitchen instead of a posh New York studio with two of the world's most elite vocalists.

Emile stroked his trim mustache. "There's nothing this woman can't do. Live concerts, studio recordings, opera productions. Not to mention her jazz albums, hit television shows. The Grammy! CBS can't get enough of her, I'll tell you that. You name it, she's proven herself!"

"I simply love to sing," answered Eileen. "Anything. Everything. It makes me happy. And if sharing a song makes others happy too, then I'm all the better for it."

Here Fred sat in a Sutton Place high-rise, in a space where money and fame seemed to be the norm, and yet the world's premier opera soprano was just as grounded as the people he knew back in LaGrange.

Maybe even more so. If an Irish girl who grew up in the world of vaudeville could perform at the Metropolitan Opera, then maybe, just maybe, Fred had a chance to make it big too.

As Eileen gathered her belongings and headed for the door, Fred dared to ask if she had any advice. Emile tilted his head as if he, too, wanted to hear her words of wisdom.

"Honestly, honey, I have no idea how I ended up in this position. Little bit of talent. Lot a bit of luck." She shrugged as if her one-of-a-kind abilities were not such a big deal and that the countless hours of training were just par for the course. "But if nothing else, I suppose I'm proof that anyone can make it in this business." She laughed again. Then she sighed and looked Fred in the eye. With a more serious tone, she added, "I guess my best advice would be that you can't let success wreck you. That's the trick. Keep your head clear. And leave it all on the stage. If you cheat an audience, they'll never forgive you. So you give 'em all you got. Every time. No excuses."

With that, she delivered motherly hugs to each of the men and was on her way.

"Wow," Fred said, feeling the entire room deflate once Eileen had departed.

"You got that right," Emile said. "Now aren't you glad you followed up with me, son?"

Yes, Fred was more than glad he had followed up with Emile. This was the life Fred wanted. For the first time, he had been in the room with people who shared his creative drive and vision. This was the kind of place where ideas flowed freely, where no one would question the constant brainstorm of creativity that swirled within him.

This was the beginning of everything.

---

After a few audition run-throughs, a proper mentorship was established. Convinced he had found "the next big thing," Emile agreed to take young Fred under his wing, teaching him everything he knew about the business. Just as Madame had arranged an even trade during Fred's high school and college days, Emile recognized Fred's talent and arranged to give him free lessons. In return, the young musician would work as an accompanist for Emile's students.

The offer seemed too good to be true. Fred had barely planted his feet in New York and he was already signing on to accompany some of the world's most accomplished vocalists during their private studio rehearsals. Surely, there had to be a catch. But Emile eased Fred's suspicions, insisting, "It's not complicated, Fred. I know talent when I see it. Give me a chance. Let's see where this takes us."

Emile quickly became the most trusted of companions. He expressed sincere care not only for Fred but for his family, welcoming Winnie and Allison into his home at times and giving Winnie a few vocal lessons too. With Emile's steady guidance, Fred was accepted into the New York opera and theater scene, building a reputation as a well-liked and easy conversationalist who was said to exude an authentic down-home charm. The time the two men spent together often led to deep, personal conversations and musings on life. No topic was forbidden, and Fred began to rely on Emile as the father figure he'd always needed.

Back in Bernardsville, choir members became increasingly impressed by Fred's uncanny ability to stretch their talents, pushing them to levels of performance they'd never imagined possible. Despite his frantic schedule, Fred never shorted them on time or attention, and he felt tremendous pride as their vocal skills improved dramatically.

As he played the organ and directed the choir, Fred took particular notice of a tenor named Mac, who exhibited great vocal strength. One day, after rehearsal, Fred commented to the minister about Mac's musical gifts. "You do know who he is, don't you?" The minister arched his brows, surprised to see Fred had no idea of Mac's profession. "That's F. L. McClure. Vice president of RCA Corporation."

Fred already had met many powerful people by that time, but he still could not hide his surprise. He couldn't believe the many coincidences he'd experienced since daring to leave Georgia. Doors seemed to be opening for him at every turn.

Not long after that conversation, Mac approached Fred with a cheerful handshake. "The choir has never sounded better, Fred. Glad you're with us."

"Ahh, well,"—Fred shrugged—"it's easy when we've got this much talent to work with."

"You've really got quite an ear. You know how to place people where they perform best. Get quality sound out of each of us. You have to be born with that kind of instinct. Can't be taught." Mac rolled his thumbs, pondering. "I've been thinking . . . you'd make a fine A&R man."

Fred was too green to know what an A&R man (artist and repertoire producer) was exactly, but he wasn't too naive to recognize a good opportunity when it came to him. While he certainly had no time to take on a new position at that moment, his friendship with Mac continued to develop as he pursued his studies, and every now and then Mac would shake Fred's hand and say, "Let me know when you're ready for that job at RCA."

One Sunday in December 1963, Allison and Winnie traveled to Bernardsville to sing in the special Christmas cantata. With Fred at the helm, the choir had already grown exponentially, with as many as forty singers now filling the small loft. Winnie and Allison had attended as frequently as possible throughout the semester. The people there were always kind to them, welcoming the trio into their homes for lunch after morning services. The choir families had become a tight-knit group, with their many children forming close relationships as well.

This particular Sunday, Jack and Mimi Rush suggested they stay to see the Christmas lights, an annual delight for their two children who were close in age to five-year-old Allison. The cobblestone streets glistened beneath strings of glistening white bulbs, and while the sidewalks weren't yet covered in snow, they held a magical holiday glow. The downtown shops had been draped in evergreen garlands, and candles illuminated nearly every windowsill.

"Reminds me of home," Winnie said, admitting the swells of homesickness sometimes got the best of her. "Fred used to lead the music program for the schools there. He had them perform the most beautiful Christmas show. The parents loved it, didn't they, Fred?"

Fred nodded but remained quiet. That life felt far removed from this one.

"So you and Fred met in college?" Mimi asked.

"We did," Winnie said, telling them about their old radio show and Fred's stellar reputation back in Georgia. "No one quite knew what to do with all his talent. He was a step above the rest of us, always."

"We feel the same way," Jack said with a smile.

Having never lived south of the Mason-Dixon Line, their hosts were intrigued, asking many questions about southern culture, food, and the landscape. When they learned that Winnie had left Columbus to attend LaGrange College, they wanted to know more about the school.

"It wasn't my first choice," Winnie admitted. "I didn't even want to go to college. I was ready to head straight to Broadway or Hollywood." She laughed. "But Mother and Daddy had always emphasized the value of an education, and there was no way they were letting me leave home without it."

"Sounds like my parents," Mimi said, sharing stories of her own Ivy League studies.

As they made their way into a downtown café, Winnie followed Mimi to a back table where she gathered the kids with a story. "I'll tell you something funny," she began. "At LaGrange, we were all expected to dress for dinner. The girls had to wear heels and crinolines. It was top-notch."

"What's a *crinolines*?" Allison asked, claiming a chair near her friends.

Winnie laughed, "Oh, you know, sweetie. Those big slips that make my skirts stand out."

Allison smiled. She'd spent many days playing dress-up with the silly hooped petticoats back in Columbus, but apparently she couldn't imagine her mother wearing them to dinner every night.

"Anyway," Winnie continued. "We had to wear those big, fancy crinolines and high heels, and we had to walk down a set of very steep stairs to go into the dining hall. At the foot of the steps was one of those waiter doors—you know the kind that swing both ways?"

The children nodded.

"So it was my first day, and I was feeling pretty upset that Mother and Daddy had left me. In LaGrange of all places. Plus, I know you probably won't believe me, but I was shy. Very shy."

Mimi's brows lifted as if she definitely didn't believe her.

"I had moved in a couple days before my roommate, so I had to go to dinner by myself. I was feeling very nervous as I walked down those stairs. Of course, you probably know what happened next."

No one answered, but the kids' eyes held Winnie's, eager for the rest of the story.

"I tripped, of course. Fell against those swinging doors with a ridiculously loud crash. The doors went flying open, and out I came, rolling into the dining hall like a flop doll."

Everyone around the table laughed, albeit politely.

"I was horrified, I tell you. There I sat on the dining room floor, my skirt all puffed out, and every eye right on me."

Allison's brow furrowed. "Then what happened?"

"No boys were allowed in the dining hall, thank goodness. You might think the girls would have rejected me from the start. But you know what happened instead? I looked up and saw a friend I had known since childhood. She walked over and helped me to her table, and she never left my side. That's what's special about the South. You kind of get used to the feeling that someone's always looking out for you."

"That would be a comfort," Mimi said.

"Yes," Winnie answered. "Yes, it was."

# Eighteen

Since moving to New York in September, Allison's health had been failing. It all started with a weekend visit to the Statue of Liberty, where she led her father by the finger, pulling him up the narrow stairwell to take in the view from Lady Liberty's crown. As Fred followed his five-year-old toward the top of the statue, her nose had begun to bleed. They were only about halfway up the stairs when, worried, Fred pulled his young daughter into his arms and carried her back to the ground level, fighting against the thick summer crowds. He assumed the higher altitude was affecting her sinus pressure, but then it happened again weeks later, when Allison rode on her father's shoulders to see the city sights. She was laughing, listening to a jazz band play in the open air, when the blood began to flow.

In the months since, Allison had begun to suffer chronic sinus infections, with nosebleeds that were becoming worse by the day. Due to painful relapses of strep throat, she had taken numerous rounds of antibiotics, but nothing seemed to help.

Because Fred's internship was unpaid and Winnie's job was the primary income source for the family, it was difficult for her to leave work every time Allison needed extra care. Of course, skipping class was not an option for Fred either, so juggling their busy lives was becoming more complicated by the day. Winnie tried to stay positive, but she missed having her extended family nearby to lend a hand.

One frigid January day in 1964, a blizzard dropped more than a foot of snow on the city as Allison's nose began to hemorrhage profusely. Winnie and Fred were at home due to snow closures, and both parents tried their best to stop the bleeding, but nothing worked. Not ice packs. Not pinching. Not warm towels. Nothing. Still at five years of age, months of illness had transformed Allison from a healthy and vibrant kindergartner to a pale, thin version of her former self. Her immune system had become weak and her body frail. Winnie's worries intensified as her daughter now struggled to swallow even the smallest sips of water.

The seminary had a staff physician who had treated Allison's infections in prior months. But when Fred called for help, the doctor explained that the snowdrifts were waist-deep and the entire city had come to a rare standstill. "I can't get out tonight," he insisted. "I'll see her when the roads are cleared."

Fred explained the dire situation, his voice cracking with intensity. He begged the doctor for assistance, fear shaping his words. Behind him, Winnie tried to comfort their daughter, swaying her in the rocking chair and singing sweet songs to try to ease their worries. But as the hours ticked away and the blood continued to spill, Winnie was beginning to panic. She pinched Allison's wrist tenderly, distressed to see her child's skin remain peaked, a sure sign of dehydration. "Try again, Fred. She's got to see a doctor!"

Deep furrows formed across Fred's brow. As the blood still streamed from his daughter's nose, he could barely keep his composure. He was a sensitive soul who felt what she felt—fear, pain, exhaustion. And he could not bear knowing Allison was suffering.

He dialed again. This time, the doctor made it clear he did not want to be disturbed. "It's just a nosebleed," the man said in an even voice.

"No," Fred argued. "It's much worse than that. She's lost a significant amount of blood and it's not slowing. You know she's been sick for months, and she's running a high fever again. Burning hot."

"Then take her to the hospital," the doctor said. "Emergency room."

As Fred dropped the receiver back in place, he gave Winnie a hopeless grimace.

Winnie's lips drew tight and tears pooled in her eyes, a rare sign of distress from his optimistic partner. When he explained how rudely the doctor had responded, Winnie became livid.

"Unbelievable," she said. "What kind of doctor would behave this way? Dr. Dillard would be over here to help us in a split second!"

The reality hit hard. They were a thousand miles from home, their daughter was in danger, and the doctor hired to help didn't seem to care enough to do so.

Fred moved to the chair and pulled Allison into his arms. Her skin hot to the touch, her eyes sunken and dull, his little girl had become too weak to press the dish towel to her nose without assistance.

Many thoughts crossed Winnie's mind as Fred tried unsuccessfully to phone for a cab. Finally, after several attempts, he hung up and looked out the window for at least the tenth time. With white-out conditions, not a living soul was seen. "Grab a coat," Fred said as steadily as he could manage. "We'll have to walk."

Winnie gathered all the winter gear they had, hoping it would be enough to make it through the blizzard. Fred cradled Allison in his arms just as he'd done many times before, but this experience proved so much bleaker in the dark, with Allison's eyes closed and her weak body lying limp against his chest as he carefully navigated the snow-packed sidewalks. Winnie kept close beside them, shadowing Fred's steps and pulling the blood-soaked scarf around her daughter's fa̧ce as the wind gusts blasted them all. Now the parents' fears were getting the best of them as the entire city seemed cloaked in an eerie, white silence, an ominous reminder that despite the millions of people who called this place home, the worried young couple would be facing this challenge on their own.

St. Luke's Hospital was just five blocks from the seminary, but by the time they reached the emergency room, their faces were numb and chapped. Winnie and Fred had lost all feeling in their damp feet, and Allison collapsed onto the registration desk, too spent to lift her head. Still, the medical staff did not call them back for treatment as the young couple had expected. Instead, Fred and Winnie took turns holding Allison in the waiting room, watching the dark hours creep by as her body fought a fever-induced sweat. They did not sleep at all, and their worries grew by the minute. They begged the admissions clerk for help, but the blizzard had left the unit short on workers, and while the stranger seemed sympathetic to their situation, she offered no solution.

It wasn't until the following morning that a red-eyed intern finally examined Allison. By that time, she'd lost so much blood that her skin held little color. "We need to remove her tonsils," the young surgeon explained, suggesting they schedule the operation for that very day.

Winnie was a wreck. "She's so weak," she insisted. "And isn't it a bad idea to cut when there's an infection?"

Fred, too, expressed concern, and as the intern's words became somewhat erratic, Fred and Winnie began to lose confidence in his expertise. Allison was quite small for her age, even in her healthiest state. Aside from running a fever and losing blood for more than twenty-four hours, she hadn't been able to eat and had barely accepted any fluids. As Winnie questioned the plan of treatment, the doctor's opinion gradually shifted. Finally, he yielded. "I understand," he said, agreeing to postpone the surgery and focus on healing the infection first.

With great relief, Winnie and Fred watched as the medical staff gave Allison intravenous fluids and a strong course of antibiotics. The next day, once the streets had been cleared by snowplows, the family left in a cab with prescriptions to keep the bacteria at bay.

After two long and sleepless nights, Fred went to class, and Winnie called her mother.

Mrs. Langley tried to calm Winnie's nerves, but having worked for an internist all those years, she, too, was worried about her granddaughter's health. She listened patiently as Winnie shared her frustrations over the phone.

"I don't want to lose another day of pay, but I can't send Allison to school like this. I've called the entire list of sitters. No luck."

"Oh, honey. I should be there," Nell said. Then, after a pause, she added, "How would you feel about me coming up for a while?"

Winnie's tone lifted. "You'd be able to do that?" As much as she prided herself for being independent, she couldn't hide her relief.

"Well, I'll have to talk to Dr. Dillard, of course, but you know how good he is to us. Surely I can arrange a leave of absence, long enough to help you nurse her back to health."

After the hospital visit, Allison's infections continued, and the stress continued to build for Fred and Winnie. Stretched thin under the increasing life pressures, they were relieved when Nell booked her flight to New York.

"Six weeks' leave," Nell said, throwing her arms around her daughter and holding Winnie tight at the airport. They had always maintained a close relationship, but now Winnie needed real help, and her mother was there to deliver. There were no questions asked. No guilt imposed. Nell was genuinely happy to spend six straight weeks with her granddaughter and eager to help the young couple.

With her mother in town, Winnie was able to focus on work and catch the family up financially. Fred was able to put his full attention back on school and church, and all seemed to be in balance again, even if precariously so. As those days turned to weeks, Allison slowly showed signs of improving. Then before they knew it, Nell's leave was nearly up, and it became time to decide the next steps.

One evening, Winnie and Nell were organizing Allison's toys. "I'm so happy you've been here, Mother. I can't even think about you leaving."

"She's getting better now, honey." Nell stacked puzzles onto a shelf. "Everything's going to be fine, I promise."

Winnie sighed. "I'm worried, Mother. She still has nosebleeds, and I just can't shake the feeling . . . she could have died!" This was the first time she'd voiced those fears, and the truth pinched her words to a low, soft place. "Crazy thing is . . . my whole life, all I ever wanted was to move somewhere like this. And now that I'm here . . ."

Nell listened patiently.

Allison's laughter flowed from the living room, where she and Fred were playing a new card game. Winnie leaned from the tiny bedroom, observing how Allison worshipped her father and feeling grateful Fred never shorted her his affection or attention.

As Winnie returned to sorting a cradle of dolls, the church bells rang from Riverside. "It's not that I don't like it here. I do. Truly, I do. Allison loves her school. The kids are cultured and advanced. She's seen so many things already. Museums and performances and all the new foods. It's been a good experience for her. Don't you think? For all of us?"

"Honey, of course I do." Nell put the final puzzle box into its proper place and began to rearrange the picture books. "You know what your daddy always says. If you ever have the chance to get an education or to travel, you best take it."

"Exactly. And that's why we're here. To make the most of these opportunities."

Nell sensed the sadness behind Winnie's tone. The somber notes said more than the words that carried them. "But?"

Winnie sighed and placed Allison's favorite doll atop her pillow. "But . . . we never imagined Allison would get sick. I don't know if it's the germs at school or just city life in general, but she was never ill back at home."

Her mother nodded. "Something to think about."

"Well, that's just it. I *have* been thinking. And I'm thinking that maybe Allison and I should move back to Columbus for a while. Fred and I have discussed it. As much as we don't want to be apart, we think it might be best if I find the right care for her back there, where the doctors know and love her."

A long pause settled between them as Winnie leaned through the doorway to take another peek at Fred and Allison. They were telling jokes and playing cards as if all was safe in their world. But Winnie couldn't quiet her fears. That night in the emergency room still haunted her.

"You know you're welcome to stay with us, sweetie. If you think that's for the best."

Winnie turned off the lamp on the nightstand, her eyes still locked on Fred and Allison. "I don't know what's best, Mother. All I know is, we want our daughter to be well again. She's our whole world."

Nell brushed Winnie's hair back with a tender hand. "Talk it over a little more with Fred. Maybe you can get Allison through the school year and then come home, even if it's just for the summer. Might lift your spirits a bit and give her health a boost."

Between Fred's studies, her job in Dr. Seaver's office, and Allison's ongoing health issues, as well as her own schoolwork, the end of May came all too soon for Winnie. Before she knew it, Winnie found herself holding close to Fred in the airport lobby, wishing she had another solution.

"How am I going to make it three months without you?" Fred asked, handing Winnie her carry-on bag.

Trying to stay positive for Allison's sake, she spoke with a perky smile. "We'll write. And we'll take pictures so you won't miss a moment."

Fred nodded, accepting a sweet series of kisses on his cheek from his frail daughter.

"And we'll call once a week. Every Saturday." Winnie's voice caught, revealing she wasn't as certain of their decision as she pretended to be and wishing long-distance calls weren't so expensive.

"Yep." Fred brushed Allison's hair back from her eyes, tucking the soft brown curls behind her little ear, trying to focus there so he wouldn't look at his wife and show her the tears in his own eyes. If he did, he knew he'd likely beg them both to stay right there with him.

Winnie gave Fred a kiss. Then a long, tight hug. "We'll be back in time for school to start."

"Promise," Fred said, able to hold her eyes with his once he heard the resolve return to her voice.

"Promise." Winnie kissed him again, both saying "I love you." Then the attendant made the final boarding call, and it was time for Fred to let his family go.

# *Nineteen*

By the time Winnie and Allison arrived at the Langley home, a handwritten letter was already waiting, addressed "Dear Partner." Winnie held the note to her heart and hoped the separation would not weigh too hard on their marriage. She was a practical person who'd watched other families deal with much harder conditions, so she focused on all that was positive in their relationship and did what needed to be done. For Allison.

Throughout the summer of 1964, letters came and went between Fred and Winnie. One sentence at a time they declared their devotion to one another while Winnie reassured Fred that Allison's health was improving steadily under Dr. Dillard's care. Her strength and complexion were slowly returning to normal, and the chronic infection that had attacked her immune system for nearly a year was finally beginning to clear. Much to Winnie's relief, she was starting to see their daughter thrive again.

Back in New York, Fred was lonely but flourishing too. He was developing closer friendships with his classmates and choir members, yet he was also feeling restless. He wasn't himself without Winnie, and while the extra hours allowed him to focus on his many endeavors, the time in between was too vacant. Too quiet. Too still.

"I'm feeling unsettled," he wrote to Winnie. "Just once, I'd like to be pushed, challenged."

In addition to the dual music program at Juilliard and Union, he was also a doctoral student in the psychology department of Columbia University, one of the oldest and most influential programs in the country. But even with the grueling academic demands, his position with the church in Bernardsville, and his work with Emile, Fred was still left with too many nights alone in his quiet apartment. With Winnie and Allison still down south, the lonely hours elevated Fred's anxieties. He had never felt so troubled. His sleep had become fraught with nightmares, and he'd begun suffering severe insomnia. Trying nearly everything to control his thoughts, he worked around the clock to rehearse, study, accompany, conduct, and compose. But it wasn't the same without his family.

"The only way to cope with the loneliness is to avoid being alone," he wrote to Winnie. His classmates and choir members had been especially generous to the young musician while his family was away. But with little sleep, the days became long and the nights even longer, especially with the haunting dreams. His nightmares returned again and again, always playing out the same recurring scene. In it, a church steeple shone above Fred, waking him in fear and leaving him disturbed every morning. He had begun paying close attention to steeples around town, hoping to find clarity, but none resembled the unique form that continued to disturb him in the early hours—a tall, narrow, brown-shingled spire with a bright golden cross.

Trying to quell the spin, Fred had begun to walk along the Hudson River during short breaks between classes. He would watch the ships, recalling the whimsical conversations he'd shared when Allison was still in New York. With his daughter on his knee, they'd sit and laugh, imagining all sorts of fantastical cargo. "See that one there," Fred would say. "That captain sailed all the way from Yippi-skippiville." The silly word would draw an eruption of giggles from Allison. "It's true," Fred would tease, as the two pretended together. "He's carrying crates of purple turtles. And they can fly! But that's top-secret information, so you can't tell anyone. Not a soul." He'd make her pinkie promise to secrecy before he'd tell her about the turtles' private island in the clouds. Finally, he'd ask, "Do you know how to say 'I love you' in Yippi-skippi?" Allison would make a string of ridiculous guesses, all in the make-believe language. There was no end to their fantasy and fun. But watching the ships now wasn't at all the same. Without his little girl, the magic was missing.

One afternoon, while quietly observing the ships slide downriver, Fred took a seat on one of the park benches. A young man sat on the other end of the bench. Fred had seen him there before, walking the same path beneath the shadows of Riverside, Juilliard, and Union, but he had never come across him on campus, much less in class.

The guy had a kind disposition, greeting other park visitors with small talk, just as he had offered a friendly "Good afternoon" to Fred. His accent revealed traces of the Caribbean, making Fred think of Desi Arnaz and the many nights he, Winnie, and Allison would laugh while watching episodes of *I Love Lucy.*

From the opposite end of the bench, the man stared out at the water and said, "It's really something, isn't it? How big and deep the river is. How small and insignificant we are in comparison."

It was rare for Fred to meet anyone who sat and pondered things the way he did, much less one who expressed such deep thoughts on a whim. Perplexed, he extended his hand. "Fred Allen."

"I'm Pete," the man said. Then he looked back to the water. "Ever wonder where those boats have been? Where they're going?"

Just like that, Fred exhaled. It was a moment of connection, a comment that made him feel as if there were other people who saw the world as he did. Their conversation started slowly, with general talk of the weather, the ships, Fred's work, and Pete's new job as a professor at Columbia.

Then the strangers went their separate ways, but each day when Fred walked by, there was Pete, and in time a friendship began to form between the two scholars. It was a comfortable fit and one that filled some of the gaps between school and church while also giving Fred the deep intellectual conversations he craved. And, of course, there was also Emile. Rather than return home to his empty seminary apartment, Fred was spending more and more time at Sutton Place, working to perfect his craft and building a broader circle of friends who made their living in the arts.

But by summer's end, the pangs of separation had grown even more intense as Fred made a call to his family back in Columbus. "Allison is doing so much better," Winnie said. "Honey, we definitely made the right choice by coming home. They said she should be strong enough for surgery by Christmas. Maybe sooner. Dr. Dillard's trying to increase her weight and keep her temperature down for more than a couple weeks at a time."

Fred's voice grew heavy. "I miss you both so much. Are you saying you can't come back until after Christmas? We're a family, Winnie. We belong together."

"We miss you too, honey. More than words can say." At that Winnie bit her lip to keep from crying, as there seemed no better option for keeping Allison healthy.

After an emotional discussion, the couple agreed. Winnie stayed in Columbus, strengthening Allison's energy for the bilateral tonsillectomy that took place in October. Fred flew down for the surgery, giving the family a much-needed reunion, albeit a brief one. As his little girl opened her eyes, still groggy from anesthesia, she reached for Fred's hand.

Then he flew down again for Christmas, relieved to find his young daughter out of pain for the first time in more than a year. Bright-eyed and full of energy, she bounded toward him with a big hug.

While he was due to return to New York for his final spring semester, Fred agreed with Winnie that Allison should stay and complete her first-grade year in Columbus. She had been so happy in Georgia, surrounded by friends and family, and her health was finally returning. Plus, Winnie had taken a job teaching kindergarten in order to help support the family. Fred and Winnie knew all the reasons why this arrangement made practical sense, but emotionally they were struggling with the plan to spend another semester apart.

At the request of the family minister, the couple had agreed to sing for the church Christmas program before Fred's return flight to New York. Since it was a last-minute addition, they had gone to the sanctuary for a quick rehearsal. The annual holiday concert had become a community affair, with children dressed as haloed angels and a steep competition among the mothers who wanted their infants to land the part of baby Jesus. But for the moment, the sanctuary was quiet, with only Fred at the piano as Winnie prepared her voice for song.

With his eyes on his wife, Fred began to play and sing one of her favorites:

Have yourself a merry little Christmas,
Let your heart be light.
From now on your troubles will be out of sight.

Winnie joined in, their voices lifting in tenderhearted harmony as the evergreen garlands filled the air with the crisp scent of pine. Red poinsettias captured the holiday mood, as did an ornamented tree standing next to the piano, its lights twinkling their sentimental glow.

Yes, Fred and Winnie were still completely in love. They were still a perfect match, and music still served as the bond that kept them both in sync. Fred's heart pounded as she offered him her bright and loving smile. Together, they sang:

Through the years we all will be together
If the fates allow.[1]

When Fred struck the final notes, Winnie slid close beside him and pulled his hand in hers. "We're better together," she said softly. He gave her a kiss and agreed.

In the morning Fred would board a plane for LaGuardia. Winnie and Allison would wave goodbye again. His wife and daughter would finish the academic year in Columbus. Fred would wrap up his graduate studies at Union and Juilliard while continuing his doctoral work at Columbia. Then when the semester ended in May, Allison would be healthy, he would find a job in New York, and they all would be together again. Fred thought, *If the fates allow.*

# *Twenty*

Back in New York, Fred was developing closer friendships not only with his Bernardsville choir members but also with his Union classmates. They had become a tight-knit group, but they all had families of their own. Pete, a self-professed womanizer, was Fred's only friend who seemed to have hours to spare. The charming bachelor spent most of his time at bars, mingling with beautiful ladies, so Fred began to meet him for drinks—an option that seemed better than wrestling loneliness in the empty apartment. Other university scholars would frequently join them, making for a diverse crowd of academics who enjoyed sharing ideas more than anything else. Fred felt safe and comfortable in their circles, and he'd learned to look forward to the deep conversations and debates. Most nights, he'd stay until the others had found their evening match. Each couple would make their way home in one another's arms, and Fred would go back to the seminary to compose songs or write in his journal, a practice he'd maintained since childhood.

In time Fred had established a trusting friendship with Pete, and the two intellectuals slowly began to share their difficult pasts—in Fred's case, truths he'd only confessed to Winnie.

"I don't know, Fred," Pete confided one night. "I doubt anyone can understand, unless they've lived it." He took a beer from the bartender.

"Try splitting one egg to feed your family. My sister, my mother, and I would take about one bite each, and that was all we'd have. The whole day. Talk about hungry."

"I never had it quite that hard," Fred admitted. "My sister used to warm a can of stewed tomatoes or open a can of fruit. It was never enough to stop my stomach from growling, but . . . we ate."

"We weren't always poor," Pete explained. "That's what made it even harder, I think. My family had owned a major company in Havana. We were upper crust, man. Big house. New cars. You name it. But then Castro took over and . . . everything changed."

Pete took a sip of his beer and stared off into the distance. It was a disconnected gaze, the kind that Fred knew all too well. One that signaled pain and suffering. And stories too dark to share. But Pete shared them anyway.

"My father was killed. Castro's guys were after us, and we had to run. Leave everything. Everything. You know what it's like to run for your life? I was just a kid, really. Sixteen when I finally landed here in New York. All alone. Had to start over from scratch. I know people say that all the time, but I'm not exaggerating when I tell you I didn't have a nickel to my name."

Fred listened, realizing that, by comparison, his own experiences may not have been all that bad. He drifted back in time, remembering his parents giving him the keys to their old Ford. It wasn't much of a wedding present by some standards, but it was the most valuable thing Grady and Velma had to offer. And they had given it to Fred. Sure, the engine stalled when he came to a stop, and the muffler rattled as he drove around LaGrange, but looking back now, Fred could see the sacrifice his parents had made for him, even if it was too little and too late.

As Pete and Fred shared stories, they built an understanding. Winnie had always been a compassionate soul, but she didn't know the pain Fred carried. How could she? She'd lived a different kind of life, one without trauma. But Pete? Pete knew suffering. And that was enough to start Fred's healing, a journey that would prove to be much more challenging than anything he had ever done.

Back in Columbus, Winnie continued to teach and care for Allison until the summer rolled around and Fred's studies drew to a close. After two years of graduate work, his chance had finally come to perform his master's recital at Riverside Church, where six of Dr. Coci's students presented their masterpieces for the city's top scholars and musicians.

In May 1965, as Fred took his place at the organ, he could hardly contain his excitement. He had long dreamed of playing this instrument—considered by many to be one of the best organs in the world. Now he gave his all to Louis Vierne's Organ Symphony No. 1 in D Minor, a powerful piece Fred had perfected under Dr. Coci's careful instruction. As his hands and feet mastered the stops and pistons, the instrument became Fred's voice. Just as he had been moved to tears as a younger man when he'd first entered this beautiful sanctuary, his body now hummed with the tonal vibrations, his heart throbbed with deep emotion. When he reached the powerful crescendo, the applause of the audience washed over him. He looked out at the many friends and mentors he had gained in the two years since leaving Georgia, and his spirit filled with pride. He had done it! He had dreamed of playing this organ, studying at Union, working with a gifted choir, creating music in New York City . . . and he had achieved every one of those goals! The only thing missing was Winnie.

With Fred's graduation on the horizon, it was time to make a career decision, but first, the Bernardsville congregation surprised the young couple by hosting a graduation party. Like all things with the elite community, the party was no small affair. They flew Winnie up for a champagne celebration at Lincoln Center, which in the next year would become the breathtaking new travertine home of the Metropolitan Opera House. The generous hosts had filled the room with floral centerpieces and delicious hors d'oeuvres. The choir members, their families, and nearly the entire church congregation gathered in the solid-glass building to celebrate.

There, they offered Fred a permanent position as their part-time music director and organist. In addition, Mac McClure again insisted Fred was the man for the A&R job with RCA. And when another friend recommended an almost-unheard-of affordable rental in Bernardsville, it became evident that the family was meant to stay up north.

After the party Fred and Winnie took their time as they walked the long way back to their seminary apartment. Strolling alongside Central Park in the crisp night air, Winnie leaned close to her husband, and Fred draped his arm around her shoulder. Together they reminisced about their romantic weekend away from Chautauqua all those years ago. How free they had felt then. Full of dreams and summer love.

"I've always believed you could do anything you set your mind to," Winnie said, turning to reveal the streetlights reflecting in her bright eyes. "And now look at all you've accomplished, Fred. A master's degree from Union, not to mention the one you already had from Auburn. Plus your studies at Juilliard and Columbia."

"Now a job offer from RCA." Fred smiled, the good news still sinking in.

"And . . . leading a church in one of the most affluent suburbs, a choir stacked with talent. Your work with Emile that seems to be leading you straight to the top."

Fred, too, felt proud. As a boy, his life had centered on meeting his basic needs and doing whatever it took to survive. He'd always been determined never to let Winnie and Allison know that kind of suffering. Now with two jobs on the table, he'd found a way for him to continue exploring his musical talents while also providing his family the security he'd always craved. Plus, Winnie would be able to pursue her own talents in the choir and continue lessons with Emile. Maybe they really could have it all.

It didn't take much to convince Winnie this was the best decision. After all, she, too, loved New York and had grown close to their many friends from the Bernardsville choir, but she was a mother above all else, and she feared bringing Allison back to the city that had made her so sick, not to mention her original concerns about someday rearing a teen so far from the safety of their southern community. While she didn't voice any of these thoughts, Fred knew her well enough to know what she was thinking.

Pulling her close, he aimed to reassure her. "Don't worry. We won't be here forever."

# *Twenty-one*

During the summer of 1965, Winnie, Fred, and Allison quickly settled into a comfortable new rental home in Bernardsville. Allison soon started second grade and was instantly accepted by her peers, many of whom she'd already gotten to know at church. Winnie focused her efforts on the family, and Fred launched his career with RCA while continuing to lead the choir on Wednesday evenings and Sundays.

The prosperous Bernardsville community was filled with the kind of people who had big ideas and even bigger wallets, so when Fred suggested rebuilding the church's organ, the congregation came through with a resounding "Amen!" plus the funds to get it done.

Winnie took pride in helping Fred with the music program and performing in the choir under his direction. She was once again singing solos, much to the admiration of the church members, who became increasingly impressed with the family's extensive talent. Allison, too, was becoming a gifted singer whose abilities were being refined. With one foot in the bustling cultural center of New York City and the other planted within the quiet New Jersey suburb, the family had found their fit.

Each weekday Fred would tackle the commute to RCA Recording Studios on 23rd Street in downtown New York. His new position seemed a world away from the public schools he'd left in Columbus, and he couldn't have been more excited to see what the future might hold. Knowing Fred's talents, Mac had hired him at a higher level than the typical entry role, so Fred was given his own office suite, a personal secretary, and a hefty expense account. Of course, he had a lot to learn from the more experienced producers who had worked with a plethora of talented stars, but Fred was an eager study and determined to rise to the challenge.

As one of the gatekeepers, Fred would help decide if a singer should be offered a record deal. Then, once he signed a new act, he would work to build the artist's career. As a result, Fred heard dozens of auditions a week, but occasionally Fred found himself at odds with his fellow producers and executives. One day those in power listened to one of the new artists being pitched. Excited, Fred raved to the other producers, his enthusiasm palpable. They all agreed the young woman presented unusually tremendous vocal talent. But unlike Fred, they took one look at her and said no.

"Admit it," Fred argued. "She's got one of the strongest voices you've ever heard."

"Doesn't matter," another producer said. "She's got no sex appeal. We sell a package, Fred. A fantasy. Someone who can grace an album cover and bring fans to a frenzy from the stage. This," he said, pointing through the glass at the woman, "won't do."

As Emile had said back in Atlanta, many people have one, maybe two star qualities, and unfortunately for the gifted young vocalist, there was nothing Fred could do to convince the executives that she was worth the gamble. Even when he played the track back and said, "This . . . this is stunning!"

Like many times before, Fred left the room greatly disappointed, convinced they were letting a superstar walk away. And a few times he was right. Some went on to sign with other labels, becoming successful recording artists with Gold and Platinum Records.

Such frustrations became common in his new position, with Fred frequently at odds with the traditional ways of thinking. Much to Fred's surprise, he soon realized he was one of the few A&R guys at RCA who could read music. Thanks to the perseverance of his high school teacher, Mrs. Dudley, Fred now had a skill many others in the industry lacked. In combination with his natural ear, these gifts proved beneficial beyond the recruiting stage, allowing him to provide valuable input as a physical producer on many projects, creating music in the recording studio whenever given the opportunity.

Soon Fred was instructing musicians and tweaking the roles of various instruments during sessions. The only problem was that A&R men were expected to stay in the control room. Fred was the producer, and, as such, he could give direction, but he was asked to remain behind the glass. To Fred, a man with proven musical genius, that restraint became difficult to tolerate.

One day proved particularly trying. The musicians were not in sync. The pianist was missing his mark, and by the seventeenth take, Fred had lost patience. He'd been warned never to enter the studio midsession, but he defied protocol and left his designated place. He moved to the piano bench, where he took a seat.

"Listen," he said matter-of-factly.

The musicians were stunned. He was the A&R guy, the producer, not the musician. Yet here he was playing the piece better than the studio pianist who had landed the gig. The pianist was not offended. He was inspired and interested in improving his work, but his union boss was having none of it. The burly man stomped toward Fred and slammed the cover over the keyboard, missing Fred's fingers by a hair.

"You do that again, I'll break both your hands," the man shouted, acting more like a mafia boss than a union rep.

With tense situations occurring more frequently, Fred began to feel hemmed in, and he yearned for more control in the creative aspects of the business. When he expressed his frustrations to Mac, his superior explained, "You probably have more talent than all of us combined, Fred. And, I agree, you could work wonders with these musicians. However, you were hired to manage. To collaborate. To seal the deal and keep more coming down the line. If that's where they want you to spend your time, you'd better do it."

In the RCA Camden division Fred was also responsible for coordinating cover songs or rerecordings. He found this work inspiring, staying full nights in the studio with leading artists such as Perry Como, John Kerry, Ed Ames, Sam Cooke, and Nina Simone. One record at a time, he was learning the music industry and finding joy in working with the talents on his roster.

Because many of the artists had expressed interest in creating albums for kids, RCA Camden soon launched a children's division and promoted Fred to head it. While still managing his other roles within the corporation, the new opportunity excited him, as he would now be working closely with artists the likes of Arthur Godfrey and Rosemary Rice—the entertainer he'd long admired for her role in *Mama*, with "I Remember Mama" as the TV show's theme song. Rosemary had played the spunky oldest daughter, Katrin, and if there had been one entertainer who had meant the most throughout Fred's teen years, it was Rosemary. Now she was working side by side with him! He couldn't believe his luck.

A mother of two, Rosemary especially enjoyed it when Fred would bring Allison to visit the studio. Mesmerized by the city, Allison liked to see the iconic statue of Nipper the dog before riding the fancy elevator up to her father's sleek executive office. Along the way she'd count the Grammys and Gold Records displayed throughout the building. She'd then stretch to peer over Fred's oversize desk, examining the state-of-the-art sound system that never failed to delight. She loved sharing that cherished time in the dimly lit chambers with her father where, through her child's eyes, Fred spent his days making *magic*. The wonder was real, and the possibilities felt infinite, not only to Allison but to Fred as well.

With Fred being a teacher at heart and a father above all, his happiest days at RCA were spent helping Allison learn the ropes. She was beautiful, with big blue eyes and angelic features that drew sweet compliments from the secretaries and studio hands. At only seven years old, Allison was already getting to know the many musicians, producers, engineers, and others in charge of moving a song from an artist's mind to the listener's ears. Winnie, too, had become friends with many of Fred's coworkers and clients, and soon the talented family had made a strong impression.

Rosemary was a good-natured soul who not only became Winnie's best friend but also became another mother figure in Allison's life. People sometimes joked that, like Rosemary, Allison had been "born singing." She'd been performing for church and school since she was a very young child, and with so much talent around her, she seemed to process the world through song, just like her father. With Fred producing children's albums now, it only seemed natural for Allison to begin singing on studio recordings, especially with her father working behind the glass. To no one's surprise, she was a natural at the microphone and quickly developed a reputation for being a "one-take wonder." This rare ability made her a studio favorite, as no one wanted to waste time or money on multiple takes.

With Fred and Winnie's careful supervision, Rosemary took Allison under her wing, not only featuring her on her own albums at RCA but connecting her with other leading artists as well. Like Rosemary, Allison soon expanded her work beyond record albums. She began singing jingles and taking part in film shoots around the city, entering America's living rooms through radio, TV, and print as she became the face and voice of many major brands, including Mattel, General Mills, Mighty White Toothpaste, Kleenex, and her favorite, Suzy Homemaker. It seemed an ideal balance, as Winnie was able to protect her young daughter within the safe and stable family life in Bernardsville while traveling with her to record in the city when the right opportunities arose.

One night, Allison and Fred were the only two left in the studio, wrapping up a late session for an album, *The Wonderful World of Children's Songs.* Fred took a seat at the piano as his daughter collected her score. Fred smiled as his talented little girl twirled and hummed to herself, fearless and free. Had he ever known such a feeling? Had poverty and dysfunction robbed him of this? He never wanted Allison to know the dangers and struggles he had known. He never wanted her to feel unseen, unsafe, unwanted. Unloved.

The magic of the moment overtook him, and he began to play "Honey Bun," the playful tune from *South Pacific* and one of Allison's favorites. She moved to the piano and lifted her voice across the empty room as if the whole world existed only for her and her song.

By the time the music ended, Allison was seated next to Fred on the bench. He let his hands rest on the keys as he turned her way. "You're my everything," he said softly.

She looked up at him and smiled.

"You really are," he insisted. "You've got the most wonderful spirit inside you, Allison. I love you more than you could imagine"

She laughed. "I love you too, Daddy."

"You're one in a million, you know? Recording music with people who have Gold Records and Grammy awards. You're holding your own with some of the biggest singers out there."

"It's fun."

"It's fun because you're a natural. You've got a real gift, Allison. Don't ever doubt that." Then he looked her in the eye and said, "You can do anything you want in this life. Anything at all."

# *Twenty-two*

Fred's position at RCA was becoming a family affair, and it was a positive experience for all. Along with the many glamorous benefits of Fred's job came plenty of nights on the town funded by the company. Winnie frequently accompanied Fred, as he could acquire tickets to any show they wanted to see. Whether in a grand concert hall, a Broadway theater, or on a smaller stage, the couple experienced it all. In between shows they would socialize with the leading talents, Fred trying to discover the next new star to sign with RCA while spoiling the clients he'd already secured.

In the evenings Winnie and Fred often joined A-listers at trendy hotspots such as the Gaslight Club, a throwback to the Prohibition-era speakeasy, where guests had to provide a password and drinks were served in coffee cups. One night they were meeting friends there when Fred leaned in and whispered, "I've got exciting news."

Winnie smiled. Unlike Fred, she loved surprises. She tugged his dinner jacket, barely able to handle the suspense.

"You know that album I produced last year, *How the Grinch Stole Christmas*?"

"Sure. Dr. Seuss?"

Fred's eyes twinkled. "It's been nominated. For a Grammy."

"Oh, honey!" Winnie cheered, just as their friends were arriving. They prodded her to share the news. "He's been nominated! For a Grammy!"

Fred brushed away the praise.

"Always so humble," Winnie beamed, giving him a celebratory kiss. Elaborate toasts began to circulate, and a festive night followed in honor of the creative work Fred's team had produced. In the early hours of morning, when the couple finally worked their way out of the party, they buzzed about the Grammy all the way back to Bernardsville. Once at home, Winnie sent the sitter home and turned on the radio, low enough not to wake Allison. Through the speakers, the voices of Barbra Streisand and Judy Garland filled the room, singing "Get Happy." Winnie smiled as the lyrics to another song summed up her thoughts: "*Happy days are here again.*"[1]

Fred moved in for a kiss, wrapping his arms around Winnie as she kicked off her heels. Together, they danced across the living room. "I'll need to buy a dress," she said over the music.

"Buy one." Fred smiled. "Anything you want."

"And we'll need a driver. A big, beautiful car."

Fred gave her a spin. "Consider it done."

"I can't believe this," Winnie said. "Big things are happening, aren't they, honey?"

Fred gave her another kiss before dipping her back for a romantic ending. "Big as we can dream, my love. Big as we can dream."

---

Soon it was time for the Grammys, and Winnie made the most of the experience. She wore a stunning floor-length black-and-white evening gown with long silk gloves that reached above her elbows. The sleek dress had been custom-made to fit every perfect curve, and when Fred first laid eyes on her, his knees went weak.

"Knockout." He smiled, still proud to call her his.

He pulled a small box from the pocket of his tuxedo jacket. As Winnie untied the delicate ribbon, she couldn't stop smiling. She opened the velvet-hinged box to discover a dazzling new pair of chandelier-drop earrings.

"Oh my goodness. Fred!" She pulled one from the case.

"You deserve the very best, Winnie. And now I can finally give it to you."

Fred, handsome as ever, served as Winnie's esteemed escort. The studio hired a driver to pick them up from the luxurious Waldorf Astoria, where they had booked a room for the late night. From the back seat, Fred poured two glasses of bubbling champagne as the limousine made its way toward Times Square. Then he toasted, "To the life we've dreamed."

Winnie clinked her glass against his. In silence they sipped and smiled nervously. The driver pulled the car around to the ballroom at the Hotel Astor, where the stars were making their entrance for the rows of photographers and cheering fans. Time seemed to slow when the glamorous duo stepped from the limousine. Fred took a look at his breathtaking partner, and with his dark hair and gleaming smile, he extended his arm her way. Winnie placed her hand in the warm crook of his elbow, enjoying the way her palm fell into the crisp fold of his black tuxedo. She remembered the time they had pretended such an act, back at the old Metropolitan Opera House when they were young and naive. Now they glided together down the famous red carpet, smiling and waving in the line of glamorous superstars. The flashbulbs snapped from every angle, and one of the reporters compared Winnie to Audrey Hepburn, complimenting her gorgeous gown.

Once inside they both exhaled, laughing. "Oh my goodness," Winnie said, pulling her hand to her heart as she was still abuzz with adrenaline. "That was so much fun!"

The entire evening was enchanting. Between the live acts, tableside chats, and after-parties, Winnie and Fred spent the hours deep in conversation with the world's most successful musical artists as well as with the people who worked behind the scenes to get them there, including Mac McClure and his wife, Fran.

At one point Fred and Mac had made their way to the balcony for some fresh air. Mac took in the view of the city lights, admiring the beauty. Then he turned his attention to a famous singer struggling to hold his liquor. Stumbling through the words, the star shouted at Mac, "What? You ain't never seen a winner before. Take a good look." He raised his fists in the air and shouted, "Winner!" Then he lost his balance, falling against a circle of admirers who laughed and cheered him on to another drink.

Mac watched the drunk entertainer collapse at the bar. "This industry is brutal," he said. "They all start out bright-eyed and full of dreams. And then we take and take until they have nothing left to give."

Fred shook his head. "They can't all end up like that."

"Most," Mac insisted. "I try to warn them. I tell them how important it is to have one person, an anchor, someone to hold the truth so they don't get lost in it all. But then I watch them slowly break. It's as if they can no longer tell the difference between what's real and what isn't. Who's on their side and who's out to get them." Mac nodded toward the bar. "You see?"

Fred studied the popular entertainer. Two scantily dressed women were now propping him up for photos, and no one seemed interested in stemming the flow of vodka heading his way.

"I'm telling you, Fred. It's as if a fog rolls in and they lose all sense. The only chance they have of making it is if they have one honest person to point them home again when the world goes gray. But when all is said and done, most of these guys don't have anybody."

By then Winnie and Fran had tracked down their handsome husbands and were giddy with gossip about the big-screen actress they had met in the powder room. In the excitement of it all, Fred quickly forgot all about Mac's warnings, and the remaining hours floated by seamlessly, with night soon turning to day.

Back at their hotel, Fred and Winnie watched the sunrise from the lush rooftop gardens of the Waldorf Astoria, still too excited to sleep. With the morning mist burning off the towering high-rises, Winnie looked out over Madison Avenue and said simply, "We've made it."

# *Twenty-three*

As Fred continued producing music for RCA, where his daughter was becoming a star and Winnie had begun writing children's stories for audio recordings, he was also leading his beloved choir at Bernardsville Methodist. Plus, he was wrapping up his doctoral coursework in psychology at Columbia while also trying to maintain his mentorship with Emile, hoping to land a lead role someday. By that time Emile had put him on a training regimen that included almost daily vocal lessons and work with a strength and fitness coach to get Fred's body in peak form—a definite plus for men on stage. He was also taking classes at the famed Actors Studio, where he was studying directly under Lee Strasberg. Emile had been pressuring him, insisting that he was certain to become a Broadway star, maybe even more, if only he would prioritize his time and focus on his own talents instead of building, as Emile put it, the careers of "far less-gifted entertainers."

Emile didn't seem to understand the many pressures Fred was under or that there were only so many hours in a day. One complication was that in order to manage his RCA position, the couple had become well-known regulars at the 21 Club, Playboy Club, Diners Club, and the like. Many opportunities came their way, and Fred and Winnie had begun to fully embrace the jazzy lifestyle. Not only were they growing accustomed to the finest quality food and entertainment, but they were also surrounding themselves with the most influential movers and shakers of the entertainment industry. It was an addictive routine, one that had both pros and cons.

With so many late nights in the city, the couple had grown weary of the back-and-forth travel between Bernardsville and Manhattan. They decided to rent a spacious apartment on the Upper East Side, allowing Fred to avoid the long commute when work kept him late in the studio or the clubs. But even with the new apartment, Fred still struggled with terrible insomnia, and when he was able to sleep, he suffered those same awful nightmares about the steeple—the haunting dream that would leave him shaking, soaking the sheets in a cold sweat. Despite all that was going right in his life, he'd been feeling more anxious than ever.

After years of running on fumes, he was suddenly having trouble keeping it all together. Mac noticed the shift in Fred's demeanor and warned him again about the burnout so common in their industry, but Fred had always been one to push his own limits. He'd never required much rest and had long thrived on the challenge of spreading himself thin. He brushed off Mac's concerns and assured him, "I can handle it."

One evening, dressed to the nines after dropping Allison off for a sleepover with close friends in Bernardsville, Fred and Winnie waited to meet more friends at the Playboy Club, a controversial gathering space where beautiful women, wearing nothing more than bushy-tailed corsets and perky bunny ears, served trendy cocktails from silver trays. The duo headed up to the VIP room for dinner before moving to the upper-floor nightclub to scout a singer. There, the owner, Hugh Hefner, chatted with Fred about one of his models, trying to convince his new acquaintance that the young woman was prime for a record deal. As the conversation ended, they were escorted to a private booth. Along the way, the popular couple shared friendly hellos around the room before ordering their favorite drinks: an Old Fashioned with Maker's for Fred and a Manhattan for Winnie.

They frequently socialized in Bernardsville with choir friends who had already become close companions, but their city life brought them an entirely different experience from the suburban dinner parties and family-friendly weekends. The club was a place to escape all stress, a fantasy forum with live jazz and high-heeled hostesses giving their customers personalized attention, a venue where Fred should have felt on top of the world. Only a few weeks earlier he and his team had received their second and third Grammy nominations for two more Camden albums, and *The Wonderful World of Children's Songs*, featuring Allison as one of its leads, was becoming one of the top-selling children's records. He also had been discussing a collaboration with good friend and world-renowned composer Henry Mancini, and just the day before he had turned down a personal request from country-music star and guitar master Chet Atkins, asking Fred to move to Nashville and produce his next album. He was quickly becoming one of the young darlings of RCA. But despite having every reason to celebrate, Fred was distant, lost in a daydream and barely listening to Winnie's updates about Allison's latest school project.

Winnie paused midsentence. "What is it, Fred? Why do you seem so troubled?"

With a sigh, he struggled to explain, fumbling a bit until he finally said, "I love my job. Most of it is great. But . . ." His voice faded, leaving her wanting more.

"But what?" Winnie's brow ruffled. Wasn't this the life he had always wanted? Across the room she spotted the actor Peter Falk. Two tables down sat entertainers Sammy Davis Jr. and Dean Martin, two friends the couple had socialized with the previous weekend. They were living the life of their dreams. And still, he wasn't happy?

"Sometimes I wonder if I'm heading down the wrong path." Fred sipped his drink. "And hell, Winnie, you should be performing too, using your voice. You had dreams like me. Don't you remember?"

Winnie tried not to overreact. "I *am* happy, Fred. This is enough for me, being a mother. And a wife."

Fred shook his head and his voice stayed tense with frustration. "Look around us. Don't you see? It's a game, Winnie. I don't want to be the producer, the salesman, the manager. I want to be the performer, the one at the piano. I have so much music in me, and yet I'm still being locked away from the instruments. The damn union bosses won't even let me touch the keys. It's . . . it's maddening."

"You're an incredible producer too," Winnie said, trying to calm him.

"And I love it. I really do love helping others shine. I guess I just . . ."

"You want to shine too," Winnie finished his sentence.

Fred took another sip and looked away. "I want to make my own music. I want to play the instruments, compose the songs, sing the notes. I want the music to come through me to the audience."

Frustrated and exhausted, Fred took Winnie's hand and said, "I'm a point man for the artists. I wrangle with the engineers, I schedule studio rentals, I arrange for the orchestra to show up on time. I give my advice and input, and they take it, but ultimately . . . I'm forbidden to touch a string, hit a key, compose, conduct. Everything I've studied, everything I am . . . it's being silenced. I'm not happy, Winnie. I know I should be, but I'm not."

Winnie ran her fingers across the new diamond clasp that hung from her grandmother's pearls. Fred had given it to her as a surprise. Truth was, Winnie had grown accustomed to five-star dinners, expensive evening gowns, and company-sponsored nights on the town. What would it mean for Fred to leave his job at RCA? Even then, would he be happy?

Fred's eyes were pleading with her to give him some sign of release from his role at the studio. Still, Winnie hesitated. Fred sighed and turned away again, scanning the room for the friends who were running much later than usual. Winnie sipped her drink and weighed her opinion as the band played "Why Was I Born?"

With the lyrics drawing a sting, Fred drained his Old Fashioned and signaled for another. Winnie reached again for her necklace. This time, she moved beyond the expensive clasp and rubbed the heirloom strand of pearls instead. They'd been passed down through three generations and had long served as a calming touchstone when life became too out of sorts.

"I don't know what lies ahead, but I want you to be happy, honey," she said. "Whatever it takes."

Fred shook his head. He saw no easy way out. How could he justify leaving the influential position? The extraordinary salary, the endless perks—most people would never throw that away.

As his brain puzzled for options, their guests arrived, apologizing for being late and asking the waitress to bring a fresh round of drinks to make up for their delay. Fred gave Winnie a sad look as he stood to greet them. Then he flashed his winning smile and went back to playing the game.

# *Twenty-four*

Despite Fred's increasing angst, he didn't resign from RCA. Instead, he continued to devote his best efforts to producing quality records while trying to give Emile even more time in the off hours. Nights and weekends were often consumed with work events or private parties with the A-list crowd he was now calling his own.

While Winnie enjoyed the lavish lifestyle as much as Fred, her priority was being a mother. Concerned they had been leaving their daughter with friends too frequently, she began staying home with Allison instead of joining Fred for every social invitation. She had hoped he would follow her lead and slow down. Instead, he was spending more time at their Upper East Side apartment while Winnie and Allison were miles away in Bernardsville.

To make matters worse, Fred had begun hosting regular parties at the apartment, inviting not only fellow RCA executives and recording friends but also Broadway stars and opera elite. The glamorous lifestyle was becoming a lure Fred couldn't resist, especially now that some of his wealthier celebrity friends were elevating the excess. It was as if they'd taken a *Great Gatsby*-esque hold on Fred's life, and it didn't take long for the balance to swing.

Winnie began to tread cautiously. As eager as she was for Fred to return home each night, she was careful not to say anything that might push him further away. Sure, the treks back and forth to the city had long been wearing on him, but it was more than that. Something had changed between them, and Winnie wasn't quite sure what to do about it.

In spite of his newfound playboy lifestyle, Fred always made it home on Sundays and Wednesdays to lead the choir. In between, Winnie would drive into the city to dine with her husband or take voice lessons with Emile while Fred accompanied her. She also brought Allison into the studio for recording sessions and advertising jobs, but no matter how hard she tried to maintain the strong connection she and Fred had always shared, a significant divide was staking claim between them.

Then everything shifted.

It happened as Fred was attending a psychology seminar at Columbia, wrapping up his final coursework before writing his doctoral dissertation. The professor was leading an emotional exercise for the small group of students, teaching them a new method of therapeutic intervention. As part of this task, Fred and his peers were instructed to close their eyes as he guided them back to their earliest memories.

Led through a form of hypnosis, each participant tried to tap into any unresolved childhood wounds. The theory was based on the controversial belief that the fragile human psyche will self-protect by burying the most traumatic moments that happen in life.

"Research suggests that while we may not consciously remember these wounding experiences, the original memories can still be reached, deep within the subconscious," the professor explained. "In other words, the files are still there. They've simply been blocked from our conscious retrieval system, much in the same way we might archive our old tax forms and tuck them away in a box rather than keeping them accessible in our everyday cabinet. We still have them. Somewhere. It just might take a bit of work to find them again."

Suspicious by nature, Fred doubted the exercise would be effective. Nevertheless, he followed the professor's instructions, respectfully closing his eyes as he focused on the meditative cadence of his soothing voice. Slowly Fred began to travel through time, reaching deep into his childhood memories. Breath by breath he was leaving the dimly lit university classroom and working his way down to Georgia, all the way back to a little white house in the Dunson Mill Village, where he saw eight-year-old Fred and his uncle Dirk, the baseball player.

Much to Fred's surprise, the exercise had him in a sweat. His breath grew rapid and short, and his heart began to beat so fiercely he wasn't sure what was happening. He gasped for air as waves of anxiety washed over him. None of his regular tricks seemed to work. He tried counting backward from ten, then twenty, then ten more. He tried switching his mind to positive thoughts, imagining the sound of Allison's giggle and the warmth of Winnie's embrace. He even sang a few lyrics silently to himself, trying to quell the nausea that was enveloping him. Then he looked around the room, naming objects, determined to ground himself back *here* in this time and space.

No matter how he tried to bring his mind back to the here and now, he was stuck in that little back bedroom, pretending to be asleep, hoping this would not play out the way it had the last time Uncle Dirk had entered his room. And the time before that. And the time before that.

Never before had he experienced such a rush of panic, but now, as adrenaline surged in his veins, there was only one thing left to do. *Run!*

Fred bolted from the classroom, fighting the urge to scream. Like a madman, he raced full-speed from the building, but even the fresh air couldn't tame his rage. Still running, he gasped, clawing at his collar, pulling at the buttons as he tried to shake his overwhelming fears.

He ran from the seminar at Columbia all the way to Morningside. Then he turned away from the river and ran the rest of the mile to

Central Park. The entire route a blur, Fred had no awareness that he was crossing lanes of traffic and shoving pedestrians. He didn't even realize he was running until the pavement hit the lawn and the streets disappeared from view.

In his panic Fred had ripped his shirt completely from his sweat-soaked body and now stared at the crumpled fabric in his hands. He fell against a grassy knoll, shivering and moaning in utter shock. Then he sobbed. Right there in the middle of Central Park, where anyone could see, he had an absolute breakdown.

He couldn't erase the memories, and no matter how hard he tried to claw his way free of them, he was that eight-year-old . . . seven-year-old . . . six-year-old boy, shaking in fear as Uncle Dirk moved closer to his bed, a drunken stupor hardening his steps. He stood over young Fred as a lion over its prey, enjoying the surge of power and conquest as he had done time and time again for more than three years. Three years!

Every memory resurfaced with a fiery explosion of disturbing images. His conscious mind couldn't process the truth of it all. It was as if someone had removed a blindfold, and years of abuse by Uncle Dirk played out on-screen. It was all there. Every gruesome detail. Every twisted assault. Every threat. Every secret. Every shame. And with that truth came a burden too big for any man to bear.

*How could he have forgotten such abuse? Did it really happen?*

Yes. He was certain it had happened. He knew it as well as he knew he was Fred Allen, husband to Winnie Langley and father to Allison. He knew these truths as well as he knew his eyes were blue and that his sister was named Novis and that he was the only son of Grady and Velma Allen. The truth was that Uncle Dirk had abused him in horrific ways when he was just a boy. And sometimes other ballplayers had their part in it too.

Around him the park was filled with ambitious joggers and emotional street poets. Children climbed boulders while college kids spread blankets across the grass. Beneath the shade tree, they strummed guitars and braided flowers and pointed out pictures in the clouds. It seemed the world was divided into two halves: the broken and the whole.

As he watched the world float around him, hours seemed to pass and yet time stood still. His new Rolex watch, a gift from a famous friend, had become meaningless, a melting haze of movement that no longer applied to him. In fact, nothing seemed to carry any worth anymore. When the sun began to set, Fred had to make a move. But where to go?

Still fumbling to grasp the full reality of his memories, Fred managed to find a pay phone, and then he made one call. He did not call Winnie. Nor did he call Emile. There was only one person who would understand this kind of trauma. Fred called his best friend, Pete.

Pete came straight to the park without question or hesitation. He rushed to find Fred still a wreck. Immediately he wrapped his arms around his friend and held him steady, saying again and again and again as the truths surfaced, "You're going to get through this, Fred. You've already survived the worst of it."

Fred's instinct to call Pete had been the right choice. As the night went on, Pete divulged that he had suffered his own form of abuse. When he was just a teenager, frightened and destitute in this new country, ravaged by the psychological abuses of war and suffering the devastating plight of a refugee, he'd arrived in New York only to endure more abuse by his predatory landlady, a much older woman who forced Pete to pay her more than rent to keep a roof over his head.

Together, Pete and Fred sat on a well-lit park bench and shared their deepest wounds. Unlike Fred, Pete had learned to cope with his own past by facing it head-on. He had found no benefit in burying it.

"Listen," Pete said. "You know the answers now. You know. All those nightmares? Those terrible times waking up, soaked with sweat and too scared to breathe? Your constant drive to prove yourself? To never be quiet? Never be still? Now you know why you've been struggling. This has been trying to surface for some time."

"But why now?" Fred gritted his teeth. His fists were clenched. So much anger welled inside him. Too much.

"Because now you're ready," Pete said.

Fred wrung his hands, suddenly realizing what they were capable of doing to a man like Dirk. "He's lucky I'm a thousand miles from LaGrange."

Pete nodded but said nothing. Clearly, he understood the rage.

Fred shook his head. His heart throbbed against his ribs. His whole being felt caged in. He needed to hit someone. To throw this pain right back to his uncle. To kick and punch and watch him suffer as he had.

Fred's pulse spiked as he imagined choking Uncle Dirk. Bashing that baseball bat against his skull the way Eleanor had threatened to do all those years earlier, when she had been the only person to protect that scared and fragile little boy.

"You know what's the hardest part?" Fred asked. "That uncle . . . he built a home next door to us. His son . . . my cousin . . . grew up with me. Served as a groomsman in our wedding. My parents must have known."

Pete listened respectfully.

"Even if they hadn't been smart enough to notice, Aunt Eleanor had never been one to mind her tongue. She would have told them, don't you think?" Then, after a pause, he added, "Maybe she did tell them. Maybe that's why she left!"

These thoughts spun wildly, sending Fred into the darkest depths of maddening fear and confusion. Hour by hour, memory by memory, Pete sat beside Fred, allowing his friend's boiling anger to simmer to a slow, cool burn. It took half the night, a long walk, and a move to a quiet bar, but when Fred had released his final tear in a back corner booth of their favorite haunt, he put his head in his hands and said, "I don't know what to do. What am I supposed to do?"

"Whatever it takes," Pete said. "As long as you don't let this take you down."

"How can it not?" Fred asked, defeated.

"Look at me, Fred." Pete held his friend's gaze. "You're not alone in this fight. I'll be with you all the way through it," he said sincerely. "And I'll still be there when you get to the other side. It won't be easy, but believe me, you *will* get through to the other side."

# *Twenty-five*

For the first time in Fred's life, the music stopped. He breathed no melody, heard no tune. The deep taproot of creativity that had long sustained him was now an infinite and empty abyss.

Since the sudden surfacing of his traumatic past, he had been feeling nothing but a heavy sense of loss, as if he were dead inside, numb. Even Winnie and Allison were unable to bring him back to life. While he had been able to confide in Pete, he had not yet found the words to tell Winnie the truth. How could he? She would never understand the horrors that had shaped him. And worse than that, Fred feared she would judge him. Maybe even leave him. She may even begin to see him as his family must have seen him—as nothing worth loving at all.

He conquered his fear of losing Winnie the only way he knew how, by pushing her away. She represented everything he wasn't, and maybe everything he would never be again. She and Allison were still the innocent, trusting, openhearted souls of his world. Now, as the beautiful mother and daughter laughed together, swimming laps in their Bernardsville pool, it pained Fred to watch them, as if their light was so bright it hurt his eyes.

Fred was shutting down, just as he had done in his youth. Only now he could not cover himself in baggy clothes and sink into silence to keep others at bay. Instead, he limped through life, hour by hour, trying his best to keep up the act, determined not to cave. Because the memories had destroyed his self-worth, he sought to prove himself at every turn, keeping later and later hours at the studio, determined to produce perfect albums and find a way to attain the happiness that had been stolen from him.

In the meantime Winnie was watching her husband unravel and had no idea how to save him. Knowing nothing of the internal battle he was fighting, she blamed their struggles on his full schedule, the late nights, the falsely fulfilling celebrity life. In some way Fred was making Winnie his enemy. She loved him more than anyone, and, unknowingly, because love was what had wounded him to begin with, Winnie had become his greatest threat.

He began countering her every move. If she reached for him, he'd pull away. No matter how hard she tried, she couldn't break through. As a result, Winnie's frustrations grew. A devoted wife, she was no pushover. Fred had fallen for this spunk and strength in the first place, loving that she was nothing like his mother and that she was the kind of woman to hold him accountable when he got out of line. But the fire he'd found so appealing in the beginning was proving more than his weakened psyche could handle.

Day after day Winnie kept trying. But she didn't know how to pull her husband back. All she knew was that she loved Fred Allen with her whole heart. He had been her best friend, her soul mate, and she was not going to give up on him. *In good times and in bad*—to Winnie, those vows meant something. In fact, they meant everything.

As she pleaded for Fred to let some of his responsibilities go, to step away from the chaos and focus on their family, Fred's walls grew higher. He turned away from the healthy parts of his life. His inner child took the wheel and functioned in survival mode again, so Fred did whatever it took to escape the pain. That was all he could manage to do.

After months of Winnie's pleading, Fred finally agreed to spend the entire weekend in Bernardsville, two solid days at home. Friday afternoon Winnie and Allison prepared Fred's favorite dinner and set the table. By evening they were eagerly watching the clock for him to walk through the door. Hour after hour Winnie came up with every excuse for his delay, determined to preserve his character before Allison as she'd always done. Eventually, the phone rang. "Stuck at work," Fred said. "Trying to wrap up this session. Looks like I'll have to spend another night in the city."

Once again Winnie covered for him, assuring Allison that he would be home by morning. But the following day, still no Fred. And this time, no phone call.

By the time he finally showed up to lead the choir Sunday morning, Winnie was at her wits' end. Others may not have noticed the glaze in his eyes, the extra shot of mouthwash on his breath, but Winnie no longer recognized her husband. His tie was crooked. His face unshaven. This was not the man she knew.

After church Fred entered the kitchen with his head down and didn't speak. Instead, he kissed her softly as if that were enough to say "I'm sorry."

"We need to talk, Fred." Winnie took a seat at the kitchen table, hoping he would join her.

He did.

After she brewed some coffee, Winne poured a cup for Fred and passed it to him. As it cooled, the two sat in silence, watching Allison jump rope with friends outside. When he finally lifted his mug for a sip, Winnie took the first turn. "I can't do this anymore. You have to tell me what's going on with you."

Finally he stuttered through a vague response. "I don't know why, but . . . I've got to find myself, Winnie. I'm not happy."

"Fred, please talk to me." Desperation clenched her throat. "I don't understand what's happening. I feel like we're losing you."

After a sigh Fred said simply, "I can't be who you need me to be."

"What on earth does that even mean, honey? You're not making any sense."

He said nothing. Winnie's palms turned to the ceiling, giving emphasis to each word. "I want you to be yourself, Fred. That's all I've ever wanted. You. Not this other man you've become. This isn't you."

Fred leaned his head against his hand. Then much more softly he said, "Maybe I'm not who you think I am."

Winnie stood from her chair. She wanted to scream. But she mustered all her resolve, pacing back and forth beside the table.

"I've got to have some time," Fred continued. "Or something. I don't know. I'm lost, Winnie."

"*Time?*" Her pitch rose despite her best efforts to stay steady.

"I can't be the right husband, the right father. I don't know what else to do, Winnie. It's just . . . something . . . something's broken in me."

"You aren't broken, Fred. You are the most wonderful person I've ever known. Can't you see that?"

Again he said nothing.

"Look at all you have overcome. Achieved. You have more talent than half the artists in this city combined. And the way you are with Allison. Show me another man who loves his daughter more than that. I dare you."

Fred stared vacantly out the window as if nothing she said mattered. As if she could never out-love this pain.

"I resigned from RCA," Fred said flatly. "It's not the job for me."

"All right," Winnie said, exhaling. "We'll figure it out, Fred. That's a problem we can solve."

He recoiled. "Nobody asked you to solve my problems, Winnie."

"We're a team, Fred." She moved her hand to his arm, hoping to calm him. "That's my job, to help you."

"No!" he said too loudly, pulling away. "My problems. My decisions. My life!"

Stunned, Winnie's spine stiffened. Never had he spoken to her so harshly. They had always shared everything, a cohesive unit since college. She helped him, and he helped her. It worked, and they were both better together. What had changed? Was he feeling smothered? Wanting out? What exactly did he mean by needing to have some time?

Winnie tried for days, weeks, months to reach him. He couldn't make her understand that he loved her—but he was tired. He could no longer keep up all the roles he was playing, and it was easier to avoid her completely. Also he was locked in a cage of shame and could hardly bear to face his own truth, much less share it with the woman he loved.

So he turned to the safest place he knew to turn—music.

With so many hours free from RCA, Fred now devoted all his time and energy to Emile's intense training regimen, determined to see his dreams through to fruition and to land a lead on Broadway. He longed to create, to perform, to give a crowd the emotional energy they craved and in return to find the path that would finally satisfy him. He needed approval, applause, stardom. He wanted it all.

By summer's end Winnie had gained little ground. School would be starting soon, and she'd made up her mind. It took her two days to track Fred down, and when she finally got a message through to him, it was simply "Come home. Now."

Fred knew he had pushed her too far, but he never expected to find her with her bags packed. When he questioned her, Winnie interrupted. She had rehearsed her speech, and now it was finally her time to talk. "I don't know what else to do. You say you need time. I'll give you time."

She had planned a response to counter any argument Fred might present. But he said nothing. He didn't beg her to stay or ask her not to give up on him. He didn't take her hand or pull her close or tell her he was sorry. He didn't as much as look at Winnie. Instead, Fred remained numb. Silent. And disconnected. His apathy told Winnie everything she needed to know.

# *Twenty-six*

Allison entered the fifth grade in the fall of 1968, back in Columbus. Fred, having left RCA, had given up the expensive Upper East Side apartment and moved out of the family's nice home in Bernardsville. He had accepted a teaching job at the Lincoln Center School and was staying with Pete for the short term while he looked for an affordable rental. Winnie, determined to fight for her family, continued to travel back and forth for frequent visits, never giving up on her husband despite the increasing distance between them.

She could neither understand nor explain Fred's erratic behavior, and she had no idea what to do about it. She only knew she missed him more than she could bear. Allison did too, which only added to Winnie's heartache.

Fred was living faster than ever in New York. But without Winnie's unwavering support, he floundered. He also had to deal with a steep cut in pay. Having grown accustomed to the large expense account at RCA, and given that Winnie had always been the one to manage their finances, right-brained Fred was facing some harsh realities.

Once again Winnie tried to help. The Langleys were still friends with the generous benefactor, Mr. Banks, the same man who had sponsored Fred and Winnie's summer experience in Chautauqua all those years earlier. It turned out that he had a friend in New York who worked with Macmillan Publishers, and, after a few dinner meetings, Fred was offered a job.

When the semester ended at Lincoln Center, Fred transitioned to his new position and rented a small apartment in Greenwich Village. He proved to be a gifted wordsmith with an intellect to carry him through the editorial job with ease, but while he remained professional in the office, he couldn't pull himself together after hours. He continued to socialize nightly with his many prominent connections, and he relied heavily on his friendships to pass the time. This reckless lifestyle was consuming him. Even Pete had grown worried, warning Fred about the negative influence of a few acquaintances and trying to steer Fred back to center, back to his family. Back home.

Yet slowly but surely Fred's show business career had begun to take off. With Emile's help, and with no demanding RCA or academic commitments on his calendar, he had landed a few supporting roles on Broadway. Now the city's top producers were expressing real interest in the up-and-coming tenor.

By late spring Winnie flew up for another of her frequent visits. Fred took her out to her favorite Italian restaurant where he asked for the corner table, bathed in candlelight. When the band struck up "Taking a Chance on Love," the timing seemed right, so Fred took his chance.

"Emile got me a big audition. Next week."

"So you're staying," Winnie replied sadly. "I'd hoped you might be ready to come home. It's been nine months."

Fred was quiet now. He had struggled with this for so long, and he had yet to come to terms with an answer. He held Winnie's hand gently atop the soft linen tablecloth. "I know how lucky I am to have you in my life, Winnie. I do. I know."

"But?" Her patience waned.

He sighed. "I've always said you are the we of me."

Winnie nodded, fighting tears.

"But there's a *me* of we too, Winnie. And I've lost that."

The next morning they took a stroll through Central Park, passing the very spot where Fred had experienced his breakdown. Winnie still had no idea any of that had happened, and he planned to keep it that way, those secrets buried deep. As they walked, Winnie couldn't help but stare at the families enjoying the beautiful spring day together. It was painful to see how happy they seemed, knowing such simple moments had failed to hold Fred's heart close to her. With tender mercy, she leaned against her husband, letting his strong frame steady her. "I love you, Fred Allen."

"I love you too, Winnie."

"I've loved you since the first time I saw you. In the quad. And I'm always going to love you." She released a heavy sigh, looking up at a bright yellow kite before turning her attention back to her husband. "This is the hardest thing I've ever had to do, Fred. But what you need and what Allison and I need have become two very different things."

She pulled her wedding rings from her finger and placed the set in Fred's palm, closing his hand softly around them.

"You're going to make it big," she whispered. "I've never had any doubt you could do it." A single tear rolled down her cheek, and Fred moved a finger to catch it. He didn't make any more promises he couldn't keep.

The following day Fred took Winnie to the airport. After she crossed the terminal and disappeared from his sight, Fred looked down at her wedding rings in his hand.

*Oh, God*, he thought. *What have I done?*

# *Twenty-seven*

With Winnie and Allison away in Columbus, Fred continued living life as a playboy, hanging out backstage with the stars and hitting all the after-parties. He flirted and hobnobbed, determined to make the most of his newfound freedom. His dedication to his craft had begun to pay off, and with Emile's help he had made significant strides with some directors and producers.

One afternoon in 1970, Emile burst into his Sutton Place studio, where Fred was preparing for another lesson. His mentor was unusually elated, with an excitement he couldn't seem to contain. "Here's our chance!" He passed a piece of paper to Fred. "I've done all I can do here. Now it's on you, son. Go get this part!"

Along with an address Emile had scribbled one word on the handwritten note: *Company*.

Fred was a firm believer in discipline and had trained rigorously in order to be prepared when the big opportunity finally presented itself. Now that day had arrived. In fact, *Company* was as big as it gets. The play was Stephen Sondheim's new musical comedy based on the popular book by George Furth. Fred had been socializing in Stephen's group for the last year and knew the lead role of Bobby was currently played by Dean Jones, a Hollywood star who had gained fame by acting in a wide range of roles, from grittier Broadway plays to blockbuster Disney comedies. Dean was truly top tier and excelling in the role as Bobby, but now, Emile explained, personal issues had left Dean no choice but to step away from the show.

A replacement was needed as soon as possible; the competition would be stiff, especially with murmurs of Tony nominations. "All the top entertainers are vying for the audition," Emile said. "But thanks to me, you have something they don't have. A slot of rare airtime in front of the producers."

"No!" Fred yelled with excitement, truly shocked.

"Yes!" Emile countered, his eyes lit with excitement.

Fred's first thought was to call Winnie and share the big news, but he resisted the urge. In fact, he no longer answered most of her calls. Instead, he'd learned to pretend his hurt away, still the sadness, shift the blame.

Fred's absence was having a devastating effect on Winnie back in Columbus, and her family had been watching her wither in grief. Recently her brother, Bill, had given Fred a call, urging him to do the right thing and put his family first. Fred had been defensive, roaring back, "Winnie left. Not me!" But now, as Fred's big chance had finally arrived, he could no longer silence Bill's voice: "Winnie needs her husband, and Allison needs her father. And truth is, Fred, you need them too. It's been long enough. Come home."

"What do I do?" Fred asked his reliable mentor. "Winnie's brother called me. She needs me home, Emile. And to tell you the truth, I'm not sure she'll wait much longer."

"She's waited this long, hasn't she?"

Fred sighed. It had been more than a year since she'd returned to Georgia. While she'd come and gone several times since, and they had never officially separated, he knew he had pushed his wife far beyond what most women would have tolerated.

"Look, Fred. I like Winnie a lot. You know I do. She's one of the most talented young women I've seen. But you could land this lead, Fred, and then you're golden. You can't give up now. Not after all we've done to get you this far."

"But I'm no good without her, Emile. You see that. I can't eat. Can't sleep. And Allison . . . God. I don't know if it's worth all this."

"Shake some sense into yourself, son. They should be *here*, supporting you. You're not just some lowbrow singer with stardust in his eyes."

That same evening, after journaling about his conversation with Emile, Fred joined Stephen Sondheim and his friends for a private party. Behind him, in the upscale apartment, a row of awards lined an entire wall. In a corner, framed photos captured smiles from countless red carpets and encore performances. One of Broadway's leading ladies caught Fred's eye as he took in the room.

"I don't know if I ever really believed I'd end up here. Did you?" She smiled flirtatiously, a siren in the midst of the chaos surrounding him.

With Winnie away, Fred and the songstress had been circling a flame for weeks, and as she gazed up at him with a sultry stare, he knew he was a half step away from crossing a line.

"Play something for us," she said, tugging Fred's arm to the grand piano where only a few nights before he had accompanied his friend Bernadette Peters. With this woman's body now close to his, Fred fought against her seductions. Outside, the city lights were a blur as he took a seat at the keyboard. Here he was in a Manhattan penthouse, at a piano that had been played by some of the most talented musicians in the world. He was surrounded by fame and excess, the glamorous life he'd always wanted. And yet . . . he felt emptier than ever before.

As his hands struck the notes, Fred tried once more for the music to erase his past, to help him escape his heartache. But as the starlet leaned over the piano, requesting he play one of her hit numbers, he paused, then pulled his hands from the ivories and shook his head. No. He had circled the sun and howled at the moon far too many times without the love of his life. Now a clarity overtook him, as if coming above the surface after swimming underwater all this time. His heart could no longer deny the truth. Winnie could never be replaced.

"Then give us something else," she said.

With a distant gaze Fred started to play a song that he and Winnie had sung together many times. It was sad, slow, and beautiful, a jazz ballad that Bobby Darin had been known to deliver with a melancholy sense of loss. But Fred took those emotions even deeper as he crooned, drifting back in time until the room faded away.

Once upon a time
A girl with moonlight in her eyes
Put her hand in mine,
And said she loved me so
But that was once upon a time
Very long ago

Once upon a hill
We sat beneath a willow tree
Counting all the stars
And waiting for the dawn
But that was once upon a time,
Now the tree is gone

How the breeze ruffled through her hair
How we always laughed

As though tomorrow wasn't there
We were young
And didn't have a care
Where did it go?

Once upon a time
The world was sweeter than we knew
Everything was ours
How happy we were then
But somehow once upon a time
Never comes again[1]

When the song ended, the woman's eyes glistened with tears. Without a word, she nodded slightly and gave Fred a gentle kiss on the cheek before leaving him alone at the keys. She understood.

From the bench Fred sat apart from the others and looked around the room through a clear lens. A famous film director was passed out drunk across the sofa. A highly esteemed actor worked his way through a line of cocaine. Couples of every orientation were tangled together, only half clothed and half aware. It was not so unlike the party scenes of his childhood, when soldiers and athletes made their way to the Allen home to pick their poison. The setting had changed, but the pain remained the same.

As he stared, clearheaded, he remembered his sister's appeal: "Whatever you do, promise me you won't end up like the rest of us."

---

Back in Columbus, Winnie was struggling too. She was thin and pale and had even resorted to biting her nails, a habit she had long despised.

Jim and Nell tried to encourage their daughter by never speaking negatively of their son-in-law's choices, even as they prayed for him to find his way soon. Her brother, Bill, on the other hand, had seen more than he could stand of Winnie's heartache. He and his sister had always maintained a close relationship, but in recent years they had grown especially connected, and his protective nature was taking hold as he tried to talk sense into her about Fred's behavior.

While visiting his parents' home, he found Winnie writing another letter to Fred. "How long are you going to keep doing this to yourself? Hasn't he hurt you enough?"

"It's not like it seems, Bill. We love each other. I'm just giving him time to follow his dreams."

"Time? Maybe it's time to move on." Bill sounded tired, and he struggled to break through to her.

When she didn't answer, he tried again. "Why are you selling yourself short? You could have any man you want."

"I want *him*," Winnie said, without looking up from writing. She had no idea her brother had called Fred to intervene.

Bill moved closer, insisting she give him her full attention. "Can't you see? He's broken, Winnie. Broken."

Winnie put her pen down and held her brother's worried gaze. But instead of yielding, she shrugged and said, "Isn't everybody?"

Bill was done. He shook his head with resignation and left.

In her loneliness Winnie had begun keeping a journal of her own, filling it with hopeful words Fred had shared during their ongoing visits, letters, and calls. Now, with Allison at a birthday party, she turned to her journal, hoping to gain clarity as to where it had all gone wrong.

Later that night the house was quiet. Bill had returned to his own home, and everyone else had gone to bed. But Winnie couldn't sleep.

Her brother's words haunted her, and her journal had provided no answers. *Was Fred too broken to ever really love her?*

Determined not to let this thought consume her, she retreated to the den. Lights flickered across the living room as she flipped the television dial, struggling to find anything but static at this hour. Finally she wrangled the antennae enough to pick up an old rerun, turning the volume down low.

Moonlight danced through the window as Winnie stepped into the hallway to close Allison's door. Curled innocently beneath her grandmother's quilts, with long, brown curls billowing atop the feather pillows, her daughter dreamed peacefully, no idea her father might never return. *How unfair*, Winnie thought. *She doesn't deserve this.* And then, *What more can I do to save this family?*

Back in the living room Winnie pulled a family photo album from the bookshelf. Page after page, she ran a finger across the images, proof of happier days. There was Fred carrying Allison piggyback through the sprinklers. Allison opening presents in front of the Christmas tree. Fred laughing with strands of shiny tinsel in his hair. Fred and Winnie newly engaged, standing in the Langleys' front yard, Winnie showing off her ring. *Was it all behind her now?*

Then an old clip of Judy Garland came on-screen. Winnie had always loved her voice, the emotional way she delivered a song, the longing gaze she would offer her listeners. The music explained everything Winnie had been unable to express. She fell onto the sofa, drifting away with Judy's melancholy tone.

As long as he needs me
Oh, yes, he does need me
In spite of what you see
I'm sure that he needs me.[2]

Winnie pulled a blanket over her thin nightgown and tucked her knees in close. She let her head fall against the arm of the sofa. As Judy sang her to sleep, the moon shone silver through her tears.

---

The next week Fred was strolling back to his apartment in the Village after another late night on the town. His group of rowdy friends surrounded him, laughing and jostling down the sidewalk, reeking of cigars and scotch. When they stumbled around the corner with their ties hanging loose, Fred was shocked to see Winnie, barely recognizable, sitting on the front steps of his building.

Unlike her husband, she hadn't spent the night on the town, and yet her hair was unkempt too, her clothes wrinkled. It was a look Fred had never seen on the normally polished beauty queen who had always placed great importance on maintaining a respectful appearance. Her hollow, bloodshot eyes proved she had been without sleep for far too long, and she had lost the proper posture she had held as a token of her upbringing.

Fred recognized something familiar in the haggard look on Winnie's face. She had been broken, just as he had been when Aunt Eleanor rescued him. But now he was the one inflicting the pain on someone he was supposed to protect from harm. *Had he become the monster?*

"I'm not here to bother you," Winnie said as Fred slowly moved toward her. "I'm staying at the parsonage, and I . . . I just wanted to see if you were okay. You haven't answered my calls. I've been worried."

Fred pulled Winnie into a hug, and she let her head fall against him. Just like that, a calm settled over him for the first time in years. "The we of me," Fred whispered, exhaling.

His friends respectfully walked away, leaving the couple alone.

"Rosemary took the kids to that Japanese restaurant . . . the one where they sit on the floor," Winnie said. "She'll have Allison for the night."

With the minister away for the summer, Fred hailed a cab and escorted Winnie back to the parsonage in Bernardsville. He didn't think twice about the expensive fare. He wanted to be alone with his wife, far away from any interruptions, no matter the cost.

By the time they made it to Bernardsville, they had been reminded—if ever two people were inextricably bound to one another, it was them. After months of restless nights Winnie finally fell into a peaceful sleep. Fred stayed awake, watching her dream. And through those quiet hours, he finally realized he could run no more.

In spite of all he had done to break free of his family's dysfunction, to rise above the abuse, to form real attachments and heal the wounds of abandonment, Fred was still operating from a place of pain. He'd been moving around the world frantically trying to fill all those deep, dark holes formed in his childhood, and despite wanting so desperately to be a better man than the men in his family, he'd ended up behaving much like them.

While he'd been striving so hard to please Emile, the only real father figure in his life, he had failed to fully realize that his daughter needed a father too.

He could continue seeking the attention and approval that he'd craved since his childhood, chasing stardom at the cost of his own wife and child. Or he could dare to become the father and husband the men in his own family had failed to be.

The choice became suddenly clear. Yes, he had talent. Yes, he longed to see where his gifts would lead him. And, yes, he had an insatiable desire to create, to express himself, to make an audience *feel something.*

But when it all came down to it, Fred loved Winnie and Allison more than he loved his career. He loved them more than he loved Emile. He loved them more than he loved himself.

As the sun began to rise, soft light filtered through the frosted panes and Winnie woke. Fred struggled to find the right words. There was so much he needed to say. "I can't live without you, Winnie. You can't possibly understand what I've been . . ." He wiped his hand over his face and finally broke down.

Syllable by syllable, Fred tried to express all that had happened. He told her about the horrific memories that had resurfaced during the seminar at Columbia. He confessed about his emotional breakdown, how he collapsed in Central Park, how Pete came to his rescue, and how he'd been struggling with the pain, trying to drown his shame and anger at any cost.

"It isn't just the abuse," he explained. "It's that my family—and God knows who else around me—knew it was happening. They all knew, and they didn't protect me. They let that man live right beside us. They protected *him* instead of me! Every single thing I knew about my family, my life . . . it was all a lie. I've spent years trying to forgive them for not being better providers. And turns out, that wasn't the half of it."

He grew quiet again, and Winnie sensed his pain was far greater than anything she could ever understand. She knew in that moment that his entire ability to trust or even process had been broken. After all, if you can't trust your own parents to love and protect you, who can you trust?

The truths surfaced slowly, and in time he discussed his relentless pursuit of fame, finally understanding that it had all been a hopeless effort to fill a dark, empty place in his soul.

"Bill was right. I'm broken," Fred sobbed. "And I've been running away from the only people in the world who truly mean anything at all to me."

Winnie had no idea how to process the news Fred had delivered. Nothing in her life had prepared her for this. There was no script to follow, no safe response. She did the only thing she knew to do. She reached for the man she loved and pulled him to her. "It's not your fault they hurt you, Fred. It's not your fault." Then she kissed him and said, "I'm with you, honey. I'm on your side. Always."

The unconditional love Winnie offered in that moment broke Fred in two. He had hurt her deeply, and yet she was still willing to stand beside him. What had he ever done to deserve a love like this?

"I want to fix it," Fred said, pleading forgiveness. "I'm no good without my family, no good without you. His mind was racing, trying to work out a plan. Then, after hours of wrestling with the options before him, he finally exhaled and said, "Winnie . . ." His voice was soft, almost too quiet to hear. "I need to go into the city." He pulled her close again, covering her hands with his. "It's time I have a talk with Emile."

# *Twenty-eight*

When Fred arrived at Emile's apartment in Sutton Place, it was beginning to rain. He didn't stop to chat with the familiar doorman or visit with acquaintances in the lobby. Instead, he made a beeline for the elevator and nearly ran to Emile's door. It was the only way to beat his nerves. *Don't stop. Don't think. Just do this.*

Emile greeted Fred with unusual excitement, pulling him into a fierce hug and leading him directly to the bar where he added a generous pour of Macallan to a pair of crystal-cut highballs. He handed one of the scotch whiskeys to Fred and raised his own for a toast. "To us!"

Fred tapped his glass against Emile's but did not take a swig.

"What's the matter?" Emile sat back, eyeing his pupil with pride. "You better get to looking happier. I have *big* news. Big as it gets."

Fred placed his glass on the side table and claimed one of the two familiar wingback chairs. He and Emile had spent many a night in these seats, sharing their hopes and dreams as the fire roared between them. Now, as the city skyline gleamed from beyond the rainy upper-floor window, Fred realized this apartment represented everything he'd been chasing: creativity, talent, wealth, success. A father.

"All our hard work, finally paying off." Emile beamed. "You are one meeting away from the *Company* role! Can you believe it? You've done it, son!"

"I have news too," Fred said, his hands shaking.

Emile's smile flattened. Fred's tone was too somber. Too deep.

Outside, the storm was getting stronger, an ominous sign that seemed to add to Fred's confusion. "It's Winnie."

"Oh, to hell with Winnie," Emile said forcefully. "Do you have any idea what I've done to get this for you?"

Fred's throat tightened.

"I miss my wife, Emile. I miss my daughter. I miss my life with them, and they need me."

"Then they can come back here to New York. Where you need them. What kind of woman makes you walk away from this? You call that love?"

Suddenly a deep sense of peace moved through Fred. The vision of the steeple rose again from his dreams. It was not a steeple he recognized from any church he had visited in real life, but for some reason, the image was clear in his mind, a beacon of light in the distance, shining, the cross a symbol of the crossroads he was facing.

Then he remembered the tired, sunken look in Winnie's eyes when he saw her on the front steps. And the tender forgiveness she'd offered him in the parsonage despite all he'd done to hurt her. He remembered the fragile shell of a broken little boy back in LaGrange, barely surviving all the pain that had been inflicted on him. Fred had been seeking his entire life for someone to love him, someone to care. And God had given him Winnie and Allison.

"Pull yourself together and go get this role, Fred. There's no debate here." Then his voice sharpened, and he glared with eyes of steel, the way Fred had seen him look when his ego had been ruffled or he hadn't been given what he wanted. "You owe me this."

Fred eyed the drink, fighting the lure to numb himself again.

Resisting the pressure to follow Emile's direction all the way through to the stage and the spotlight . . . to become a star.

"Isn't this what you always wanted? What have you been working for, if not this?"

Fred cleared his throat. "I don't want to live my life without my family."

"So that's it?" Emile stood, his neck tensing, his veins bulging. "That's your choice?"

Fred nodded. "I choose them."

"You can't be serious!" Emile was shouting now, red-faced and enraged. "You really want to run back home with your tail between your legs? Scramble around trying to keep your small-minded wife happy?"

Fred tensed, ready to defend the woman he loved.

"And how long do you think you'll be happy there? You give this up, you're probably giving up a Tony award. Is that not too high a price to pay?"

Fred stood and moved closer. He wanted to express his gratitude, to let Emile know that he loved him like a father and he was sorry to let him down. But as Fred opened his arms to embrace his mentor, Emile drew back his hand, slamming his glass of scotch into Fred's face and slashing a deep and painful gash across his cheek. Fred pulled his hand to the stinging wound, shocked as Emile's fury continued to boil. Before Fred could react, Emile, a former competitive boxer, swung a second time, this round landing a bone-crushing strike against Fred's nose.

Fred fell, stunned and heartbroken. Outside, lightning flashed as Emile grabbed Fred by the collar and jerked him up from the marble tiles.

"I gave you everything!" Emile's voice boomed as he dragged Fred toward the door, a bright streak of blood trailing behind them.

"Emile," Fred said. "I love her."

"And I loved you. Like a son." Emile spat the words, shoving Fred toward the elevator. "I never want to see you here again."

# *Twenty-nine*

As Fred arrived back at the parsonage, Allison stepped out to meet her father, holding her own conflicted emotions about his inconsistent presence in her life. She'd spent the last two years only seeing him for holidays or while visiting friends in Bernardsville, and now at twelve years old, she was no longer buying into Winnie's story that he'd only been away for work. But as Fred stepped out of the car, Allison gasped at the sight of the wounds. "What happened, Daddy?"

Just then Winnie came out from the house, her face full of questions. Fred eyed the nearby church and said, "Can we talk?"

Allison reluctantly returned alone to the parsonage as Winnie led Fred to the old stone sanctuary for their private conversation. Inside, the organ's brass pipes shone from the center of the room. Fred took a moment to admire the magnificent instrument he'd created. Through the seven years since his family had left Columbus, this organ had been the one consistent part of Fred's life. He'd been through many homes and jobs, Winnie and Allison had come and gone a few times, but through it all, the organ had been there, a safe and reliable outlet for his pain. He had tended it with care, working countless hours with Dr. Coci to leave a legacy for Bernardsville. In return, this organ had taken all his hurts, fears, and sorrows and transformed them into sacred songs, delivering prayers through the pipes and sustaining Fred's all-too-fragile faith when life had become too much to bear.

As sunlight streamed through the stained-glass windows, illuminating that same red cross that had welcomed him there all those years before, Fred lowered himself on bended knee beside Winnie. With tears in his eyes, he pulled the set of wedding rings from his pocket and placed them back where they belonged, on Winnie's finger.

It was time to begin again.

Winnie remained guarded, hoping for the best but fearing yet another heartbreak once Fred's creative genius took hold again. She glanced down at the rings, snugged comfortably where they should be. She'd never adjusted to the feel of her bare finger and had spent many sleepless nights fidgeting with the empty place where the bands belonged.

Now, as Fred moved to the organ bench, Winnie claimed the front pew, watching carefully as her husband's hands began to stir with trepidation across the rows of keys. With passion he struck the notes of Organ Symphony No. 1 in D Minor by Louis Vierne. It was his signature piece, the one he had performed for the Riverside Church recital and a song that had lured several audiences to their feet in applause. But now Fred seemed to be in a world of his own, playing solely for the heavens.

The sound filled the room with pristine reverberation. Fred was a master, pulling magic from the keys in a way few could. Note by note, he layered the sounds into a grand combination of stops and flows, overlapping the rich, deep tones to form a soulful symphony.

As his notes became louder, more intense, more emotional, Fred's tears began to flow. He was a man of great depth, tremendous passion. In that moment, as the music reached a powerful crescendo, Fred surrendered. It was a soul-deep submission. A genuine cry to God, a more wholehearted version of that familiar prayer from his younger years: *Thy will be done.*

Winnie moved carefully toward the organ and placed her hands atop Fred's shoulders. He was shivering, sobbing, sacrificing.

And then, after a long and mournful release . . . rebirth.

Fred held the final chord until the sounds dissipated and all the echoes fell to silence. Then he closed the organ and said simply, "Let's go home."

# *Thirty*

In 1971, Fred, Winnie, and Allison returned to Columbus as a united family. From the Langleys' living room, they watched the 25th Anniversary Tony Awards. Stephen Sondheim's *Company* received a record-setting fourteen nominations and took home six wins that night, including Best Musical. Larry Kert, the actor who'd accepted the lead role, was nominated for Best Actor in a Musical.

As Fred watched the show with Winnie, he knew how close he had come to being in Kert's place. But he swallowed all regrets, reminding himself he had not settled for this life. He had chosen it. So there was only one thing left to do. Just as his friend Carol Channing was singing on-screen from her flashback role in *Hello, Dolly!*, he would find *a new goal, a new drive.* He would feel his *heart come alive again*, with Winnie and Allison at his side.

As the couple searched for jobs from Columbus, Winnie tried to bolster Fred's confidence. While he'd struggled on a private level, he'd always been professional and disciplined when it came to his career, and he'd maintained several close relationships through it all. As word spread that Fred was looking for a job near home, offers began to come in from across the South.

In West Palm Beach, Florida, a large congregation was looking for someone to launch a forward-thinking musical theater program that would extend well beyond the typical church choir. It seemed like a good fit, and while the couple knew no one in that area, the city was below the Mason-Dixon Line, at least—even if it was an eight-hour drive from Columbus.

As Fred loaded the family's convertible for a week in the Sunshine State, the local postal carrier eyed the car. "Cutlass convertible. Nice. What is that, a '68?"

"Sure is," Winnie said with a friendly smile. "Fred got it as a surprise for me a few years back. I love the color. Reminds me of my grandmother's pearls." She reached to touch the heirloom beads around her neck before taking the daily delivery from the carrier.

As Winnie brought the letters to her mother, a bold ad from the United Methodist bulletin caught her eye:

Music Director Needed
Thomasville First United Methodist Church

Curious, she plucked the newsletter and put it in the Cutlass's console for a later look.

By now Nell was leaning over the driver's door and talking to Fred. "Are you sure you don't want to wait and leave in the morning? You're already so far behind schedule."

Fred smiled and cranked the engine, his final say in the matter.

"Don't worry, Mother." Winnie gave her the mail and an extra hug. "We'll find somewhere to stop for the night, and I'll call as soon as we get there." Then after plenty of farewell kisses for Allison, the couple was on their way.

From the passenger seat Winnie peppered Fred's ear with a string of random thoughts about sharks and palm trees, alligators and bikinis. Then she pulled the bulletin from the console. "Did you see this?"

He gave it a quick glance as Winnie explained, "A church. In Thomasville. It's practically on our route. Maybe we should swing by and take a look."

Fred grimaced. "We've all but accepted the job in West Palm Beach." He set his eyes on the road, focused on getting to Florida as planned.

"I know, honey, but Thomasville is so much closer to home, and I really would love it if we could stay in Georgia."

No answer.

"We sang there once. Back in college, remember?" Winnie adjusted her silk scarf, securing her now bleach-blonde locks as she tried to remember anything she could about the community. "I've heard Jackie Kennedy went there to hide away after the assassination. She could have gone anywhere in the world, but she chose Thomasville. That says something, don't you think?"

Mile after mile, Winnie searched for memories about the south Georgia town, sprinkling any facts that surfaced into the conversation. According to the map, it was only about 150 miles south of Columbus, a much easier commute than West Palm Beach, and the idea of being that much closer to home appealed to her.

"Do you remember Madame's story about the trains?"

Fred shook his head.

"Supposedly, wealthy northerners wanted to come south during winter, so they took the train to the end of the line—in Thomasville. Then they bought up a bunch of land and built those beautiful hunting plantations. She told us they still come there today to play polo, shoot quail . . . those kinds of things."

Fred responded with statements to contradict each of hers. "I'm not a hunter. I can't play polo. I don't eat quail."

"Oh, honey, I know that," Winnie said, frustrated with his negativity. "But I'm just thinking this place may have more to offer than we think." With a smile she reminisced. "Remember those big, beautiful oak trees? It really *is* such a sweet little town, Fred. I bet nice people too."

When Winnie pointed to the exit and said, "Last chance," Fred sighed and turned the car toward Thomasville. As Winnie had suspected, it was a surprisingly vibrant community perched just north of the Florida-Georgia line. With nearly twenty-five thousand residents, it seemed to be the kind of place where you not only knew the names of many neighbors, you likely knew the names of their parents, grandparents, and even their dogs. In spite of the extreme wealth and lush plantations that surrounded the quintessential Old South town, it was a family-centered community where nothing seemed to rise higher than the steeples. A place where people held the door open for others, business deals were made with a handshake, and the aroma of pastries filled the air as even the flagship Flowers Bakery fostered an atmosphere of sweetness.

It was 1971 when the dapper thirty-six-year-old musician drove the family's pearl-white convertible into town, admiring the beautiful antebellum homes and the impeccable landscaping. "Picture perfect," Winnie said as Fred navigated the red-brick streets. He wore a crisp sports jacket and stylish striped tie. Winnie donned classic shades and wore a well-fitted dress that complemented her Jackie O scarf. The fashionable duo turned heads as they explored.

Church bells rang across the venerable moss-draped oaks, drifting like whispers among the bright pink azaleas. They had arrived during what some would call "the magic hour," that brief window of time when the afternoon rays come through at an angle and the day shifts to a warm, amber glow. A perfect scene until, without warning, Fred pulled the car to a sudden stop right in the middle of Broad Street, and his face turned pale.

"Fred, honey? What is it?" Winnie reached for his arm, concerned.

Aghast, he pointed to Thomasville First United Methodist Church. "That's it, Winnie. That's the steeple."

Winnie followed Fred's gaze to the top of the church's tall, shingled spire, where an unassuming cross overlooked the blossoming dogwoods below. "What do you mean, that's the steeple? The one from your dreams?"

"The exact one. I'm sure of it." Fred was unable to turn his eyes from the slatted white belfry. "And they weren't dreams, Winnie. They were nightmares."

She held up the ad from the Methodist bulletin, confirming the job announcement was for that very church. "Maybe it's a sign," she said, ever the optimist.

Spring had just burst through, and leafy shadows danced across the grass as Fred pulled into a parking spot. The couple then wended their way up the steps to the beautiful nineteenth-century sanctuary. It was a unique building with ornate brickwork and layered angles, an impressive Victorian design unlike any church Fred had ever seen—except in his dreams.

Fred's throat tightened as they entered the vast expanse, where a man called from across the vaulted nave, "Come on in." He walked toward the vestibule carrying a stack of bulletins. When Winnie realized he was the minister, she put on her best smile, introducing her husband and making a point to mention they'd just moved back from New York, where he'd earned a master's degree at the School of Sacred Music.

Quickly explaining they were just driving through from Columbus, Fred added, "On our way to interview with a church in West Palm Beach."

"You know, we've been trying to fill a position here too," the pastor said, a hint in his voice as he introduced himself. "George Zorn.

If you'd like to stay, you could lead choir rehearsal tonight. See if it's a fit. Starts in less than an hour."

"Oh my goodness, Fred! Wouldn't that be wonderful?" Winnie beamed. Then she told the pastor, "We do have a few extra days built into our trip."

"You'd be a tremendous help," said the Reverend Zorn.

Fred glanced toward the choir loft where the entire wall held an elaborate series of pipes from one of the most impressive organs he'd seen since leaving Riverside and Union. As he examined the full display, he gasped, suddenly realizing that this scene had also appeared in some of those recurring dreams.

Winnie asked if she could use the phone. "I think my mother has friends here in town," she explained. "I bet they would be happy to let us stay for the night."

As the reverend led Winnie to his office, she leaned toward Fred and whispered, "Let's just keep our options open. We never know what we're going to find when we get to Florida."

While Winnie headed toward the phone, Fred made his way through the sanctuary, hoping to give the organ a try. He tested the resistance of the pedals, the keys. Then he began to play Bach's Toccata and Fugue in D Minor, a classical composition testing the full range of the organ. Fred needed to learn the limits of this instrument, weigh the sound, explore its tone. He thought back to all the choirs he'd led, all the songs he'd performed. This was one of his favorites, and the familiar melody helped to ease the anxiety he'd felt since seeing the steeple.

By the second stanza Rev. Zorn returned. His brows were bunched, heavy with emotion. "I've never heard the organ played like *that*."

Within the hour choir members began to arrive. The reverend introduced Fred and Winnie, explaining the church's good fortune at "having such a talented duo drop by out of the blue."

As more than a dozen members trickled in, they were friendly and engaging. The singers not only impressed the couple with their chic style and impeccable manners, they were eager to share their hopes for an invigorating music program. The group had big ideas, and when they discovered Fred had directed a section of Handel's *Messiah* with the Bernardsville choir, the vocalists reacted with a flurry of excitement, asking if they, too, could tackle the challenging performance.

Fred had his doubts. Even Beethoven had considered Handel to be the greatest composer who ever lived, and all would agree that *Messiah* was his masterpiece—a powerful series of baroque arias and rousing choruses, including the famously emotional "Hallelujah." The music was no small feat to perform, even in Bernardsville where the talent seemed to be without end. He would be wrong to even tempt this small choir with such an idea, so he tried to steer their hopes back to a more realistic goal—Sunday morning services.

"Ready for rehearsal?" Fred asked, opening his hymnal.

Throughout the session, Fred offered tips they'd never been taught, tricks he'd learned from his own instructors through the years. "Make sure you pronounce every sound. Don't let the middle get blurry. Sing all the way through each word. Careful not to drop the end." When they were unable to hold a note steady, he taught them they could sing on the inhale, a fact that went against everything they had ever known. "You need to have a pear-shaped tone, like a fruit. Large, open-the-back-of-your-mouth sensation like you're yawning. Lift that soft palate. Then focus and round the front of your mouth. That's how you get that very mature, heavy, full tone like opera singers."

By the end of the hour, Fred closed the hymnal and smiled. "I have to admit. I'm impressed."

The singers were equally enamored, asking a string of questions about technique and performance, hungry for all the knowledge they could gain before Fred and Winnie took their leave. They all stayed long past dismissal time, sharing ideas and vocal strategies while getting to know more about the people of this community, including a particularly engaging couple, Tom and Janice Faircloth.

Finally, when the choir members had gone home for the evening, the Reverend Zorn thanked Fred and Winnie for their time. "I've never seen a spark like that," he said. "I don't know how to describe it, but . . . if you'd be willing to accept, it would be my pleasure to offer you the position."

Fred shook the reverend's hand and said he'd give it some thought. Then the couple headed toward their friends' home for the night. As Fred opened the Cutlass's door for Winnie, he said, "I figured I'd never find another choir like the one I had in Bernardsville."

Winnie smiled. They had finally found their place.

# Thirty-one

Throughout their first summer in Thomasville, Fred focused on building a strong church choir. He held rehearsals on Wednesday nights and quickly grew the number of vocalists from fifteen to forty. He also was in the process of securing funds to restore the pipe organ of his dreams. Any remaining hours were spent managing the construction of the family's new home, as all three were eager to escape their temporary apartment at first chance.

One of the many bright spots of Fred's job was that the choir members were exhibiting talents parallel to those of the people in Bernardsville. The singers were hardworking, dedicated, and passionately committed to elevating the music program, even learning portions of *Messiah* as they prepared a special Christmas program.

Nevertheless, while the adult choir was off to a powerful start, the youth chorus was basically nonexistent. Each week, Allison sank in humiliation while a handful of bored teenagers half-heartedly sang through the old-fashioned hymns.

Determined to bring something new to the youth of Thomasville, as well as create an opportunity for Allison to continue developing her talent, Fred remembered the music that spoke to him as a young performer. Then he recalled his days on Broadway and at Union Seminary and even further back to the years he had spent building the outstanding youth choir in Columbus. At that time he had taken a group of middle-school girls, most of whom had never received vocal training on any level, and he had built a choral group that earned praise and awards. He'd had zero budget, but in the end that "little choir that could" had left a longstanding positive impact across Georgia.

If he'd done it once, he could do it again.

That next Sunday evening, as the few familiar teens ambled in for rehearsal, Fred played the piano with vibrant energy, singing through the rock-style "What's the Buzz / Strange Thing Mystifying." The music had been written by Tim Rice and Andrew Lloyd Webber for the rock-opera *Jesus Christ Superstar*. It was scheduled to debut on Broadway just that year, but Fred, still on the cutting edge of music trends, already knew the songs by heart. The young singers appeared to have never heard a song like it, and by indication of their big smiles and wide eyes, it became clear Fred was delivering something new and exciting to these Thomasville teens.

As Fred belted out the catchy rhythm, the teenagers gathered around the piano. Allison held back, observing nervously and hoping her new peers would accept her dad's out-of-the-box approach without laughing behind his back. Sensing he was onto something, Fred slid right into the fast-paced lyrics as a couple of the members began to dance around the room. By the end of the chorus, the teens were hooked. This was nothing like any church choir rehearsal they had ever attended. They were actually having fun! As they made their way out of the choir room that night, Allison smiled. And Fred exhaled.

The following Sunday, the young singers had not only returned, they had brought friends. Where there had only been a handful of teens the first week, a dozen now flowed through the doors. The week after that, fifteen. And soon there were twenty. Even more surprising was the fact that these were some of the most social adolescents in town, the kind of kids who had several other activities to choose from, but they were showing up to sing.

After several months of weekly rehearsals, it was time to show the adults what the youth had been learning. That Sunday morning, Fred assembled the young vocalists at the front of the sanctuary to perform his unique composition of the song that first caught their interest, "What's the Buzz." The children dressed in quirky homemade costumes, adding to the energy onstage as the entire chorus lifted their voices to tell the familiar story.

At the end of the song, the congregation applauded, a gesture not usually extended during formal Sunday service. This fun and unusual experience drew the youth choir participation levels even higher, and Rev. Zorn could not have been more pleased. When he thanked Fred after church one Sunday, Fred shrugged and said, "I just know what music meant to me as a kid."

Unfortunately, while one might assume the adults would be thrilled to discover their teens were spending Sunday nights at church, Fred had unintentionally stepped on a few toes. One evening the family had just sat down to dinner in their small second-floor apartment when they were interrupted by a rapid knock. Fred opened the door to find a gray-haired man standing tight-lipped with a forced smile. Winnie joined Fred at the stoop, and the visitor introduced himself as the head pastor of one of the other churches.

"Sorry to interrupt your supper," he said, adjusting his wire-framed glasses. "I just wanted to stop by and welcome y'all to town."

"Oh, how kind of you." Winnie beamed, inviting the gentleman in for a serving of her signature dishes: country fried steak and green beans with a hot-buttered slice of corn bread. "Melt in your mouth." Winnie smiled. "Promise."

"Thank you, ma'am, but I don't want to keep you. I was hoping to have a quick word with your husband." He looked to Fred and fidgeted with his tie. "About the youth choir."

Fred got the hint and stepped outside, closing the door behind him. In the dining room, Winnie and Allison waited patiently to continue supper, discussing another invitation for Allison to fly back to New York and record with Rosemary. It was the third one they'd declined in recent months, not to count the calls for commercial shoots. While Allison agreed it was time to focus on her new life in Thomasville, she remained reluctant to completely surrender her own career.

Within a few minutes, Fred was back in his seat, and the minister was long gone.

"Something wrong?" Winnie asked.

Instead of answering, Fred lifted his fork to his mouth and said, "Best dinner ever."

Winnie smiled, taking a sip of iced tea. Drops of water were already pearling on the humid glass when Allison prodded, "Tell us, Daddy."

"He's upset because the kids have stopped coming to choir rehearsals at his church. Apparently, they've joined ours instead."

All were quiet as they gave this news a moment to sink in. Then Winnie adjusted her napkin across her lap. "Well, gosh, that means we're onto something. Of course, it won't do us any good to cause trouble."

"I never intended to pull singers from their own churches," Fred explained.

Winnie nodded. "Maybe we could push the rehearsal time back an hour? Let them meet with their own choirs first. Then they can walk over to ours."

Fred took another bite and said again, "Delicious, Winnie."

"You really think they'll go to both rehearsals?" Allison's face pinched.

"As long as we keep it fun, they'll keep coming back," Fred assured her.

After some thought, Winnie offered another idea. "What if we create a community choir instead? Something apart from the church."

Fred pulled his chair closer to the table, intrigued. "Could keep our rehearsals set for after-hours. Make them nondenominational. Open to everyone."

"I like the sound of that," Winnie said with a nod.

"Even if we meet at the church," Fred continued, "how can they complain about us practicing on, say . . . Thursday nights?"

"They can't!" Allison grinned.

Fred served himself a slice of corn bread.

"We'll need a name," Winnie said. "So no one confuses it with the church choir."

The family began shooting ideas across the table: concert choir, choral group, Thomasville singers.

"What if we do more than just sing?" Fred suggested. "The students are loving these show tunes. Maybe we could bring a taste of Broadway right here to Thomasville."

"You mean, perform musicals?" Winnie's pitch elevated. She was eager to put her creative skills to the test again.

"No. Not exactly. There are too few parts in a show. We wouldn't be able to include everyone." After another swig of tea, he explained. "I'm thinking we teach them a combination of styles, everything from show tunes to pop songs. Kind of like what you and I used to do on the radio."

"A revue, of sorts?" Winnie looked off to the side, ideas already flowing. "I love it!"

"I do too." Allison grinned.

Winnie leaned over the table, excited. "I could help jazz it up, you know. And Tom Faircloth is great with choreography. Could find an artist to design a set. Some volunteers to help sew costumes. Tackle it the way I produced those plays with Dr. Seaver back at Union."

Fred agreed. "Take a little of everything we've learned along the way. We can put it all together here, help these kids see what they're made of."

"Exactly," Winnie said. Then she fanned her hand through the air and said, with flair, "The Thomasville Music and Drama Troupe."

"That's it," Fred said, assuredly. "The Thomasville Music and Drama Troupe. Perfect!"

Allison took her final bite and sat back against the chair, satisfied. A long wave of silence settled among them. Then Winnie tilted her head toward her pensive daughter. "What are you thinking, honey?"

The teen was all smiles as she looked at Fred. "I'm thinking if anyone can do this . . . Daddy can."

Winnie with Nell, Jim, and Bill after winning Miss LaGrange

Fred accompanying Winnie during their first year at LaGrange College

Winnie and Fred performing on their radio show, *Songs for You*

Winnie and Fred at their wedding

In Chautauqua, New York

Winnie and Fred in the early '60s

Preparing for a spring concert in the late '70s

Before a concert performance in 1972

The Music and Drama Troupe perform at the White House for President Jimmy Carter

Velma at the family's old upright piano

Five-year-old Fred

Fred with baby Allison

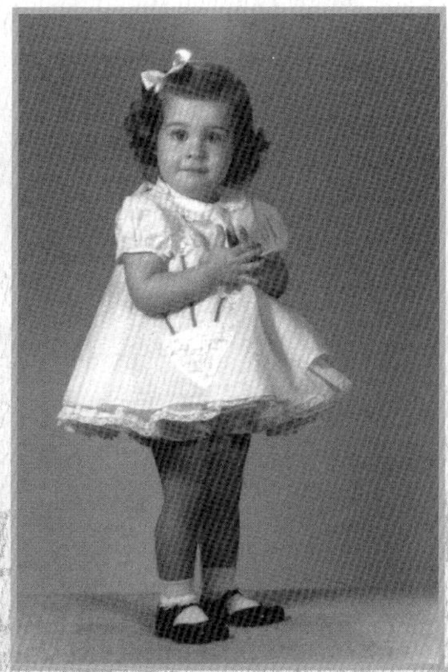

Allison at sixteen months old

Troupe dress rehearsal in the early years

# Troupe's Spring Concert delivers dazzling magic in Rose City

By PATTI WARD
*Times-Enterprise News Editor*

Two things are givens in springtime Thomasville: Pollen and Thomasville Music and Drama Troupe's Spring Concert.

The dreaded first aggravates and never seems to go away. The second, with the capacity to sooth, calm and thrill, arrives and departs all too soon.

This year's concert offers yet another aspect — dazzling magic that may be witnessed tonight and Saturday night at Thomasville Municipal Auditorium, 144 E. Jackson St. Curtaintime is 8.

Act I opens with highlights from the Walt Disney film "Aladdin."

A musical revue — Rock the Jukebox — is a nostalgic blend of music, drama and dance. The high-energy hit parade's tunes include big band, country and western, rock 'n' roll and easy-listening songs by Troupe singers and dancers.

One eclipse of the musical provides the audience with a tongue-in-cheek retrospective of music that made listeners chuckle through the years.

Act II of the 21st annual Spring Concert, as is the event's tradition, salutes the best of Broadway. In addition to standard Broadway favorites, the act includes music fron current musical productions, such as "The Most Happy Fella," "The Secret Garden," "The Will Rogers Follies" and "Jekyll and Hyde."

Another Act II attraction is a medley of songs from "Guys and Dolls," which will showcase singing, dancing and comedy.

The grand finale is a salute to Troupe seniors, during which Lyn Deringer will present a slide show about seniors. Slides are comprised of photos provided by senior Troupers' parents, friends and teachers.

Senior Troupe members will be recognized at the end of the Saturday show, when Troupe awards and scholarships are presented.

Troupe was organized in 1972 by Fred Allen, who continues as director. Troupe today has 151 teen members from Thomas and surrounding counties.

Troupe members rehearse weekly year-round for the group's Christmas and Spring shows. This week, they've rehearsed nightly for hours, including dress rehearsals Wednesday and Thursday.

**Troupers Christi Spann and Robert Williams rehearse country and western-style in 'Rock the Jukebox' during Thursday dress rehearsal for tonight's and Saturday's annual Thomasville Music and Drama Troupe Spring Concert. (Greg Bryant/Staff Photo)**

Saturday's Troupe concert is a sellout. A few tickets remain for tonight's. performance. Tickets are available at the door.

Concert musicians are Bobby Dollar in percussion and Allen as pianist. Staging is by Becky Sellers, Denny Blair and a committee of Troupe members' parents. Choreographers are Leigh Brandenburg and Allison Cheney. Costumes are by Sue McAnnally, with technical lighting by Ken Lanter. Rose Marie Robbins is Concert coordinator.

Newspaper coverage of Troupe's 1993 Spring Concert

Allison with her grandparents Nell and Jim

Fred playing with a young Allison

Fred, Winnie, and Allison visit Madame Elizabeth Gilbert

RCA
FRED ALLEN
ARTISTS AND REPERTOIRE PRODUCER
RCA VICTOR RECORD DIVISION
RADIO CORPORATION OF AMERICA
155 EAST 24TH STREET
NEW YORK, N. Y. 10010
(212) 689-7200


Fred's business card from RCA Victor

Allison with Ed McMahon

Allison in ninth grade

Magazine articles

Just a few of the numerous letters sent to Fred and Winnie over the years (see Coda to read excerpts from some of them)

Winnie and Fred as honorary grand marshals of the Thomasville Rose Parade

Early 2000s Music and Drama Troupe

2004 Troupe dance rehearsal

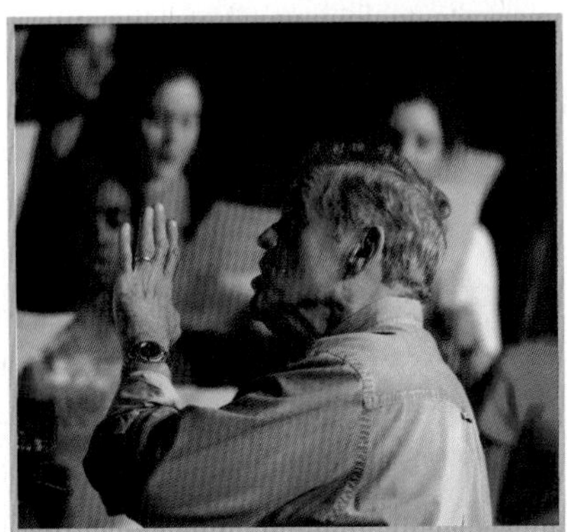

Fred in Troupe rehearsal, 2006

Encore at the 25th anniversary show

Fred and Winnie in 2012

# *Thirty-two*

Throughout that first year the family focused on building the kind of deep, trusting friendships they had established in LaGrange, Columbus, and Bernardsville. Eventually they traded their temporary apartment for a beautiful new ranch home in the Country Club neighborhood. And after years of consecutive transitions, they finally began to plant deep roots. They were done with relocations, separations, and farewells. Whatever challenges this new life delivered, they would face them together right here as a family. Thomasville, they decided, would be their forever home. Reconnecting with his childhood memories of Papa Noah, Fred filled the family's new yard with camellias and roses, all anchored by a sturdy magnolia tree much like the one that stood guard over his bedroom window at Highpoint—the Lewis home he had called his own as a teen back in LaGrange.

Because Fred's music director position was part-time, Winnie had begun working at the church too, helping with secretarial tasks to supplement the family income. In the meantime, Fred had convinced both the public and private school districts to add music appreciation to their course load. Now, he would be splitting his weeks between the two campuses while continuing to expand the music program at church.

As Allison finished her breakfast before her first day of high school, Fred poured a thermos of coffee and asked, "Ready?"

"Let's go," she sighed. The many moves had begun to weigh on her, and while she had enjoyed a wonderful year of eighth grade in Thomasville, entering yet another school was no small challenge.

"It won't really feel like a new school, honey. You've already got a good group of friends who'll be there." Winnie smiled reassuringly. "And the rest will want to be your friend as soon as they meet you."

Allison looked down shyly, adjusting her outfit one last time. She tended to be an introvert, like her father, sitting back and letting others come to her rather than reaching out to meet new people. This had always enabled her to form healthy friendships, but such relationships would take time, even with the help of her growing circle of friends.

"Just remember who you are." Fred hugged his daughter. "Be yourself. That's the best you can give to the world."

Allison exhaled as Fred gave Winnie a quick kiss and headed off to Thomasville High with his daughter. When they pulled into the faculty parking lot, a group of girls met Allison at the car, giving her a smooth transition into ninth grade. Fred, on the other hand, sat for a minute before cutting the engine. Around him, a few educators scrambled to their rooms, but Fred took a deep breath, closed his eyes, and thought about what he was about to walk into—a job of low pay and high demands, far removed from any spotlights or prestigious accolades. *Who in his right mind would leave RCA or Broadway . . . for this?*

As doubts began to resurface, Fred cleared his head. He had loved being a teacher in Columbus and again at Lincoln Center, and his work with the youth church choir had proven successful. If this was what he had in front of him, then he was determined to make the most of it. No one had impacted his life more than his musical mentors, and now he would be in a position to do the same for these students in Thomasville. With time ticking, he finally left his car and made his way to the green space. Much to his surprise, a few students greeted him, following as he moved toward his assigned classroom.

"Is it true you sang on Broadway, Mr. Allen?"

Another chimed in, "Did you really win a Grammy?"

A third added, "I heard you know Elvis! What's he like?"

The questions whirred, with the huddle of excited teens eager to hear every detail about New York City. Fred recognized this desire to sneak a peek at a world beyond rural Georgia. It didn't seem so long ago when he was their age, desperate for someone to understand his big dreams and his never-ending desire to create. When he looked into the eyes of these teens, he knew them. He really knew them.

As Fred made his way through campus, he could see why the school had been coined "Pizza Hut High" by locals. Its odd octagonal pods resembled the distinct design of the popular restaurant franchise, with awkward roof angles leading to a flattened surface at the top. Two teachers stood near the entrance of his assigned pod, watching all the commotion with interest. The older one was pale, thin, and looked as if she put more cigarettes in her mouth than food. Her sidekick was stockier, with a strip of bright gray roots that contrasted with her long red locks. They smiled when Fred said, "Good morning." But as he walked to his room, he overheard one whisper to the other, "He can't be *that* talented. Why else would he be *here*?"

When the students filtered into his classroom, he greeted each one with a firm handshake, drawing from his psychology training to gauge personalities. Those who spoke clearly, made eye contact, and responded without hesitation were the self-confident leaders. He would call on them to set the example. Others shuffled away with their heads held low or giggled as they looked to their friends for direction. These followers were likely to be afraid of criticism and would do anything to fit in, so Fred would boost them with just the right amount of praise. Finally, there were those whose cheeks blushed red at the unexpected attention. Fred would not call them out, even for positive reasons, as their insecurities would likely get the best of them.

So far Fred had seen nothing he couldn't handle, but there was one young man who avoided interaction altogether, sliding past the new teacher with a shy, fatigued look on his face. Fred carefully eyed him. He was an attractive young man with an athletic build that likely could have landed him in the role of the all-American homecoming king if he hadn't chosen to wear layers of baggy clothes as if he didn't want to be seen. His hair was long like most of the boys, but unkempt, hanging down over his eyes, and he was the only guy in the room not watching the beautiful girl who was the last to enter.

"Hi. I'm Laura," the girl said, shaking Fred's hand with a steady confidence. Her long blonde hair and golden summer tan were an irresistible magnet for her peers, but her bubbly personality seemed an equal draw. She claimed a seat on the lowest of the three-tiered rows and said, "We heard you were rich and famous, Mr. Allen. Is that true?"

The others stared wide-eyed, eager to hear their teacher's backstory.

In educator mode, Fred stayed serious, setting a disciplined tone. "Laura, right?"

The girl beamed, apparently happy he had already learned her name. The students would soon realize he had memorized all of their names, his photographic memory being one of his intellectual gifts.

"Surely you aren't the kind of girl who believes everything she hears," Fred said with a playful smile. Holding everyone's rapt attention, he asked the group, "Why are we here?"

It was an unusual way to start class, one that made the students look at each other quizzically, trying to gauge reactions. Fred walked along the front row as they pondered his question. He took time to give eye contact and then said, "Think about it. Why even have a music class? Of all things you're at school to learn, why music?"

He let the pause do its work, as the students shifted in their seats, studying his every move.

"Because music . . . music can change the world. Or at least change your life. I can tell you that it completely changed mine." He spoke with passion.

Laura smiled. The boy in the back stared blankly out the window. He was the only one not engaged with the lesson.

"And yes," Fred continued, eyeing the young man. "You matter too. Because you, too, can change the world." After a small pause, he continued, "And maybe music can help you do it."

He stopped near a girl with freckles and braids, leaning in as if speaking only to her. "And another thing that matters is that you keep showing up every day." He looked around at the others who were all processing their atypical new teacher. "I *will* notice when you aren't here. I'll notice, and I'll care. Why?"

Fred pointed to a boy in the middle who was laughing. "Because you get paid to," the youth answered, trying to be funny.

The music man swung his arm charismatically, as if the answer was correct. "Because it's my job," he echoed dramatically. "Yes. Yes, it is."

Everyone laughed.

Then Fred grew serious again, lowering his voice to make them listen even more closely. "But it's also more than just a job to me. I don't care what test score you earn or how we decorate the classroom. Those things are irrelevant to your quality of life."

His volume increased gradually, along with emotion, and he gestured with emphasis to land each point. "I care about how you treat one another. I care about you not selling yourselves short. I care about you getting through high school without being devoured by the struggles of life. I care about you not falling through the cracks."

Then he stepped back, remembering his elementary principal, Mrs. Duncan, as he took in the entire group of students from the front of the room, near the piano. "I care about *you*. Every single one of you. That's why we're here today. And that's why it matters. Because if we don't find a place where it's safe, even encouraged, to care for one another, then we're all just a bunch of animals. Music . . . music reminds us to care. And just as importantly, it's fun!" He added a wink.

The students still engaged, Fred sat at the piano bench and began to play Buffalo Springfield's popular protest song, "For What It's Worth." It had found its way to the pop charts years before, and as Fred rounded out the first verse, he lifted one hand toward the class, signaling the students to join in for the familiar chorus. He then instructed Laura to take the lead. She stood, hesitantly at first, but then kept singing as she stepped toward the piano.

At Fred's invitation others followed, building the energy as they gathered around the choppy old upright. Its top had been scratched and worn from years spent in the school's dusty storage room, but Fred had given it a fresh tune, and so far it had held. As the small group of teens sang along, others began to mouth the words softly from the safety of their seats.

By the ending notes nearly every student was smiling. Just as with the youth choir at church, Fred had won them over with a song.

Fred eyed the teens and asked, "Now tell me, what do you feel?" The students waited for him to tell them the answer. Again, he pressed. "What does that melody, those lyrics, make you *feel*?"

He scanned their faces for answers, and the pensive expressions suggested they were giving this serious thought. The class was a music appreciation class, not a singing class, but Fred knew he first had to get them to care about music before he could teach any hard-core theory. He began calling them out by name, pushing them to give words to their emotions. They were each in awe when he identified their names correctly, and his questioning yielded replies such as, "I feel happy. Inspired. Hopeful."

With each answer Fred responded with animated expressions, encouraging them to share openly, without a filter. Without fear. Reminding them, "There are no wrong answers here."

Then as the students began to talk with one other, he clapped once, loudly, resulting in a sudden return to silence. "Ahhh . . . you see? Sound is power," he explained. "When you hear a sound, or a song, you're actually receiving energy. And that energy affects you. It all comes down to physics." He snapped his fingers and added, "Sound waves."

He stood, and the students walked back to their seats. Fred began to identify various instruments he had in stock, showing the different sounds made by each: cymbals, drum, flute, violin. All were participating, except the boy in the back of the class, a teen who clearly wanted to be anywhere but in a high school music appreciation class singing from the Billboard charts and learning about sound waves.

"Now think about this. There is only one instrument in the world that is capable of both words and melody," Fred said, waiting for the boy to make eye contact. When the disgruntled student finally looked up, Fred added, "We create sound with our voice. And, as I said, sound is power."

He emphasized these last three words, sensing the boy had been feeling, above all else, powerless. Just in case he had not gotten the message the first time, Fred repeated each word emphatically. "*Sound. Is. Power.*"

The rest of the session Fred spent getting to know his students. He led them through a few fun team-building exercises, trying to establish trust and respect within the classroom. The only resistance came from the young man in the back, who seemed to shift back and forth from an underlying rage to numb disconnect.

The class period passed quickly, and when the bell rang to signal dismissal, the students left the room in a flurry of enthusiasm, chatting to their friends about their cool new music teacher and jokingly chanting down the hallway, "Sound is power!" They sang this with the passionate flair Fred had exhibited when teaching, which only seemed to add to the envy of the two teachers who had side-eyed Fred that morning. They stood at the end of the hall and barked at the students to "Hurry" and "Get to class." Fred watched, hoping he wasn't destined for the same burnout so many teachers seemed to face while also wondering how he might ease the tension.

Those two may have been suspicious of Fred, but a third teacher smiled warmly from the doorway to her special education room. Fred had interacted with friends from all ethnic backgrounds in New York, especially while living in the Village, but he was surprised to see this African American teacher working in the public schools of Thomasville. When he had left Georgia, the schools had been segregated, and despite a large percentage of minority residents in the community, he'd never had a teacher with skin darker than his own part-Native American tone. As the woman greeted Fred from the adjacent classroom, he took it as a sign of hope, proof that Thomasville would be a progressive-minded place, even here in the Deep South.

Smiling back at the teacher, Fred noticed a frail, sandy-haired young boy with an obvious disability leaving her classroom. In that same moment a group of boys forced their way through the pod, laughing and mocking the young guy.

"Hey!" Fred said forcefully.

The teachers observed, curiously, as the boys turned toward Fred. He gave them a long, commanding stare that clearly directed them to cut it out.

With broad shoulders and a thick neck, the bully strutted toward the exit, and his posse followed. They were not yet out of earshot when the aggressor huffed, "He thinks we're one of his little songbirds."

Laughing obnoxiously, one of the others sang out, "Tweet! Tweet!"

Fred was reminded of his own childhood days, trying to avoid Uncle Dirk and the abusive ballplayers. He was fighting the dark flashback when the kind special education teacher sighed and said, "Thank you."

"Some things never change," Fred said, his voice carrying both sadness and frustration.

"Most people around here aren't that way," she said. "Some just don't know any better. Those boys think that's how to act like a man. Be tough, loud, abrasive. Like a bunch of animals smashing their antlers together." She shook her head, welcoming students into her classroom. Then she looked at Fred and continued. "That's why they need strong, stable role models. If they had more of that, maybe they'd know how to behave." She extended her hand with a smile. "Frances Williams."

Fred shook Frances's hand and said, "Sure am glad to meet you. I was beginning to fear I might have landed in the wrong pod."

She laughed and glanced down the hall toward their jaded coworkers. With a softer volume, she said, "Change scares a lot of people. Don't let 'em get to you."

Then the bell rang, and all four teachers returned to their classrooms. As he closed his door for his next group of students, Fred was grateful to have been placed next to someone who seemed to be gentle and clearheaded. If the morning was any indicator of how this year would go, he certainly was going to need an ally.

# *Thirty-three*

While teaching music appreciation in the schools, Fred continued to grow the choral program at the Methodist church. In hopes of keeping young people involved in their own churches, he pushed his youth choir rehearsals back an hour on Sunday nights, but he had not yet gone as far as launching the music and drama troupe the family had discussed over dinner. To everyone's surprise, most of the teens had been returning each week after their own church rehearsals were complete, suggesting the teens of Thomasville might actually support the idea of a community youth choir. Soon the group had outgrown the small choir room and relocated to the congregation's fellowship building for a larger space.

By October it was time for something more.

After running his idea by Rev. Zorn, Fred tacked a sign-up sheet outside his classroom. At the top of the page, Winnie had typed: Thomasville Music and Drama Troupe. Laura and a few of her friends filled in their names to get the list started. As students began to filter in to music class for the day, they noticed the sign-up station and began buzzing about the clipboards, building excitement. Fred stood back and let the students take the lead. He listened quietly as questions filtered through the group: *What if I can't read the music? Do we have to wear a costume? How much does it cost?* These queries were countered by comments of all extremes: *Can I sing a solo? Oh, I hope he doesn't make me sing a solo!*

As the bell rang, Fred nudged the teens to their seats and moved to the piano. His presence hushed the room, and the students immediately settled in, giving him their full attention. He was a quiet man, not like the teachers who would sometimes yell at their students, and his class had quickly learned to respond accordingly.

Now that he had their focus, he explained his plans for Troupe. "We'll invite students from the county school and the private school to join us."

"Oh joy," one of the girls said with a smirk, drawing laughs from all sides of the classroom.

Fred had expected that kind of flare-up. The region had long been divided by class, race, gender, and religion. As far as he knew, Troupe would be the first activity that dared try to bridge all these groups.

"You are far smarter than the people who believe in stereotypes," Fred said in response. Then he added, "Respect others. Respect yourself. I expect nothing less."

Launching such a troupe would be no small undertaking, but Fred believed wholeheartedly that the people of Thomasville would rise to the challenge. Nevertheless, bridging cultural divides wasn't his objective. Fred's goal was to give young people a positive creative outlet, as his musical mentors had done for him. And most of all he wanted to help them make beautiful sounds, satisfying his burning desire to create.

"Look around this room," Fred instructed. The students complied. "Every person you see here today has something to offer. Something you can't."

A few of the kids kept their heads low, seeming to lack the confidence of others more affluent or popular.

Fred noticed and spoke directly to them. "It doesn't matter where your parents work or what kind of house you call home. Talent doesn't see any of that. Talent comes from somewhere deeper, somewhere pure. It's in your bones, in your blood. In your heart. And it's begging you to let it out."

He stood and walked near each chair, holding everyone's attention. "When someone we know starts to forget they have something to offer, it's our job to remind them. Remind them there is something truly unique in them. Something unique in each of us. Something no one else can ever take or destroy, no matter how hard they may try. And yes, there are people out there who will try."

The air was charged as Fred moved back to the piano. Slowly, students began raising their hands, and Fred answered questions about Troupe: "Rehearsals will be held two nights a week, Thursdays and Sundays. . . . I have very high expectations, but this group is open to anyone willing to give your best efforts. . . . No, you don't need stage experience. You just need to enjoy music and come ready to learn. . . . Can't sing? I bet you can sing better than you think. You might surprise yourself."

Most of the students expressed interest, except Paul, that one annoyed kid in the back who always wore baggy clothes and seemed to lack any real friends. Fred had tried to reach him countless times, to find out what was causing such angst, but he hadn't been able to break through, no matter how hard he had tried. If he called on him in class, Paul stared silently and refused to answer. If he tried to have a private conversation, Paul wouldn't even make eye contact. He was so withdrawn, Fred was beginning to worry. Anger was one thing, but numbness? Emptiness? That only happens when all hope has died.

When the bell rang, Paul prowled the hall like a ticking time bomb. No one spoke to him, and he seemed intent on keeping it that way. The thin teacher at the end of the pod saw Fred's attempts to reach the troubled teen. She rolled her eyes and said, "Why bother with a kid like that? He'll end up in jail someday. Wait and see."

Her unhappy cohort shook her head and said, "Lost cause."

Frances defended the wayward student to Fred. "He wasn't always this way."

The redheaded teacher smirked. "Maybe he should be in your class. He is *special.* That's for sure."

Just like that, Fred was transported back to his own childhood, hearing that he had been born with "special" gifts, a misunderstood outsider who felt he didn't belong. While most people at Thomasville High looked at Paul and saw only his troubles, Fred looked at him and saw some part of himself.

That afternoon when school released, teens stirred around planning weekend dates and talking about homecoming. A small group of Fred's students began playfully singing one of the songs Fred had taught them from the brand-new Broadway musical *Pippin.* Spirits ran high, and he was happy to see the music's positive impact already taking place.

Join us, leave your fields to flower
Join us, leave your cheese to sour
Join us, come and waste an hour or two[1]

Of course, the two resentful teachers shot scornful looks.

Fred was trying to ignore them when he noticed Paul getting into a car with an attractive older woman behind the wheel. Dressed in a scant low-cut blouse that covered barely more than a halter top, she looked to be at least two decades older than Paul but exuded strong sensual energy even from the driver's seat. On first glance, the situation may have seemed like any of the other teens being picked up by their mothers, but Fred quickly sensed something uneasy in the way this woman leaned over to embrace the young man. Something unnatural about the way Paul smiled at her, then looked away.

Frances's car was parked next to Fred's in the faculty lot just outside their classrooms. She eyed the bizarre exchange and then said, "That's not his mother, you know."

After all Fred had experienced, he had learned to sense predators a mile away, and now Frances had confirmed his suspicions. As the car left the lot, he was certain. Paul was more than just a troubled kid with a bad attitude. He needed help.

"What do you know about him?" Fred asked.

"All I know is his parents don't seem to take much interest in him. It's obvious he needs somebody in his life who really cares." Francis gave Fred a knowing look, as if to say, *somebody like you*.

# *Thirty-four*

One fall weekend, as the temperatures were dropping, Fred called Winnie and Allison to the living room piano. Outside the winds had picked up, sprinkling leaves across the lawn like confetti. Inside, Allison had been doing homework while Winnie was scheduling a few events for the women's ensemble she had launched under Fred's direction. While his wife and daughter were focused on their own projects, Fred had closed his journal and began to jot down song ideas for Troupe. His musical genius had long enabled him to play without sheet music, and his photographic memory allowed him to memorize the scores for thousands of songs. For that reason he had been dubbed the "walking jukebox" and was able to fulfill nearly any musical request on the spot. Now it was time to put his skills to the test.

Having finished her calls, Winnie joined Fred sitting at the black Steinway concert grand piano they had moved with them from New York. "Why so serious?"

"I'm trying to choose music for the troupe," Fred explained.

"It might be nice to pull some classic show tunes," Winnie suggested. "Give the adults in the audience a nice stroll down memory lane before introducing them to the modern shows. Maybe you could compose some kind of unique arrangement of all our favorites?"

"I like that," Fred said, scribbling across one of his many note cards as Allison looked up from her studies.

"How about some new songs too?" Allison suggested. "Stuff from the radio. With your own spin."

"Of course," Fred said with a wink. Ever the creator, he loved to rearrange scores, which he'd spent a lot of his time doing while working at RCA.

As the evening stretched beyond sunset, the rippling leaves tucked under the blanket of night, moonlight began to shine across the polished piano. It created a mesmerizing glow, reminding Fred of the big city lights that still shone back in Manhattan, where Mac had given Fred this rare Steinway model, an instrument that was more than a hundred years old. Recognized by professional musicians as "the perfect piano," it had been a meaningful gift to recognize their special friendship and show appreciation for all Fred had done at RCA and Bernardsville Methodist. From the bench Fred recalled the shabby upright he'd first played from his mother's lap, out of tune and missing a few keys.

Now Fred looked around the room, tracing back through the years and realizing how many meaningful relationships music had brought him. Since leaving New York, he'd tried to reach Emile several times. Sadly, those calls had been unanswered. The letters returned unopened. Like Emile, many of Fred's high-life friends were gone with the wind. But the true friendships remained—Pete, Mac, Rosemary, and others from Union and Bernardsville who had never tried to lead him down the wrong road or profit from his talent.

Atop the piano sat a stiff cocktail, the trace of his old vices still used at times to calm his anxious mind. Now, as Winnie's image reflected in the windowpanes, Fred's heart warmed. Winnie had been that one true voice when he had gotten lost in the fog—just as

Mac had said he'd need. Like so many other stars, Fred had come close to losing it all, but now, in this room, it seemed he had beaten the odds.

He had the moonlight, the stars, the home on the hill. He had his piano, his music, his daughter, his wife. And here they were on the verge of creating something new together, something only they could offer the world. After all these years, Fred was finally overcoming the shame and insecurities that had caged him most of his life, the wounds that had driven him toward more, more, more! Now, with Winnie and Allison at his side, he sensed a newfound peace forming within him. A feeling of wholeness, or at least as close as he had ever come to it. The nightmares about the steeple had stopped, and the agony of constantly feeling unsettled had begun to dissipate. He might not be completely healed, but he was on the right track. And for that he was grateful.

With a tenderness, he began to play one of Winnie's favorite songs. He offered her a sweet, sensitive delivery, crooning romantically through the loving lyrics of "That's All."

I can only give you love that lasts forever
And a promise to be near each time you call,
And the only heart I own
For you and you alone,
That's all, that's all.

With the final verse, Winnie leaned close, wrapping her arms around Fred's neck as she took the lead.

All I have are these arms to enfold you
And a love time can never destroy.

If you're wondering what I'm asking in return, dear,
You'll be glad to know that my demands are small.
Say it's me that you'll adore
For now and ever more,
That's all, that's all[1]

---

Back at school Fred was adapting to his role and learning to enjoy teaching again. While he never encouraged students to turn to him as an unofficial counselor, many came to his classroom in the off-hours, hoping to discuss personal concerns. Fred's sensitive nature seemed to appeal to the teens, who one by one began to rely on him as they shared their life struggles. In time, they began to confide in him about family dysfunction, eating disorders, bullying, substance abuse, petty crimes, relationship issues, and even a few pregnancies. It seemed his training in adolescent psychology at Columbia had prepared him in more ways than one for his position in the schools, and while he always maintained healthy boundaries and rarely offered direct advice, he aimed to give as much time and attention as needed to help them feel heard and to encourage them to stay true to themselves.

One afternoon he was leaving campus when he passed a group of boys sharing a raunchy analysis of the girls on campus. Noticing Fred's disapproving look, that same burly blond who had tormented a fellow student at the beginning of the semester now sang out, "Fa la la la la," waving his arms as if conducting the others, who laughed and sang along.

Fred had been trying to reach these guys since the start of school, pulling them out of tense exchanges in the halls on more than one occasion. He'd even tried to have a heart-to-heart with two of them about maturity and what it really means to be a man. Regardless of Fred's attempts to steer them in the right direction, they seemed intent on choosing cruelty. As Fred reached his car, he suddenly had another idea.

Slipping his keys back into his pocket, Fred walked to the gym to have a word with the head coach. Behind the desk sat a middle-aged man whom Fred had known as a friend before moving to New York.

Coach Jim Hughes glanced up and grinned. "Well, look what the cat dragged in! The Einstein of Columbus." He welcomed Fred with an affectionate pat on the back, commenting on a few night classes they had shared back in the day. It was one of the many graduate programs Fred had attended through the years, always eager to learn as much as time would allow.

"It's good to see you again, Jim. I always thought you'd end up on stage somewhere," Fred said, remembering Jim's avid support of the arts.

"Yeah?" Coach Hughes's eyes glazed over with a sense of nostalgia. Then he snapped out of it and grabbed a football from his desk. "I guess the field is just another kind of stage, come to think of it. You know, I was in charge of the literary competitions here before you came on board. Football takes all my time, of course, but I do kind of miss directing those plays. We weren't too shabby, if I say so myself."

"That's what I'm here to talk to you about, Jim. I'm thinking these athletes need that outlet too. Not just sports but something creative."

Coach Hughes rolled the ball between his hands. He may have been leading his team to a championship, but it was clear he still had a heart for theater.

"I have an idea," Fred professed. "And I'm going to need your help."

The coach listened attentively as Fred explained his new creation, the Thomasville Music and Drama Troupe.

"You want the jocks to join your singing group?" Coach slapped his hand on the football to counter the sound of surprise in his voice.

"I do," Fred said with a smile. "You've got some great boys, Jim. But I've noticed a few who are . . . struggling. They bounce around the world like they're trying to shove their way toward a goal line. What happens when they start to feel vulnerable?"

Jim shook his head, as if he'd already seen it all play out. "They panic."

Fred nodded. "It comes out as anger, aggression. That may work on the field, but it won't serve them well in life."

After a long pause, Coach sighed. "Most of the fathers won't stand for 'em joining a choir. I can tell you that already." He tossed the ball to Fred with no warning.

Fred caught it. "Well, I can tell you it's not a *choir*. And also most of these young men care more about impressing you than they do their fathers." He threw the ball back to Coach as he moved to open the door.

Outside, a young assistant coach was yelling to the players, "Get moving!"

"Stay with me a second," Jim said, leading Fred toward the practice field. Then he pulled the whistle to his lips and gave it a harsh blow. "Huddle up!"

Immediately the Bulldogs swarmed, each holding a red-and-black helmet, some more battered than others.

Coach Hughes put his hand on Fred's shoulder. "I want y'all to meet my good friend, Mr. Allen," he said. "We took a few classes together back in the day, and I always enjoyed hearing him perform around Columbus."

The assistant coach sneered as if he couldn't believe what he was hearing. A couple of athletes laughed until Jim interrupted. "What's so funny? Who here doesn't listen to music?"

The assistant looked around, red-faced, finally understanding he was being seen as the fool.

"Now listen. I can't imagine my world without sports. But I can't imagine the world without music either. It all matters. That's why I want you boys to consider joining the—" He looked to Fred to fill in the blank.

"Music and Drama Troupe," Fred said. "It doesn't matter if you think you can't sing. That's what I'm here to teach you."

"And boy, will he teach you! If we were talking football, Mr. Allen would be the equivalent of an NFL pro. A true Super Bowler right here in Thomasville. You'd be doing yourselves a favor to learn anything you can from this man. That's the truth."

With that, the players scattered, half-jogging away while they strapped on their helmets for afternoon drills. Fred patted Coach's back and said, "I really appreciate this, Jim."

"Ahhh, well . . . we're lucky to have you here, Fred. And I'll be around to help with those literary competitions if you ever need a hand." Then he headed out for another afternoon of hard-hitting football.

From the parking lot Fred could see the assistant coach glaring his way. He cranked the engine of his car and thought to himself, *Victory.*

# *Thirty-five*

Within the first few weeks Troupe had quickly grown to include forty-four teens from the county, city, and private schools. Poor students sang with rich ones, extroverts shared songs with those who were shy. And thanks to Coach Hughes, a few football players signed up too, giving Fred hope that he could break through any barrier. He had certainly crossed gender lines, and Frances had promised to help recruit some African American students in time.

By December 1972, Fred and Winnie had established a highly structured routine to ensure rehearsals were run as efficiently as possible, each chair labeled to organize the kids in alphabetical order and sheet music stored neatly under each seat. The chairs were lined perfectly, with nothing out of place, and the students were expected to be seated precisely by 8:00 p.m., not one minute later. Fred didn't have to impose any significant consequences for misbehavior because he carried such a sense of respect for the students that they naturally wanted to please him in return. He set the bar high from the start, and they rose to meet it.

If anyone ever dared complain, he would remind them, "You can't have art without discipline." Then he would explain the way it worked for professionals. Fred knew all too well that some top-tier creative types were known to party hard, but he also knew that they worked even harder, understanding the long hours and the grueling demands required to refine their craft. Even if they did land one of the coveted roles on Broadway or with the Metropolitan Opera, producers were always watching, eager to replace a weak link with fresh-faced talent. Like any athlete on a professional team, performers were always one injury, one mistake, one bad stroke of luck away from losing it all, and that looming threat kept everyone on their toes.

"If anyone else can do it, then you can too, body and soul permitting," Fred would say. "That holds true for anything in life. Not just music. You simply have to be willing to get off your backside and make it happen!"

When students would offer excuses, he'd shift responsibility back to them. "If you didn't get what you wanted, it's because you didn't want it badly enough. I'm not telling you failure is not an option," he'd explain. "Truth is, we all fail sometimes. But quitting? No. Sure, other people will quit on you. Even people you think will never quit on you will quit on you. But no matter how hard life gets, no matter how scary it feels, no matter how tired you are of trying . . . you can never, never, never quit on yourselves. Quitting is not an option."

While he was always encouraging students to dream big, he also refused to coddle them. Even when parents complained that he was pushing the group of teenagers too hard, Fred never lowered his expectations. And when mothers called Winnie to complain that their child had not been chosen for a solo, Winnie also stood firm. Instead of making life easy on Troupe members, Fred instilled a strong sense of self-discipline. Week by week, he elevated them to the highest standard—not because they were being pressured to perform at their best, but because they felt better about themselves when they did. He also taught them to be accountable not only to themselves but to one another.

Fred made this clear one night after hearing about some of his singers getting drunk at a weekend party. He used the opportunity to deliver another life lesson. Stepping in front of his students at the beginning of rehearsal, he waited for the room to quiet. Then he cleared his throat and said sternly, "If you are a member of Troupe, then you represent this group at all times. Your actions. Your words. Your choices. They matter. Every single one of them. So if you choose to behave in a way that is beneath you, you need to realize you're bringing the entire troupe down with you."

He gave the kids a moment to think before continuing. They soaked in every word as if considering their own personal lists of regrets.

Fred sensed their nervousness and their remorse. "Now don't get me wrong," he said. "We all make mistakes. But *you*? You are never a mistake. Don't forget that."

The tension had not yet left the room, so the caring teacher continued. "Mistakes are going to happen, even to the best of us, especially when we're young and figuring things out. Trust me, I've made more than my fair share."

A few students giggled in nervous relief.

"But if you choose to intentionally do something foolish, or you don't rise up to correct a mistake, then you aren't letting *me* down . . . after all, who cares about me?" He smiled affectionately. "But when you make poor choices," Fred continued, "you *are* letting yourselves down. And everybody else in this room included. Personally, I think you owe each other more than that. So if that's a risk you're willing to take, then . . . well, this may not be the group for you."

As he lectured the teens, Fred realized he needed to follow his own advice. He had come so far from the broken days in New York City, but he still carried one last piece of his family's dysfunctional legacy. More often than not, the last few years had led him to stiff drinks, despite his susceptibility to the effects of alcohol. If he really wanted to lead these young singers, he'd have to do more than talk the talk. In that moment he promised himself he would never expect anything from them that he couldn't manage in his own life. It was time to break the habit, if not for himself, then for his students.

With his steady guidance Fred modeled a mature, respectful character for these teens, a path toward life-altering self-discipline. In time, he was increasing not only their musical abilities but also their self-esteem, confidence, poise, manners, and social skills.

As weeks turned to months, the leading members of Troupe were slowly beginning to make a strong impression in the community, and soon the others would follow. They took everything they were learning in Troupe and applied it to their daily lives. Because expectations were high at the weekly rehearsals and in Fred's classrooms, his students demonstrated maturity among an age group that was usually written off as being self-absorbed, immature, or careless. Parents began to notice the difference, as did teachers, ministers, coaches, and the like.

Still, not everyone offered their full support. While Allison had been thriving in Thomasville, developing close friendships and taking part in several extracurricular activities, she had become the target of a couple of teachers who seemed to resent the family's popularity.

Fred came in one evening to find Winnie preparing dinner in the kitchen. "Where's Allison?" he said, after giving Winnie a kiss.

"She's been in her room with the door shut all afternoon," Winnie said with a sigh. "She keeps saying she's fine, but clearly something is wrong. See if you can get through to her."

Fred nodded and headed for his daughter's bedroom. Winnie knew firsthand how beneficial it was for a girl to have a caring father, and she was grateful Allison still had Fred in her life. Just down the hall, he knocked while calling, "Allison? Can I come in?"

"Sure," she said flatly.

He found her sitting on her bed, listening to music, looking defeated. "What's wrong?" Fred asked, taking a seat.

"Nothing." She didn't bother looking his way.

"Allison, please don't do that. You know you can talk to me about anything. What is it?"

Her agitation increased as she stood and moved toward her window. "I already told you. I'm fine."

"Yes, that's what you said. Only problem is, you aren't saying it very convincingly."

She brewed, keeping her eyes focused on the sunset with her arms crossed tight.

"Please, Allison," Fred persisted. "Tell me."

It wasn't until Fred dared to turn off the music that she finally began to open up, still facing the window. "Word spread about *The Tonight Show*," she began. "Everyone was all excited that Ed McMahon held up that old album cover with my picture on it and said all those nice things about me." She turned partly toward Fred, just enough for him to see her brows pinched and her eyes red from crying. "But that teacher . . ."

Fred sighed and patted the bed.

Allison sat but kept a good distance from her father. "I haven't done anything wrong. I don't understand why she doesn't like me."

"Jealousy is a terrible thing," Fred said. "Oldest story in the book."

"It's not fair."

"You're right. Nothing fair about it," Fred admitted. "And I'm sure it hurts."

She finally made eye contact. "Can't you make her stop, Daddy? You're a teacher too."

"Unfortunately, there's not much anyone can do to make a person like that stop," Fred said. "All you can control is how you handle it."

"It's not that she does anything specific. She just gives me looks and talks like she's mad at me all the time. She won't call on me in class. She doesn't choose me for projects. She makes it very clear she doesn't want me there."

"But you've got a lot of friends who do want you there, and you're good at choosing people who really care about you," Fred said. "You know you're loved. Just hold on to that truth, and you'll have all you need to get through school. Through life."

Giving Allison a kiss on her forehead, Fred turned to walk out of the room when she called out meekly, "Daddy?" Fred turned to see his daughter's eyes looking down as if holding a burdensome weight, something heavier than a few school worries. "Someday will you talk to me about what really happened?"

Fred's brow furrowed. "What do you mean?"

After a pause, Allison continued. "Will you tell me why you were really gone for so long?" She looked up to reveal a deeply held pain and confusion. "I just . . . I feel like I deserve to know."

Fred walked back to his daughter and wrapped his arms around her. As she leaned into him, he kissed her forehead again. "Do you know you are the we of me? And that I love you more than I can put into words?"

Allison nodded from the safety of his arms.

"From the very first day I saw those perfect blue eyes looking back at me, and you reached up and grabbed my finger, I knew you deserved the world." He held her in silence, wanting to shield her from all the hurts of life. She had grown to become observant, like her mother, and curious, like her father, and it was clear that she had been longing for answers for quite some time. "You deserve to know the truth."

Allison grabbed her daddy's arms, as if he were her rock in an unsteady world.

"Someday I'll tell you everything you want to know. You have my word. For now, I just want you to know that everything is okay. It really, truly is."

Fred and Winnie had worked diligently to protect their daughter from the strains they had endured, and since leaving Bernardsville together, even they hadn't spoken about any of it, believing the best thing to do was to move forward in their new life. Clearly that had left Allison with nothing but questions. Fred imagined she had been equally confused by the fact that they hadn't spoken to their Allen relatives in several years, even rejecting some of their attempts to reach out and come visit. Allison was surrounded by Winnie's loving and doting family, but she knew only that they didn't talk about Fred's. She deserved to know more about her father's journey so she could understand her own. In time Fred would have to find a way to tell her everything, but for now his reassurances would have to suffice.

Not long after that day, Allison experienced another unfortunate episode at school. A different teacher had caught a few students cheating and falsely accused Allison of taking part. When he called her out with the group, he gave her a condescending stare and said, "Well, it looks like Fred Allen's daughter isn't so perfect after all."

This time, Fred and Winnie did intervene, meeting with the teacher who, upon reviewing the exam with the Allens, admitted he had been mistaken and reinstated Allison's innocence. After speaking with that teacher and sorting out the misunderstanding, Fred then experienced yet another unpleasant incident on campus. The door of the teachers' lounge had been propped open, so he'd wandered in unnoticed and overheard his two bitter podmates gossiping.

"He's so arrogant. Thinks he's God's gift," one said.

The other jeered, "I don't know why they don't just go back to New York. Or wherever they *really* came from."

They only realized Fred was in the room when he stepped toward the coffeepot for what was sure to be another weak cup of joe. He'd just given Allison a life lesson about not letting the bullies get to you, and now he realized he had to follow his own advice. It wasn't easy letting their brutal comments slide, but with coffee in hand, he glanced toward the teachers, gave a wink, and walked out.

Fred exhaled and held his head high, but by the time he reached his classroom, he was fighting that old, familiar feeling of inadequacy. No matter the age, no one wants to be on the receiving end of cruelty, and Fred was especially susceptible to its effects, having fought long and hard to find a place where he belonged.

Sensing his frustrations, Frances came into his room and closed the door behind her. "What'd they say now?" she asked, certain his grim expression had something to do with the foes at the end of the hall.

"What are you? Psychic?" Fred laughed.

"Intuitive," Frances said with a smile. "And wise. Very, very wise." Now she laughed too.

He offered her the cup of lukewarm coffee.

She winced in disgust and said, "Well, that's your first mistake right there. Never drink that awful stuff."

The two had become close friends in the months since Fred had arrived at Thomasville High, relying on one another for support through the turbulence they faced each day. In time, Fred had learned that Frances had her own strong musical talents, having trained as an opera singer and directed productions within her church community. She'd sometimes send students to Fred for discipline or support, and he'd send singers her way for extra vocal lessons or encouragement. It was proving to be a successful partnership in more ways than one, and now Frances sat at Fred's desk and said, "I avoid that lounge with all I have in me."

"You too?" Fred took a seat on the piano bench.

"People can say horrible things, Fred."

"Again, you speak truth," he said, sad to imagine Frances on the receiving end of any hate and more impressed than ever by her upbeat spirit.

"You know what this pod was like before you came?" she looked out the window where a group of students were talking innocently, causing no trouble. "I was outnumbered. Barely wanted to put my head out the door some days."

Fred's jaw tensed in defense of his friend.

"But you know me," she said, waving her hand through the air. "I just shake it off. You know why?" She held Fred's gaze, as if she were his teacher, understanding that even adults needed help sometimes. "Because I learned a long time ago," she said, "happy is a choice."

As the kids began to filter in, the two teachers moved to greet their students. Frances hugged a boy who had thick glasses and an exceptionally fragile frame. He walked on the tips of his toes, with his knees turned inward, but he wore a bright smile and seemed to not be bothered in the least by his own limitations. As he limped through her classroom door, Frances looked toward Fred again and whispered, "See? It's like I tell my sons. Some people are happy no matter what. And some people are unhappy no matter what. You gotta choose what team you want to be on."

# *Thirty-six*

By mid-December everyone at school was eager for the winter break. With exams just around the corner, holiday stress was building, and the seasonal rains were taking their toll. Frances had become Fred's closest friend. Each day they would share deep conversations nothing short of those he had enjoyed in New York with Pete and the other academics. By then their families had become close too, so in between conversations about music, history, and politics, Fred would ask about her five sons, and she'd insist Allison would wear the crown for Miss Georgia someday. "Too beautiful, that girl of yours. The perfect blend of you and Winnie. And my goodness, can she sing!"

In addition to his work with the schools, Troupe, church, and ensembles, Fred began giving voice lessons upon request. Many of his students were training to sing for literary competitions, college auditions, or the talent portion of beauty pageants.

"You're working wonders in this town," Frances said to Fred. "You think these are little things, that they won't matter in the end. But some of these kids . . . they're on life support. They'll come back and thank you one day. Watch and see."

As she said this, Fred spotted Paul in the commons area. He was standing apart from the others, arms crossed, head down. Alone.

"He's the only one I can't seem to reach," Fred admitted, drawing

Frances's attention to the troubled young man. "One minute he's cocky and bullish. The next, he's sullen and withdrawn. With his looks, he's the kind of guy who could be running this school, and yet . . . he's lost, Frances. I'm afraid I'm running out of options."

A gifted teacher with a knack for helping people find their strengths, Frances kept her eyes open. While she wasn't one to gossip, she was one to care. "He really needs someone like you, Fred. You know how I feel about these boys needing healthy male role models in their lives." She lifted her brows, as if to say, *What are you going to do about it?*

The bell rang, and Frances went back to her room as the students filtered in, complaining about exams and shuffling their backpacks until Fred closed the door. Then a sudden silence fell as they snapped straight in their seats and gave their music teacher the respect his mere presence commanded.

"How about we do something different today?" Fred asked, eager to brighten their spirits before midterms. "Paul, Annie. Come on up to the front."

The girl in braids did as requested, but the loner stared from the back row and said nothing.

"Come on up, Paul. It'll be fun. I promise."

He glared, angry at having been called out.

Laura raised her hand and said, "I'll do it," so Fred called her to the front instead, cutting Paul some slack.

From the back Paul glared at Laura and grunted, "You're not normal."

As the beautiful blonde moved enthusiastically toward her teacher, she turned to Paul and spread her arms wide open as she began to quote a line from *The Fantasticks*. Fred had introduced his class to the musical just last week, but he certainly never expected to hear any of his students quoting lines at random. Now Laura beamed brightly, lifting her voice above Paul's criticisms as she declared: "*I am special. I am special. Please, God, please, don't let me be normal!*"[1]

Fred couldn't help but smile as the students laughed in response to her performance. "You're on to something, Laura," Fred said. Then he turned to address the class as a whole. "There's already far too much normal in the world. Be better than normal!" From his desk Fred pulled out a feather. Then he told Laura to lie flat across the floor, faceup.

She did as she was told, and he then instructed Annie to stack books on Laura's abdomen. "Gently!" Laura warned, drawing more laughs from her peers as Paul watched curiously from his seat.

Fred leaned over Laura, speaking down directly to her. "I want you to lift this feather just a little bit into the air while you exhale. Remember everything I've taught you about breath control. Take a deep breath and slowly exhale, vibrating the feather without sending it flying. Then when you're a master, you'll be able to lift it just enough to let it fall back down against your lips between breaths."

Laura blew the feather a little too high into the air, but the stack of books sank low as she exhaled. "Good," Fred said. Then he turned to the class and said, "See? Only your belly should move. Do not let your chest collapse." When Laura inhaled, the books lifted, providing a clear visual demonstration of how to breathe deeply. Fred patted his abdomen, modeling for the students to follow his lead.

"Now, I'm going to give you each a feather. Find a partner and show me how a singer should breathe."

The students were allowed to move around the room as they tackled the challenge. Just as the classroom became a frenzy of feathers, one of the school administrators entered unannounced. From the doorway, he eyed Fred suspiciously.

Fred shrugged and said, "Breath control."

The administrator offered a confused grimace. Then he closed the door, causing a gust of air to scatter the feathers across the classroom.

Instead of showing his frustration, Fred used this opportunity for yet another moral lesson. "See how that wind from the door had power in this room?"

He noted a few nods.

"You've got that power too. You can either use your energy to help each other rise, like your feathers. Or you can use it to leave chaos in your wake." He eyed the feathers that had been scattered haphazardly when the administrator closed the door. "We each get to choose. How will we use what's inside of us?"

---

After class Fred was gathering his belongings when shouts rang out loudly from the commons area. "Fight! Fight!" While the kids jeered, Laura pounded on Fred's window, yelling from the green space. "Mr. Allen! Hurry! It's Paul!"

Fred raced from his room to find Paul red-faced and pointing a switchblade at another boy. Students had circled the pair in silence, their eyes wide with horror. Fred's heart pulsed as he frantically worked his way through the anxious crowd. Several other teachers had gotten there before Fred, but instead of intervening, they'd kept to the side in shock.

With urgency Fred wedged his way between the two boys, quickly allowing Paul's target to pull away. All the while, Fred was looking Paul in the eye with a calm and steady authority. Then, without so as much as a blink, Fred held out his hand and said, "Give me the knife, Paul."

Despite the December temperatures, Paul was covered in sweat. His hands were shaking.

"Everything will be okay, Paul. I promise. Give me the knife."

The troubled young man looked at Fred, fear in his eyes. It was clear he didn't really want to hurt anyone. Paul had long been the target, never the bully. But now this young man had found himself in a corner, exactly where Papa Noah had warned Fred never to get pinned.

In a panic Paul turned the knife on himself, holding it tight against his own throat and yelling, "Leave me the hell alone!"

The crowd remained unusually quiet.

Paul's face shone red with heat. His eyes darted every direction, and Fred recognized this desperate move as an act of survival. What he didn't know was whether the terrified teen would react with fight or flight. In that moment he was responding by freezing, but he couldn't stay frozen forever. Fred thought back to all his training in adolescent psychology, but he also recalled the many emotional extremes he'd experienced in his own life. The graduate coursework may have given Fred names for various conditions, but it was his personal journey that enabled him to feel empathy. To understand.

"We can get past this, Paul. Nothing is worth ending your life. I promise you that." Fred reached for the weapon. "Give it to me."

Paul could have run. He could have stabbed Fred with the blade or tried to take his own life right there in front of his peers. But the frightened teen didn't do any of those. Instead, he burst into tears and surrendered, handing the knife to the one teacher who dared to care.

It was a peaceful resolution that should have pleased everyone. But rather than thank Fred for his intervention, his graying podmate huffed, "Show-off."

Her skeletal cohort snarked back in response, "Always thinks he's the *star* of some show."

By then an administrator had arrived. "I'll take it from here," the man said, grabbing Paul's arm with forceful aggression.

Fred stood tall. This was the last thing the vulnerable boy needed. More criticism? Cruelty? Shame? Sure, he would need a serious consequence for threatening another kid with a weapon, but Fred couldn't stay silent and throw Paul to the wolves. He also knew better than to challenge a superior in front of a crowd. He followed them to the administrator's office where he asked for a minute with his superior in private.

By no small miracle the administrator told Paul, "Wait here." Then he told another teacher, "Keep an eye on him," as he led Fred into his office, closing the door behind them.

"This kid's in a lot of trouble," Fred said.

"Tell me about it." The man reached for the switchblade in Fred's hand. "The police are on their way."

"What I mean is, I don't think he's in a safe situation. Outside of here."

"I don't want to hear an excuse, Fred. He can't pull a knife on a kid and get away with it. Not in this school."

They both remained standing, and it was evident Fred's time was short. "What if you let me spend some extra hours with him? See if I can break through somehow."

Sirens rang out in the distance.

Fred tried to use a measured tone. "Aren't we here to make a difference in their lives?"

"I give you another year in this place," the administrator said with a grunt.

"Well, if that's not our goal, then honestly, I don't know what any of us are doing."

The administrator exhaled. Then he looked at the framed diplomas hanging on the wall, as if he, too, was remembering the reason he had become an educator. After a long, weighted pause, he turned back to Fred. "The police are here."

Defeated, Fred walked back to his classroom. Within minutes Frances met him at the piano, where he'd begun taking it all out at the keys.

"Guy like that doesn't stand a chance if we ship him off to the cops," Fred said. "What does it say about us if we give up on him? He's just a scared kid, Frances. Screaming for help in the only way he knows."

Frances listened patiently. Her heart had been broken for the very same reason, caring for her students as if they were her own. "He gave you the knife," she said calmly. "That's something, isn't it?"

# *Thirty-seven*

When Paul returned to school the following semester, students made a point to avoid him more than ever. He had finally accomplished his apparent goal—to be left alone.

But Fred knew it was only a defense mechanism, no different than an injured dog biting the hand that tries to help it. This boy was in a silent agony, but he was still here, in Fred's classroom, showing up each day. And, as Frances had said, he *had* given Fred the knife. That meant he hadn't given up yet.

After class was over, Fred asked Paul to stay behind. When the others cleared out, Fred sat in the chair near the quiet young man. "I spoke with the principal and a few of your teachers," Fred began. "I told them I want you to join Troupe."

Paul's brows lifted with surprise. "Why?"

Fred laughed. "That's exactly what they asked."

The boy half smiled. Another sign of hope.

"I think you might actually like it." Fred then gave Paul the power, a gift he'd been needing more than anything else. "Give it a chance?"

He shrugged.

"Unless you have something better to do?"

Paul shook his head and mumbled, "Why not?"

"Perfect. You can ride with me. Do we need to call your parents and let them know?"

Paul's defeated look made for a clear answer.

That afternoon Fred grabbed his belongings and led the troubled teen to his car. As they passed the carpool line, the familiar woman was waiting to give Paul a lift. Fred's thoughts went back to Pete and the abuse he had suffered at the hands of his predatory landlady.

He turned to his young student and asked, "You want to tell her, or should I?"

Paul nervously shrugged, and Fred took control, channeling his aunt Eleanor and hoping this would be the last either of them ever saw of the woman in the car.

That evening Paul joined Fred's family for dinner at home. Allison made every attempt to be welcoming, despite feeling deeply concerned by her father's choice to welcome the troubled teen into their lives. She knew all about Paul's reputation from school, and though she had a sweet and open spirit, Allison worried about inviting someone like him to join Troupe, especially since she was still acclimating to the new group herself. Despite her trepidations, she trusted her father and felt certain that he had a reason for this unexpected move. Still, that did little to diminish her embarrassment of walking into rehearsal that night with Paul close behind.

By 8:00 p.m., Winnie had already added Paul's name to a chair and given him a set of sheet music. A few of the students from Thomasville High raised eyebrows and whispered at the sight of their new member. Fred tinkered at the piano and organized his notebook, giving the group a minute to mingle and hoping a few kind words would be given to Paul. Then he struck his now infamous C chord, and everyone snapped to attention in their seats, spines straight, voices silenced, eyes on Mr. Allen. Troupe was becoming a well-oiled machine.

"I want you all to know something," Fred started. "I think of you as more than just a bunch of kids. I think of this group as something much bigger. We're like a family. And healthy families know how to stick together, stand up for one another. We lift one another. We celebrate each other's talents and victories. We don't break one another down, and we never stand alone."

Like the others, Paul intently watched the revered Mr. Allen, a man who had not yet realized the impact he would have on these young lives.

"Take a good look at the people around you," Fred continued.

The students did as told, and the weight of the moment was evident.

"I want you to think of each other as brothers and sisters." Then he added playfully, "Or if you don't like your siblings, try cousins."

A chuckle broke out among the group.

"Point is, we need to be a cohesive team. That starts by accepting and supporting each other to the best of your ability, and that's what I want in here. It's what I expect. I promise you're all more alike than you are different. Even if you don't want to admit it."

Then he began to lead them through his arrangement of "Corner of the Sky," their newest song from *Pippin*. The students worked through the music note by note. When he reached the lyric "*Why do I feel I don't fit in anywhere I go?*," he stopped midsong and said, "How many of us have ever felt like we don't fit in?"

The kids looked around, shifting uneasily, not eager to admit their own insecurities. But it was clear they could all relate, especially Paul and another young guy from the county, Cliff—a gifted vocalist whose rural family had all but forbidden their son's interest in the arts despite his tremendous talent and fierce determination to be a part of Troupe.

"That's what this guy is singing about," Fred continued. "He's looking for a place where he belongs. So when you sing these words, I want you to sing it like you mean it. Tell me how it feels to be left out of the crowd, to think you're different from everyone else, like no one understands you. Sing like you want your voice to be heard, like you want to find your corner of the sky."

Together they sang the next lyrics:

Thunderclouds have their lightning,
Nightingales have their song,
And don't you see I want my life to be
Something more than long.[1]

"Sing like it matters!" Fred shouted over the piano strings and collective voices. "Like you matter! Like you want *your* life to matter!" His intensity grew with each phrase.

Line by line, note by note, lyric by lyric, Fred ignited sparks in those young hearts. And the students loved him for it. He didn't talk down to them or punish them or shame them. He simply saw them. And valued them. And elevated them. He believed in them, and because of that, he hoped in time they would learn to believe more deeply in themselves.

As the last student left rehearsal that night, Paul looked at Fred and asked, "What now?"

It hadn't been all that long ago since Fred had been a scared teenager, unsure of where he would rest his head each night. Remembering the people who saved him as a boy, he grabbed his keys and asked simply, "You like cobbler?"

# *Thirty-eight*

It would not be an instant healing, and the transition would prove to be bumpy at times, but through music Fred had found a small opening, a way to reach Paul's true spirit, the one that had long been hidden behind walls too thick and high for anyone else to break through or climb.

Fred had told Paul to call if he ever needed anything, and one Saturday morning he did just that. Sensing the young man needed a safe place to land, Fred and Winnie welcomed him again to their home, introducing him to the family's expansive record collection. Thumbing through a box of albums, Paul pulled a black cover from the stash.

"What've you got there?" Fred asked with a slight smile, waiting for the young man to attempt a pronunciation of the long Italian title.

"Chee . . .chee-ge, gee-lie-da," Paul struggled to produce the first two words.

"It's '*Che gelida manina*,'" Fred said. "An Italian aria."

"A what?" Paul's brow bunched.

"An aria," Fred explained. "That just means it's an operatic song in Italian. This one is from an opera called *La Bohème*. Very famous." Fred casually organized a folder and took a seat at the piano. "It's a story about young people struggling to find themselves and make it through the hard times of life." He glanced at his student to see if the description had elicited any emotion.

Paul simply stared at the black-and-white image of a singer on the cover.

"Go ahead. Put it on," Fred said, nodding toward the stereo.

"I don't know Italian," he said sarcastically.

"That's the thing about opera," Fred explained. "It's packed full of emotion. The lyrics are sung with such power, depth, and vulnerability, you don't have to understand the words to understand the significance."

"No wonder I don't like opera," the teen responded with a smirk.

"Have you ever heard one?"

Paul shrugged. "I just know I don't like it."

Fred gave an understanding smile. "What you mean is, you haven't given it a chance." He stood and moved to the stereo, taking the album from Paul's hands. "I used to do that with people. I'd hide parts of myself or push people away completely. To be honest, the only one hurt by that was me."

Likely uncomfortable by the forwardness of his teacher's confession, the teen continued to scan the box of albums one-handed.

"I tend to believe our lives have a soundtrack, Paul. We can find a song to match any given moment in time. Every thought, every fear, every feeling—just when we think we're the only ones who could possibly understand how it feels to be us, we discover someone else has already put it to music."

Paul stayed stoic. "If this is some kind of psychological game, I don't need it."

"Ehh," Fred said, trying to defuse the tension. "Maybe you're right about opera. It's all the same anyway. There's always a guy who gets stabbed in the back, and instead of dying, he sings."

The joke failed to break Paul's scowl.

"May I?" Fred asked, reaching for the album. When Paul passed it over, Fred gently slid the vinyl from its worn cardboard and placed it on the turntable. "If you aren't afraid to hear something new, we could give it a listen."

"I'm not afraid," Paul said, a defiant snap to his tone as he looked away.

As Fred dropped the needle and rotated the volume knob to increase the sound, he continued. "It's just a simple love song, but if you're willing to give into it, the music can really carry you away."

Within seconds the gentle melody of the orchestra began billowing from the speakers. Fred leaned against the crook of the piano while the music vibrated from every surface, its tone gentle and slow. Lifting his voice over the notes, he explained. "This is a guy allowing himself to be vulnerable, daring to open his heart and hoping she'll love him in return."

As the Italian tenor Giuseppe di Stefano began to sing the emotional lyrics, Paul watched his teacher's face become animated. Having mastered the piece while studying at Juilliard, Fred mouthed every Italian word but stopped short of singing audibly over Giuseppe's beautiful vocals.

For five minutes the piece played on, and the sounds overtook the room, circling with intensity as Giuseppe delivered his powerful yet restrained vocals. Slowly Paul began to relax, sinking into his chair and giving in to the deep, glorious sounds of the aria. The young man seemed moved by the depth of emotion and the stirring accompaniment. Fred watched as Paul's forehead tensed in the soft, tender moments and again as his brows lifted with the soaring high notes. The sounds seemed to wash over the teen as he leaned his head a little farther back against his chair. By the time the song ended, a subtle shift had taken place. Paul no longer seemed enraged and defensive. Instead, he was quiet and calm.

"You know what I hear in that song?" Fred asked, lifting the needle and setting the arm back on the rest. "I hear it all. The sound of pain and desire. Fear, hope. And love."

Paul remained silent, but Fred suspected the student had never heard anything like it. With any luck he hoped the music might begin to work its magic on the young man's heart as it had his own, reminding Paul it's okay to show emotion and be vulnerable.

"Tell you what," Fred said. "I'm still short a few songs for Troupe. Think you're up to the job?"

"You want me to choose the songs?" Paul sustained eye contact for the first time since school had started. Finally, a connection.

"Sure." Fred nodded. "I can tell you have an ear for it."

"I'm not creative like that," Paul said dismissively.

"I'm sure you have no clue how much talent you have. Have you ever tried?" Fred held his gaze confidently. "Give it a shot, Paul. Pull me five songs before next rehearsal."

"Five?"

Fred nodded. "Any songs you want. Just make sure you give me a solid reason for wanting them in the show. Then, if it's a good fit, I'll choose one of them. We'll add it to rehearsal next week."

Paul hesitated, then looked back at the extensive collection. "Where do I start?"

"Don't worry. The right songs have a way of finding us if we let them." Fred moved toward the door, turning back briefly to offer final advice. "Spend as much time in here as you want, till you find what speaks to you."

Paul spent the rest of the day listening to dozens of albums. Each time Fred checked on him, he'd find his student completely engrossed in the music. It seemed this lost and broken teen had finally found a map to begin to guide him through his trauma. If he dared stay the course, the lyrics might help give him the words to process his pain, knowledge that others had survived similar wounds, and confidence that he would too.

---

The next week at Troupe, Fred started rehearsal with a simple but powerful question. "Why is it important for us to learn music?"

Then he leaned over the piano, speaking directly to each singer in an almost individual capacity, not trying to embarrass or call them out but to be personable, to connect. "As humans, we all have a primal need to communicate, right?"

The teens nodded.

"Well, think about it. Music is the language we all share. It's a language of feelings. A tool we can use to relay our deepest emotions."

He sat back down at the piano and began to play a slow song, one with a sad melody. Then he shifted to a faster piece, one with energetic pep. Next, a loud and aggressive tune, one to incite anger. He followed this with a haunting string of slow, low beats—the sound of horror. With each shift the group's emotional energy changed, and around the room, facial expressions morphed in response to the various tones.

"When you sing, I want you to consider the message you want to communicate," Fred said, pausing the music. "Pay close attention to every lyric you sing because when you are on this stage, you're telling us a story, painting a picture, and if you make the most of that opportunity, you will captivate your audience! You have the power to hold them in the palm of your hand. And once you get them there, hold on as tight as you can."

He played a few examples, showing the young singers that by making small changes in speed or volume, they could control the energy in the room. That by adjusting gestures or facial expressions, the entire message morphed.

"When you create music, you touch your audience. But it goes deeper than that."

He left the piano, moving closer to the group and lowering his voice for emphasis. "Learning to communicate better as a vocalist will help you learn to communicate better in any situation. For as long as you live, you will pay more attention to how your voice is used." Then stepping toward the keyboard, he said, "Let me go back to my original question. Why do we learn music? Why do we work so hard to go out there and share it with others?"

When no one answered, he explained, "Because we want to be better communicators. We want to connect with other people on a deeper level. We want to leave them feeling differently than they felt when they came into the room."

Moving his fingers across the keys, Fred began to play Don McLean's "American Pie," one of the five songs Paul had selected. When he glanced up from the piano, Fred saw a discreet smile spread across Paul's face as the group sang. The pride in his student's eyes gave Fred a sense of encouragement, and he realized how many young people must need this kind of support in their life. In that instant one thing became clear. Fred would start using every opportunity possible to make his students feel included and valued. To give them a purpose, a sense of worth.

Through the months ahead Fred worked to craft the rest of the lineup for Troupe's first public performance, building a sampling that would transport singers and listeners through the entire range of human emotion. As the rehearsals continued, Paul's life wasn't the only one Fred was changing. He was helping to teach these teenagers how to be the best they could be. And he did it all through the power of song.

He introduced them to Broadway show tunes, pop ballads, jazz standards, folk tracks, rhythm and blues, and operatic arias. He let them sing silly songs, using their voices in playful ways to expand their range. He countered that with sad sonnets that forced them to hold a note. And he taught them to pay attention to lyrics that were expressing thoughts and emotions they had always been taught to silence. And along the way he reminded them, "Give it all you've got and then some. Go as big as possible with your deep, resonant vocal tones. As a matter of fact, I want you to picture what you think is too much, and then go far beyond that. It's easier to pull yourself back than to push yourself forward, so don't be afraid to go for it!"

As Fred played, the students began to sing so loudly they seemed to be shouting the lyrics. They had missed the point. Adjusting his posture at the bench, Fred stopped the music and held up his hand. "Whoa."

The students grew silent.

"When I tell you sound is power, I'm not suggesting you need to yell to be heard. Whether you're singing or speaking, it's about getting your audience to listen. We live in a loud world, but sometimes there is power in restraint. You have to know what you want to say. And then say it with meaning. Now let's try this again. Let's sing with meaning."

For the rest of the spring semester, those forty-four Troupe members showed up for rehearsals twice each week. Their relationships blossomed, their musical abilities grew, and by Wednesday, May 25, 1973, it was time to put their skills to the test at the church's Family Night Supper. But first, Fred delivered a pep talk to ease the students' nerves before they sang for their very first audience.

"One afternoon in New York," he began, "this world-renowned Wagnerian soprano gave me a ride across town. She drove her own car everywhere—very unusual for a New Yorker! But that's how independent she was. Eileen Farrell. A good person. Humble. Kind. I always admired Eileen, and I would take any advice she would offer. Well, that day she taught me an important lesson. And now I'm going to teach it to you."

The kids listened nervously, trying to focus on Fred.

"She told me that when she was about your age, her voice teacher had introduced her to the Singer's Silent Prayer. It's very simple, and it will help you remember the reason we're all here tonight."

Fred took a sip of water as one of the girls hurried in from a last-minute zipper repair.

"Tonight, you will stand up there and offer your gifts to the audience. Then, when you've given all you have to give, I want you to think to yourself these words: *Thank you.* Now I'll go ahead and admit, Eileen would have said, 'Thank you, Lord.' And so do I. Of course, I'm not here to tell you what to believe, but I do hope you believe in *something* bigger than yourselves. Whatever word you choose to use for that is up to you as long as you recognize this gift that was given to you and you take time to appreciate it."

Many students smiled, which suggested Fred's inspiring words had eased their nerves a bit.

"So that's it. You sing that final note, and you offer thanks. That's the Singer's Silent Prayer."

That night the troupe performed a debut dress rehearsal for the members of the Methodist church. Winnie had ordered formal costumes, and she'd carefully measured each girl's hem to fall precisely one inch above the floor, the way it was done in New York. The well-rehearsed teenagers sang with precision and pride, producing rich vocal tones with the depth, range, and quality of professionals. After each song, the audience responded with overwhelming praise, a welcome boost as the students were scheduled to make their first official public appearance the following day.

This time the students sang for the Kiwanis Club, again performing numbers from Broadway in addition to popular radio hits, including Paul's selection, "American Pie," sung this time as a solo with the group joining in as harmonies on the chorus. As the kids circled for another preshow pep talk, Fred reminded them of how far they had come since their first rehearsal.

"Nervous?" Fred asked.

The teens nodded or said, "Yes, sir."

"Good! Use that. Every drop of it!" He smiled, funneling their nervous energy in a positive direction. "You've put in countless hours for this. But when you get out there and sing, the audience should think it comes easy for you. Remember what Frank Sinatra says: 'A true pro performs like a duck on the water. On the surface, the duck is gliding effortlessly across the lake. No one can see that underneath, he's paddling like crazy to get the job done.'"

As the students lined up for their marks, Fred looked each of them in the eye, providing an extra dose of encouragement to the few who still held pinched expressions as they waited for the show to begin.

Again, the community response was overwhelming, as the group garnered long-lasting applause and countless compliments. Now that they had seen firsthand the magic of the stage, Fred's students were hooked.

With an unstoppable passion surging among the teens, Fred began pushing them to higher and higher levels. Through the following months, Troupe performed at area civic functions, fund-raisers, church services, and community banquets. They were making great strides and honing their craft, with Fred and Winnie guiding them the way they and other professional entertainers had been directed. Fred was giving them true musical theater training and, most important, a genuine mentorship, taking time to personally relate to each and every one of his students, whether in the high school classroom, church choir, or Troupe.

As his belief in them grew, their self-confidence flourished. The students began racking up awards in regional and state competitions, literary meets, pageants, musical revues, and talent shows. Word spread and parents from across the region began contacting Winnie, hoping their children could join Troupe.

Soon the Thomasville Music and Drama Troupe had grown to ninety members. They rehearsed tirelessly, and Fred began dreaming of a much more extensive show for the following spring. "I believe they have what it takes to put on a full-length professional performance next year," he said to Winnie. "Something on a grand scale with an actual set design, costumes, and an intermission. Let's make it happen."

---

With Fred's first school year ending on a high note, Winnie accepted an invitation for the family to celebrate Rosemary's birthday in New York. It would be their first time back to the city in nearly two years, and they were excited to reunite with old friends.

In addition to attending Rosemary's party, Fred, Winnie, and Allison spent time visiting choir families in Bernardsville, caught up with colleagues from RCA, and took in a few shows in the city. After a long weekend filled with friendship and fun, Allison enjoyed one final sleepover with church friends while Winnie packed for their return flights.

Despite calling it an early night, Fred felt too nervous to rest. A subtle tension had been brewing throughout the trip, as neither he nor Winnie had discussed the pain and turmoil that consumed their last memories of the city. They had chosen long ago to let the past be the past and to move forward with their new lives in Thomasville. But now, as Fred paced the hotel room, Winnie could no longer avoid the issue.

"This has been fun, honey, so much fun," Winnie said, stepping free of her high heels for the night before removing her jewelry. "But I admit, I have mixed feelings about being back here."

"I do too," Fred said, his voice weighted with regrets.

"We need to be able to love New York again. Bring the troupe here, keep ties to our friends, all of that. But there's just something . . . still in the air."

Fred moved closer, pulling Winnie close. "You've been so good to me, Winnie. I don't thank you enough for all you've done for me."

Winnie smiled, but there was something in his tone. *Had she made a mistake in planning this trip? Was there more she didn't know?* Her mind raced as Fred seemed worlds away again. "What is it, Fred?" Through his silence her heart began to beat faster as she took a deep breath. "Tell me, please."

Understanding her fears, he nodded and said simply, "There's just one thing I really need to do."

Winnie had been expecting something like this long before they had ever reached the city. Fred had sacrificed so much for his family, for his new community, for his work with Thomasville's students. But she knew he still wrestled with his past and was in desperate need of closure. She resisted her urge to ask questions. Instead, with trust and a gentle kiss, she whispered, "Go. I'll be here."

Grateful for Winnie's steadfast support, Fred climbed into the back of a cab and told the driver, "Take me to Sutton Place."

As the taxi reached the east side of Second Avenue, where tree-lined streets crossed through quiet residential blocks, Fred straightened and said, "You can drop me here." Then he paid the fare and began to walk this familiar part of the city, taking his time to notice every new shop and refurbished restaurant, most of them closed for the night. The memories came flooding back. So much had changed, and yet he still could have navigated this district with his eyes closed. The area had always reminded the couple of London, as if they'd traveled through time to old New York for every visit.

How many times had Fred used these crosswalks, rushing back and forth to Emile's studio for a private lesson or an accompaniment job or a fireside talk with the man he'd loved as a father? Now, as he approached Emile's block, his jaw clenched, and his throat tightened.

On the corner of East Fifty-Third Street, Fred stared up at the century-old building, the one that had given the brilliant musician his first taste of opulence and a welcome into New York's in-crowd. With the curtains still open and the lamp shining brightly through the window, Fred had a clear view of the grand piano he'd played through those years. No matter how much he'd tried to deny it, the truth was that he still missed that life and the possibilities it held: the intellectual challenges, the creative circles, the constant flow of artistic energy, and most of all, his chance to truly shine.

He closed his eyes, imagining what might have been.

With the buzz of the city humming around him, the minutes passed slowly, quite like the warm summer breeze that had begun to wash over him. There, with the full moon barely visible above the hazy sea of lights, Fred debated whether he should make his way to Emile's door and try to make amends, restoring the father-son bond the men had once shared. It was this hope that had pulled him here this night, but now as Fred stood on the street corner, he once again became consumed with the possibilities that lay beyond that window. His mind lit up with those old dreams. Maybe he, Winnie, and Allison could try it again, he thought. Maybe they would get it right this time—healthier, happier . . . maybe . . . *All I have to do is go for it!*

But Fred stood frozen, unable to take one step closer to Emile's building. With a lump in his throat, his mind began to fill with thoughts of his students, of Allison and Winnie. Yes, he had loved Emile and the idea of a life in the spotlight, but his work in Thomasville had become more than just a job. It satisfied his soul, filling Fred with a purpose and joy unlike any he had found in this city.

*Why is this still so painful?* he wondered. *Why so hard?*

In the distance, the lamp dimmed in Emile's studio, a final signal that he had missed his chance. But instead of feeling defeated, Fred exhaled with relief. As he'd told his students countless times, life is all about choices. Now, looking up at the darkened window, a peace settled in his muscles and a clarity overtook his mind. The last year in Thomasville had completed him in a way that all the other possibilities here in New York could not. Yes, he thought, everything really does come down to choices. And as Fred turned to hail a cab back to Winnie, he finally knew for sure. He had made the right choice.

The next day the family was scheduled to board a plane for Thomasville, but first Fred met Mac for early morning coffee.

"We'd love to have you producing for us again," Mac said.

Fred's brows lifted. He wasn't expecting this kind of offer, and his mind began to swirl again with the possibilities.

"I know you weren't happy with so many restrictions," Mac continued, "but what would you say if I told you we'd give you the creative freedom you lacked back then? See what you can do if we loosen the reigns a bit."

"Tempting," Fred admitted, giving it serious thought. Returning to RCA would mean reintegration into the elite circles he and Winnie had once enjoyed. The executive role would place him back in a high-paying position as a top-level music maker.

"You'd be in the studio, but this time with full access to the instruments. Compose. Conduct. The doors are wide open for you, Fred. It's what you always wanted, and surely it beats this small-town work you've been doing. Plus, I know Fran would love to have you all back here."

Fred could hardly believe his luck. The two shared big ideas for at least fifteen minutes, dreaming of projects and collaborations they longed to explore. But then a youthful waiter refilled their coffee cups, and the young man's smile reminded Fred of his students back home in Georgia.

Mac's offer was incredible, too good to be true, in fact. But Fred knew in his heart he could never go back. Now, more than ever, he felt unwilling to risk the new, stronger foundation on which his family had been rebuilt. After a long pause he gave his old friend a pat on the shoulder and said, "I may sound like I've lost my mind completely, but Mac, I'm finally on the right path in my life, and I think it's time for me to move forward."

After the two men exchanged brotherly hugs and kind farewells, Fred walked to meet Winnie and Allison in the hotel lobby. He may never again be collaborating with the nation's top recording artists or winning Grammy awards for his work, but now more than ever, he felt certain he was making the music he was born to create.

# *Thirty-nine*

As soon as Winnie and Fred arrived back in Thomasville, it was time to focus on building and preparing for the big show. Fred began poring through his extensive catalog of music, spending countless nights with Winnie, listening to songs for inspiration. Using his skills as a composer, he created custom arrangements, rewriting melodies and transposing keys specifically to fit his group.

With Winnie's encouragement Fred aimed high. Twice each week the teens came together for group rehearsal, plus extra hours spent on choreography or ensembles. Additionally, they worked individually with Fred to perfect solos, duets, and quartets. And Winnie was there at every step, using her vocal talents and professional training to critique and coach the singers while overseeing the production as a whole. They were a dynamic duo, and together they were determined to dot every *i*, cross every *t*.

But, all in all, Troupe was a success because of the tremendous devotion of the Thomasville community as a whole. Numerous volunteers worked long hours to alter costumes, wire the sound system, feed the students, and donate money for the many expenses that went into producing such a top-level show. Others helped with set design, choreography, and accompaniment—adding drums and even a trumpet to Fred's piano.

Before they knew it, another school year had passed, and the night of the dress rehearsal had arrived. Nerves were high as the teens shot questions like darts.

"Do you think we'll be in the paper?"

"We've let them know about it," Winnie said, insisting they shouldn't worry.

"I keep having dreams that no one comes."

Again, Winnie countered, "You've sold nearly every ticket!"

And finally, "What if they hate it?"

She gave them an exaggerated but genuine smile. "Remember, your facial expressions are a way to offer joy and love. Give 'em all you can give. Go out there and *sparkle*!"

The students ran through the entire dress rehearsal with only a few minor mistakes. Fellow choir member and friend Tom Faircloth helped Winnie make adjustments on showmanship as Fred honed in on vocal performance. By night's end they were feeling well prepared for the big show.

It was late by the time Fred made his way to his car, only to find one of his best singers waiting nearby. "Mr. Allen, I wanted you to meet my grandfather." She introduced an older gentleman whose trim, gray beard framed a friendly smile.

Fred offered a steady handshake. "Your granddaughter's got a lot of talent. I'm sure you'll enjoy hearing her solo tomorrow."

"That's why I've driven in all the way from LaGrange. More than three hours, not counting all my old-man stops." He chuckled kindly. Then he beamed at his granddaughter and said, "I wouldn't miss it for the world, darlin'."

Fred smiled. "We appreciate your support."

"Now that I think about it," the man said, "there's a good number of Allens back in LaGrange. You know any of 'em?"

Fred pocketed his hands before the man could see them tremble. One mention of his family, and he felt like a wounded child again. *Could he possibly know of my family?* Fred thought. His heart raced; his mouth became dry. *After all these years, how could this be happening?*

"Actually," the man continued, "you do look a bit like 'em. Not your people, are they?"

Fred fought his shame, forcing another smile as he politely said, "I don't think so."

"Figures. The Allens I know sure aren't the kind of people you'd have teaching your kids," he said with a smirk. It was clear the man hadn't made the connection, but the comment had done its damage.

With that, the man thanked Fred for his work with Troupe, and he took his leave.

All night Fred struggled to sleep. It wasn't just preshow jitters that had him tossing and turning. It was the riddling insecurities the man's comments had revived in him. Maybe the man was right. Maybe Fred had been kidding himself all along. In truth, maybe he was nothing more than a fraud, just another deadbeat Allen who had no business doing any of this work, especially taking responsibility for young lives. In the end, it didn't seem to matter how much Fred had accomplished, how far he had come. He would always be that little boy from the mill village trying to prove his worth.

In the early hours Winnie noticed Fred's sleeplessness and tried to settle his nerves. He told her about the exchange, still haunted by the unexpected encounter. With gentle understanding Winnie kissed him softly and said, "You still seem to see the worth in everyone but yourself. You are absolutely wonderful, Fred Allen. Your only problem is you still don't know it."

The next day, as the students gathered backstage, Fred was still fighting a crippling case of self-doubt. He was pulling on his tuxedo jacket when a couple of parent volunteers found him in the wings. The woman spoke first. "Excuse us, Mr. Allen?"

Fred smiled politely but did nothing to encourage conversation. He needed to block out all distractions and stay focused.

"We don't want to keep you," the man hurried to explain. They were a timid couple, speaking with soft voices as they stood holding hands. "We just wanted to let you know how excited we are about the show tonight." His wife nodded.

"Well, thank you," Fred said, adjusting his bow tie with no need for a mirror. "We're all happy to have the chance to do this."

"You may not know it," the man continued, "but this last year with you has changed our daughter's life."

Fred stopped fidgeting with his tie, surprised.

"I know she's not a soloist or anything. But just being up there and learning from you . . . well, it's saved her. You've given her something. Something she needed."

Still reeling from last night's comments about his family out in Troup County, Fred's heart warmed to hear these words. "She's a bright young lady," Fred said. "We're honored to have her in Troupe."

The mother nodded. "This experience has brought out a whole new light in her. In a lot of people." She glanced around the room as the students were working through the warm-up exercises. It was clear her daughter wasn't the only one enjoying Troupe.

"You're like a minister without a pulpit," the father added. "And we can't tell you how glad we are to have you and your family here in Thomasville."

With that, the mother put her hand on her heart and said, "God bless you, Mr. Allen. I hope you know how wonderful you are."

On May 24, 1974, the community gathered at Thomasville's Municipal Auditorium. Two years had passed since Fred and Winnie arrived in town; one year since their first group of singers performed at the church's Family Night Supper. And now standing-room only with an 1,800-strong audience for Troupe's first official Spring Show, a two-hour performance called "Concert: A Night to Remember." It was to be presented with the attention to detail that Fred and Winnie had practiced during their time in New York, a truly professional production with no corners cut.

Backstage, Fred stood before the students and offered final instructions. "Remember, you've learned what it means to be '*on*.' When you're onstage, you don't move a muscle off-script. That means you don't scratch. Don't yawn. Don't touch your hair or adjust your clothes. If someone faints, don't react."

The students released nervous laughs.

"I'm serious. We've got volunteers back there to take care of it, and no one should even glance their way. No matter what happens, you just keep right on singing as if everything is perfectly normal."

"What if we have to sneeze?" asked a jokester of the group.

"Then just do me a favor and don't go for the Oscar," Fred said, smiling. "Be discreet."

Fred softened his tone and gave his final advice. "You're about to do something this town has never seen before. When that curtain rises, I want you to remember two things. One, it's not about you. It's about what comes through you. And two, it's about the light you shine for others, not the light that shines on you."

Moments later, with the curtain still closed, the singers stepped into place, fighting nerves as they quietly filled four tiers of semicircular risers. Then the charming voice of Tom Faircloth came through the loudspeakers, like a seasoned ringmaster, eloquent and clear: "Ladies and gentlemen. The Thomasville Music and Drama Troupe. In concert!"

A chipper volunteer named Shirley climbed onto a stool and pulled the lever to lift the heavy red-velvet curtain. Winnie worked the stage lights to reveal the well-dressed teens all standing in perfect position. The boys wore white trousers with red vests and black bowties, while the girls donned long white gowns. Again, every hem had been carefully measured.

In his crisp black tuxedo Fred sat at the concert grand piano, center stage, facing his performers. He had structured the show to include several acts, with costume changes, lighting effects, and an intermission. From the soundboard in back of the auditorium, Winnie called the show, controlling both lighting and sound. Backstage, a team of volunteers worked feverishly to keep the production moving through each transition.

It all started when Seva Day, a star soloist, stepped to the front of the stage with a single spotlight shining as she invited the audience to "*Join us, leave your fields to flower.*"[1] Just as she was rounding out her powerful portion of the troupe's favorite song, the lights lit up the entire group as they all began to sing the lyrics. To add a little magic to the number, set designers had crafted a special effect by attaching a large cotton bedsheet above the middle of the risers, filling it with shiny confetti. A team of volunteers gently pulled the cords, sprinkling the sparkling metallic shower over the group as the students sang passionately. Winnie smiled from the board, grateful the testy cords had worked as designed, but just as she exhaled, the sheet slipped, and the entire load of glittery confetti dumped on top of one unfortunate alto, leaving the other singers in a shimmery cloud.

Despite the failed prop, not a single student reacted. They had learned from Fred that "when you're on, you're on," and they simply kept belting out the lyrics, giving the audience their all as they delivered a power-packed show and reminding everyone in attendance, "*We've got magic to do, just for you.*"[2]

Winnie exhaled and thought to herself, *Well, that's one way to sparkle!*

After the big opening number, the first act brought the audience through a colorful revue of Broadway showstoppers. Not a sheet of music was to be seen, as the students and Fred had memorized the entire show. Because they had rehearsed so thoroughly, they nailed the first act, covering five full decades of award-winning numbers, from *Man of La Mancha* all the way through *Jesus Christ Superstar*, in a unique arrangement composed by Fred. With nothing more than a few handwritten note cards to track his set list, Fred kept eye contact with the singers throughout the show, conducting effectively with facial expressions and a few discreet hand gestures all while he played the piano. From the keyboard Fred supported his singers effortlessly, skipping along with them and transposing on the spot to cover any mistakes, just as he had done when Winnie first sang "Summertime" all those years ago.

The crowd cheered voraciously after every number, even louder as the second act delivered more solo performances and a barbershop quartet, spotlighting the standout talents with songs from *Funny Girl*, *Sweet Charity*, and more. Then, just before intermission, Allison discreetly stepped off the risers, disappearing into the wings before gracefully striding to center stage. As Fred had taught the students, she moved with purpose to a front microphone, careful not to disrupt the flow of the show.

When the spotlight found her, Fred adjusted his note cards, surprised to find Allison's handwriting across the top of this one: "I'm still holding your finger, Daddy."

Fred's heart surged as he fought the urge to smile. Of course he would never have treated her any differently than the other singers, so he stayed focused and hit those old, familiar notes, the same ones

Mrs. Duncan had struck back in the Dunson Mill Village when she seemed so determined to draw her fragile young student back to life. As Allison delivered an emotional solo of "Over the Rainbow," she had no way of knowing what this music meant to her father. Nor could she possibly have known how much it meant for him to see her there onstage, shining, singing.

She, too, had given up a career to move to Thomasville. But now, as Allison's voice rang clear and true, a flow of memories flashed through his mind: the moment Winnie had first told Fred he was to become a father; the first time he saw his beautiful baby girl; the moment he held baby Allison with Winnie, insisting they were the "we of me."

Now, as his daughter commanded the stage, all Fred could think was how much he loved his little girl. He had made many mistakes along the way, but if he had done one good thing in his life, it was choosing his family, returning to be the father she deserved.

After intermission the performers returned with more solos and small group ensembles, working through *West Side Story*, *Oklahoma!*, and *Mame*, as well as pop songs, such as "Hound Dog" and "The Way We Were." One such song was "American Pie," and although Paul didn't sing the solo, he beamed brightly as his friend delivered the emotional lyrics. Fred knew Paul's wounds were far from healed, but he also knew the young man now had a fighting chance. Music had given Paul a dose of hope when he had become broken by life, and now, after Paul's year and a half in Troupe, Fred had every reason to believe this strong young man would find his way.

Next came songs from Troupe's favorite musical, *Pippin*, a work that had connected deeply with the teens, igniting their hopes and dreams for a bright future. One piece, "Corner of the Sky," was performed by Cliff, the gifted young man from the county school whose parents had struggled with his interest in the arts, all but forbidding him to take part in Troupe despite his tremendous talents. Like Paul, Cliff had come to rely on Fred as a mentor, if not a father figure of sorts, and Winnie had also grown close to Cliff in the last year, helping to expose him to a world much bigger than the little corner of the sky he had always known. As Cliff performed the original arrangement flawlessly, Winnie fought tears, knowing his life would have been so much more difficult if he hadn't found this outlet for his gifts, knowing the difference Troupe was making for him and so many others.

Finally the singers wrapped it all together with an emotionally charged grand finale of "No Time at All." Fred had rearranged the lyrics to the solo number to fit the large group and to capitalize on the powerful message, leaving listeners with the reminder: "*It's time to start livin'!*"[3]

The crowd had given almost continuous bursts of applause from the first selection all the way through to their enthusiastic standing ovation at the show's end. With nearly two thousand attendees on their feet, and Winnie's tear-filled eyes watching her husband from behind the soundboard, Fred remained seated at the piano, shunning the spotlight and refusing a bow as he allowed the attention to focus solely on his hardworking students. As the teenagers smiled proudly in front of him, he finally understood the true purpose of his gifts.

Perhaps Mayhayley had been right all along. Yes, he was sure now. Those dreams of the steeple really had led him to Thomasville. And Winnie had been correct when she insisted divine intervention had landed them in this town. Every brutal abuse, every heartbreaking trauma, every bad choice and mistake and wrong turn had been equipping Fred for something bigger. For something more meaningful. For this.

As the students bowed in sync to the inner rhythm of the words

*Mis-sis-sip-pi-Riv-er-boat*, Fred remembered the Singer's Silent Prayer and the lessons he had learned from Eileen Farrell. He also thought back to every stage and every spotlight he had found along the way. As he scanned the students, he pictured them each as shining stars, wondering where their journeys would take them, how far their lights might shine across this great big world. Paul, Cliff, Laura, and many others had come to rely on him in the last two years, and now he recognized something each one had gained from the many lessons Fred had taught them, lessons he'd learned from his own personal experiences in LaGrange, Chautauqua, Atlanta's Theater of the Stars, Union, Juilliard, Columbia, Riverside, Bernardsville, RCA, Actors Studio, Lincoln Center, Macmillan, and Broadway.

He heard the voice of every mentor who had crossed his path: Aunt Eleanor, Mary Duncan, Mrs. Dudley, Lucy Nixon, Mrs. Lewis, Madame, Ralph Erolle, Claire Coci, Hans Heinz, Emile, Pete, Mac. And most of all, Winnie, Fred's greatest mentor of all, his dear partner who had helped him discover love, personal strength, confidence, and self-worth.

He could see it all clearly now. All those peaks and plummets, valleys and hills . . . it had all been worth it. Every one of those people had been a sound wave, a pulse point, a source of positive energy in his life, propelling his spirit upward, outward, with greater and greater purpose. And now it was rippling out toward his students, like the gradual build in a song's crescendo.

As the singers lifted from their coordinated bow, Fred took a deep breath, closed his eyes, and thought to himself, *Thank you, Lord.*

Then, realizing Shirley had forgotten to close the curtain as planned, Fred gave her a subtle nod to remind his loyal volunteer of her appointed duty. Unfortunately, she didn't notice his cue as she was too busy clapping atop her stool, completely lost in the enthusiasm that consumed the auditorium. Fred resumed playing, signaling the students to deliver an encore all while trying his best to get Shirley to glance his way. Still, she cheered so passionately, Fred was unable to catch her eye even when he attempted subtle hand gestures.

As the students finished the reprise from "No Time at All" and took a second bow, Fred resorted to bigger and bigger gestures toward the wing, but Shirley just kept right on dancing with her big cheery smile, enthralled by the powerful finale and leaving Fred no choice but to move into another round. Once again the students lit back into song like pros, never breaking character. As they took their *third* bow, Shirley finally glanced Fred's direction and realized he had been desperately signaling her to pull the lever and end the show. With a frantic gasp, she quickly stretched to close the curtain as the audience was still on their feet in loud applause.

Fred exhaled and, whispering this time, repeated, *Thank you, Lord.* Then he struck his final note.

# *Forty*

After the curtain closed, families lingered as if even they didn't want the magic to end. The performers were gifted bouquets of fragrant flowers while parents snapped photographs and grandparents wiped tears of pride. The energy in the room certainly had been transformed, morphing into something so positive, so powerful, it seemed no one wanted to leave.

The audience was especially eager to congratulate Fred and Winnie, taking time to discuss their own sentimental responses to the music and asking to sign up their children for the following year. After more than an hour Frances was finally able to get a word with Fred onstage. She gave him an affectionate hug and said, "I've been singing my entire life, Fred. What I would have given to have had a teacher like you. Just think how long all this talent has been waiting to be discovered in this little town. Completely untapped."

"It feels good to be on this side of it," Fred admitted, realizing it was never the spotlight he was craving. Instead, he had only needed acceptance, belonging. Connection. And song.

Frances took note of Paul helping to break down the set with a group of Troupe friends. She leaned close and whispered to Fred, "He's come a long way from the kid holding a knife to his own throat."

Fred turned his attention Paul's way, agreeing the young man was on the right track again, doing his best to stay above the fray.

"I told you he needed you," Frances said. "A lot of us need you."

Fred shook his head. "I don't know about that, Frances. I think I'm the one who needed all of you."

"You're just getting started, my friend." Frances gave him a warm smile. "And someday, you'll realize what a difference you've made. You'll be proof of what one little life can do."

---

It was near midnight by the time the auditorium finally emptied. In the quiet of the stage, Fred made his way back to the piano. How many years had he spent at keys like these, trying to offer the world something new—a unique melody, an original combination of notes, a never-before-seen routine? All that time he had used music as his way to say, "Don't be afraid. Dare to feel something. Feel it all." And yet he had wasted so much time running away from his own true emotions, transferring pain onto all the wrong people.

But by no small miracle he had been given this second chance.

Now shiny, colorful confetti was scattered on the floor around him, reflecting the few dim lights that continued to shine. In the solitude, Fred thought through what these kids had accomplished here tonight, the level of talent he had been able to pull from them.

Meanwhile, having seen the final guests out of the building and given Allison permission to go celebrate with fellow Troupe mates, Winnie walked back into the darkened auditorium and up to the stage. There, she gently wrapped her arms around Fred's neck. As his fingers continued to dance across the keys, Winnie kissed his cheek. "You did it, honey."

Leaning his head back against her, he replied, "*We* did it."

With only his soft, gentle medley surrounding them, Winnie exhaled, exhausted. "Well, now what?"

The two chuckled and sighed, both too tired to think of next steps.

"Any requests?" Fred asked in a half-joking manner.

After a second of thought, Winnie grinned. "Play 'Nature Boy.'"

Nat King Cole's jazz standard had been performed by a soloist earlier in the evening and had long been one of Winnie's favorites. As Fred delivered the tune, she stepped toward the piano and began to sing.

There was a boy
A very strange, enchanted boy.
They say he wandered very far
Very far
Over land and sea.

Winnie leaned near enough to see the faint line of freckles across Fred's brow. He was still a handsome man, his looks striking in a Hollywood sort of way as if he belonged on the silver screen. She didn't bother hiding her affections. She couldn't fool him even if she tried. That's the thing she'd always loved most about Fred, his innate ability to size someone up in a matter of minutes and reach them on a level no one else had ever managed to do. He only knew how to offer something deep and almost spiritual, leaving everyone he met with a sense that they hadn't only been seen but understood. And, more importantly, loved.

A little shy
And sad of eye
But very wise was he.

And then one day
A magic day
He passed my way.

While we spoke of many things
Fools and kings
This he said to me.

Fred's voice joined Winnie's, giving breath to the notes and the dreams and to all things meaningful between them. As they delivered the ending message in perfect harmony, together, they were sharing their story, their truth. Their song.

The greatest thing you'll ever learn
Is just to love and be loved in return.[1]

# *Epilogue*

The troupe's first official Spring Show was such a tremendous success, the waiting list jumped to three hundred students. In hopes of reaching more kids than the maximum that could squeeze into the rehearsal space, Fred started an award-winning competition group during one of his high school class periods, recruiting his friend Frances to help him coach the newly created Show Stoppers. Students who were not able to take part in his high school music class, his literary meets, Troupe, or Show Stoppers were encouraged to join their church choirs. And on top of all that, Fred continued giving private voice lessons, determined to mentor as many young musicians as time would allow.

Through the years Fred and Winnie would lead the troupe on many trips to New York City and beyond, having been declared "official ambassadors of good will for the state of Georgia" by Governor Jimmy Carter. The students would perform for numerous national and international audiences, including the Kiwanis International Convention, an Atlanta Falcons game, a packed Shea Stadium, and the always-energizing Disney World. They also continued accepting invitations from dignitaries, singing for members of the British Parliament in London and at the White House as guests of President and Mrs. Jimmy Carter.

After several years of operation under the umbrella of the

Thomasville First United Methodist Church, the group outgrew the fellowship hall, and the supportive community came together to offer the old television station for an unbelievable rental fee of only eighteen dollars per year. Volunteers gathered to paint the space, creating what would come to be known for decades as the Troupe Building, serving the group's needs until a storm damaged the building beyond repair. At that time, funds were raised to erect a state-of-the-art facility across the street from the town's famed rose gardens. The structure was named the Fred Allen Building in honor of the town's beloved music man, with Winnie Langley Allen Hall dedicated to his dear partner who had worked side by side with Fred through rehearsals and productions from the start. The two-million-dollar facility was paid in full with community donations by the time the ribbon was cut.

For forty-four years Fred shaped many a soul—and saved some too—as he devoted his life "like a minister without a pulpit." From the start, all were welcome at Troupe. County teens sang beside city teens, public school students danced with private school peers, and athletes who once laughed at the idea of dancing and singing onstage discovered a whole new side of themselves.

While this kind of open-minded acceptance may be a more common occurrence now, it was nearly unheard of in the early 1970s when Fred and Winnie arrived in a newly integrated southern town, drawing young people to the stage and challenging them to expand their own understanding of themselves.

It was no small goal to bring these diverse pockets of the community together for a united cause, especially bridged through music and the dramatic arts. But with brave determination, Winnie's undying loyalty, and a wave of support from Thomasville's finest, Fred did the unthinkable. He brought the power of Broadway, Union, and Juilliard to a small Georgia community where most of the youth had never heard a show tune, much less performed opera. In time the Spring Show added a second performance to accommodate the growing crowds, becoming an annual sold-out Mother's Day weekend tradition. Then a Christmas show was added, providing a cherished holiday activity for the community's families. Through the years the shows improved steadily, developing into top-notch, professional-level productions with dazzling lighting displays, intricately choreographed dance numbers, and artistic set designs.

The Langleys never missed a show, always offering full support. The Allens, however, never saw the Troupe perform. Fred had learned, in time, to forgive them, but after realizing the extent of his childhood trauma, he remained reluctant to allow them access to his life again.

Frances eventually joined the board of directors, leading all five of her sons through the Troupe program and remaining Fred's most trusted friend. Coach Jim Hughes not only saw his football team through to a national championship, he continued to attend literary meets and helped critique the one-act plays alongside his old friend and fellow teacher. Tom and Janice Faircloth, along with many others, became ardent champions of the troupe, devoting personal time and resources to support the organization's efforts year after year. Allison declined numerous opportunities to continue her career in show business, choosing instead to become a devoted wife and mother of three in Thomasville, where she remained intimately and loyally involved in the troupe alongside Fred and Winnie, contributing to music selection, set design, choreography, and helping to produce the overall show until her father's official retirement. In the end, students like Paul, Laura, Cliff, and countless others went on to lead productive, healthy lives, with many of them crediting the Allens for much of their success.

Today Fred has retired from the group that he and Winnie lovingly cultivated for more than four decades, having passed it on to new directors who have incorporated their own unique visions and styles. With him went a particular brand of magic, musicianship, and creative passion rarely seen in one person. Though it exists in a different form from Fred Allen's music and drama troupe, the group remains a point of pride for the community of Thomasville, serving as a powerful creative outlet for yet another generation who gather in the building still named after their original *music man*.

In 1935, when Fred Allen entered this world, he was called cursed, an unwanted kind of special child. Since then he has been called a creative genius, a musical prodigy, and an artistic wonder. Today he is best known as a composer and teacher who has helped lead countless young people to success through the magic of music. And because I'm one of the luckiest souls alive, my brothers and I get to know him as our grandfather, a man who has shared life lessons with me as we come together at the piano as well as in his garden, the way Papa Noah once did with him.

Above all else, Fred Allen has come to be known as a mentor. And through his selfless servant leadership, Fred's legacy has become much like a powerful crescendo. Year by year, his life has gained a loudness of spirit and intensity of purpose, broadening its reach with every passing moment. And now, as I look back at his tremendously positive impact, I have learned to answer not only *who* is Fred Allen, but *why* he is the man he is today. After hearing from countless students who crossed my grandfather's path, poring through decades of his personal journals, enjoying seemingly endless days and nights of deep conversation with both of my grandparents, and reading powerful, heartfelt letters from those whose lives he has touched, the message is clear. Not only has Fred overcome all odds to live with his heart wide open, he has shown us the value of a meaningful life, a life of purpose. A life that, as his old friend Pippin would say, is "*something more than long.*"[1]

# *A Note from Fred Allen*

What can any man say about his own life? I lived it. At times I flourished, and at other times, I simply survived, but through it all, I lived the best I knew how. Just like everyone else. While grateful and humbled for kind recognition, I don't think I've done anything more noteworthy than any other individual who has shared a moment of their own time to help another.

I hope that my life has helped others in some small way and at times encouraged young people to reach beyond their own understanding of themselves. As for my own dreams and ambitions, sure, I've had them. We all do. I've tried to help my students realize that dreams are worth pursuing if you're willing to put discipline and accountability behind them. And they are reachable, especially if you never tell yourself that you can't. Dreams are like rays of light piercing the night, shining to illuminate our way forward in the darkness of the world around us. Such goes the fragility of dreams that if we allow our hearts and minds to fear our perceived limitations, we lose trust in the light before us.

Of the life lessons I've hoped to share with my students, the most important to me are these:

1. Do the right thing because it's the right thing to do.
2. Strive to make wise choices and guard against a cynical attitude.

3. Be cheerful to everyone, and it will surprise you how many times a stranger will become a friend.
4. Enjoy the good times life brings and be at peace with the world around you.
5. Trust in God and pray to him, thanking him for your blessings.
6. Strive to be happy and never forget the world is a beautiful place.

The greatest blessing of my life has been my family. Their love and support have given me the pride and joy that I wish for the world. With them by my side, my life has been a discovery. A trust. A faith, with my heart continually daring my feet to take another step into the unknown. To anyone who's afraid of not knowing what's next, I say that's what life is for! Be your best and have faith that life is unfolding before you just as God intended.

Perhaps if I had more carefully sketched and diligently followed a map for my own life, I would have wandered a simpler, kinder, even more prosperous path, but by the grace of God, I've run, stumbled, skipped, fallen, laughed, cried, and sung along mine. And I'm better for each part.

When I was a freshman at LaGrange College, my drama coach assigned a poem for the class to memorize and recite, "Desiderata" by Max Ehrmann. The title means "things desired." Throughout my time as a teacher, "Desiderata" influenced my thinking and enabled me to be a better mentor, and, all these years later, I realize its simple wisdom has had a profound effect on my life.

> Go placidly amid the noise and haste,
> and remember what peace there may be in silence.

As far as possible, without surrender, be on good terms with all persons.
Speak your truth quietly and clearly; and listen to others,
even to the dull and the ignorant; they too have their story.
Avoid loud and aggressive persons; they are vexations to the spirit.[1]

# *Acknowledgments*

Working on this project for the past year has been one of the most rewarding experiences of my life. Not only have I been blessed to get to share such a personal story; I've been fortunate to have a wonderful support system, personally and professionally, that allowed me the creative freedom to truly explore and help craft a book that I'm proud to give to the world. Thank you, Julie Cantrell and the W Publishing Group family, for helping make this a reality.

I've always enjoyed a close and loving relationship with my family and, in particular, my grandparents. It is through them that I've developed my love of creative expression through the arts and because of them that I undertook this project to share with the world a story of selflessness, love, sacrifice, inspiration, and song.

Through the powerful work they've done and the countless lives they've positively touched, I've spent years hearing from individuals about how impactful and inspirational Winnie and Fred Allen have been. I'm grateful to everyone who takes time to share what my family and their work have meant to them.

I thank everyone who has supported and encouraged this project as Julie and I spent the last year pulling from every source we were able to find—former students, Troupe members, friends, colleagues, immediate and extended family, countless notebooks, journals, letters, newspaper articles, and so forth. We have been so fortunate for the abundance of information that allowed us to put this beautiful story on paper. Our goal from the beginning was to tell as vividly and accurately a story as possible, taking only the slightest creative liberties to allow the reader to experience the moments just as Winnie and Fred recalled them firsthand. We have been fortunate to sit with my grandparents for countless hours over the last year (along with the lifetime of moments I've been blessed to have with them), talking through their memories of the situations, conversations, and emotions that have played out in their lives. I wish this kind of precious time with loved ones for everyone.

From childhood, I've seen the journals that my grandfather has kept since he was a small boy. My grandfather has saved every one of his journals and used them to intimately write the details and thoughts of his daily life for almost eighty years. It was from these and an abundance of other sources that we were fortunate to be able to write this story.

After this incredible journey I've taken, I encourage everyone to learn as much as they can about their own parents, grandparents, and beyond. Not only can we have a better understanding of ourselves and learn from those who came before us, but we also allow their lives to continue living on.

Thank you to my hometown of Thomasville, which has been so supportive of this project. Along with my incredible family, this community has helped to nurture and raise me in a way that only it can. Thomasville is a community of values. Of substance. Of hard work and hospitality, graciousness and humility. My family has called this extraordinary place in the sun home for several generations, and it is here that we have taken great pride living and working, doing our best to support, protect, and give back to the place that has given so much to us.

I also want to thank Ryan Smith, a pillar of support both personally and professionally. You have been a beacon of selflessness, motivation, encouragement, and loyalty matched only by your own unwavering professionalism, dedication to excellence, and concern for others. This project would not be a reality without you.

In addition I want to express my heartfelt appreciation to all the members and parents of the Thomasville Music and Drama Troupe, past and present, for giving breath to my grandparents' ambitions of working with young people to make beautiful music. It has literally been your voices and support, along with the support of our community as a whole, that has allowed their work to take root and have meaning.

To Lisa Jackson, we owe you a debt of gratitude for guiding us through the process and helping make this project a reality. It has been through your enthusiasm and championship that we have this story today.

Denise Stevens at Loeb and Loeb, you have been an ardent advocate of our work for years, and we couldn't spend our time creating as we do without your expertise.

Deborah Giarratana, your friendship and mentorship have made our work so much stronger. We are lucky in life if we find people who truly believe in us, who know just what to say when we are struggling, and whose prayers can be counted on. You are a brilliant producer, and it's an honor to be able to work alongside you. You inspire me to create the best projects I can in hopes of bringing goodness in the world.

Lastly and mostly importantly, I thank my mother and father, who have given me unconditional love and support. Through the ups and downs of my life, it is the two of you who have worked to guide and lift me in hopes that I would become a compassionate, honest, hardworking citizen, just as the two of you have worked so admirably to model.

Mom, it's you who has been my biggest champion, and it's through your artistic drive and beautifully creative mind that I'm inspired every day to push myself higher and higher. I've spent my life watching your dedication to excellence, putting all of yourself into whatever it is you undertake, just as you did and continue to do for Stephen, Scott, and me. Thank you to you and Dad. I wish the world parents just like you.

—Allen Cheney

When Allen Cheney first approached me with his idea for this book, I was intrigued by his love and devotion to Fred and Winnie Allen. I wanted to learn more about these grandparents who had made such a positive mark not only on the life of their grandson but also on the lives of countless others.

Allen and I spent nearly all of 2018 sculpting this story. We decided from the start that we would write it in the tone of a novel, with the kind of visual and sensory details easily imagined in a reader's mind, as if watching it play out on-screen. In order to do this, we had to take creative liberties as we developed certain scene descriptions and dialogue. Some names were changed as well. However, the story is built on extensive research, and we made every possible effort to verify the details. We spent countless hours interviewing Fred and Winnie, examining their collection of newspaper articles and scrapbook mementos (letters, photos, playbills, etc.), while also gathering stories from former Troupe members, students, colleagues, and friends. Additionally, Allen had access to the family journals, where he was able to mine specific details that Fred had carefully documented for nearly eight decades of his life. In the end, we tried our best to thread together the countless pieces of information we had collected, hoping to give the reader open access to this extraordinary family.

Throughout the process, each draft was reviewed carefully by Fred, Winnie, and Allison (with other extended relatives and friends reviewing drafts as well). While Allen and I filled in the gaps, we were able to connect enough dots to deliver a book that is based on Fred and Winnie's life story. We are extremely grateful for the many people who worked with us along the way, including the wonderful community of Thomasville, who welcomed me with open arms as I explored the Allens' beautiful and vibrant southern hometown. One detail not mentioned in the book is that as people stroll the sidewalks of downtown Thomasville, not only do they smell the sweet dough baking at Flowers Bakery, they also hear music playing from speakers in the trees. I found this detail to be a perfect way to sum up this dream town—a place where even the trees have found their song.

To Fred and Winnie, it all begins with you. Thank you for opening your arms and lives to me and for giving me this incredible opportunity to share your many gifts with the world.

To Allen and Ryan, you have granted me the most wonderful author experience imaginable. I will forever be grateful our paths crossed and that you took a chance on me. Allen, you have made this a delight at every turn, and I'm over the moon to be called your partner.

To Allison, Amy, Anne, Bonnie, Camille, Jeff, Marlesa, Stephen, Stephanie, and every person who worked along with us, near and far, to help give voice to this story, thank you. Your love for Fred and Winnie has fueled this entire project, and your determination to pay it forward will continue building the powerful crescendo across future generations.

To the people of Thomasville, you make me want to call your community home, and you will always hold a special piece of my heart. Thank you for welcoming Fred, Winnie, and Allison all those years ago and for fostering the kind of community spirit that celebrates the arts.

Thanks also to Daisy Hutton and her talented team at W Publishing Group, who continue to believe in me as I strive to deliver stories that celebrate the healing power of love and the resilient strength of the human spirit.

And to everyone who has ever dared to dream, dance, sing, or create something beautiful for this great, big, wonderful world, you are the reason this book exists. You bravely approach life with your hearts wide open, and because of people like you, we have been granted a wonderful year filled with inspiring souls, creative spirits, tremendous love, and a dose of magic that will illuminate our paths forevermore. Thank you.

—Julie Cantrell

# *Coda*

Of the hundreds of letters Fred, Winnie, and Allison have received through the years, these are but a few excerpts that relay the depth of gratitude and admiration so many hold.

Dear Fred and Winnie,

It is so pleasant to encounter someone who understands that you can expect, even demand, excellence from our children and at the same time help those children to build a positive self-image. [. . .] Thomasville is so fortunate to have someone like you with technical ability and a genuine caring for the psychological and moral well-being of our youth.

[. . .] I am truly convinced that our boys have grown more from their involvement with you than they ever could have from any other activity, including competitive sports. We have watched [them] grow to become m[e]n that we are extremely proud of, and we are glad to say that Fred Allen was no small part of the process.

Jimmy S.

Dear Mr. Allen,

You have probably given me the best graduation gift of all, only you have been giving it to me for the last four years. Along with knowledge of music and the privilege of being a Troupe member, you have given me discipline. [. . .] You are definitely the most admirable man I have ever known, and I cherish every memory. Anybody who can do what you do with us, accept us the way we are, and be so supportive regardless of the mistakes we sometimes make, deserves much more recognition than you get.

Seth C.

Dear Mr. Allen,

You are to be highly commended for the time and effort you put into working with young people. [. . .] You have brought out a lot of hidden talent over the years. We are definitely delighted that you "discovered" our daughter. Without a doubt you have helped bring out the best of her.

Mary R.

Dear Winnie,

Regardless of what your students do with the rest of their lives, the Troupe experience is one deposit in the "life bank" that can be drawn on forever. In Lindley's solo, she sang about "never having the moon." Thank you and Fred for choosing the "moon" and for sharing it with us all.

Love, Beth B.

Dear Allison,

Spectacular music, wonderful costumes, and precise movement and timing. There were excellent individual and group performances by beautiful young ladies and handsome young men combined to provide an experience well worth remembering. Add to these qualities the capable and top-notch direction of an incomparable director, the backing and support of a group of believing and dedicated parents and friends, and you have an unbeatable combination. That's what the entire performance was—unmatched and unbeatable. [. . .] Even though the Music and Drama Troupe is not a school-sponsored activity, it serves as a medium through which you and many of our pupils have an opportunity to grow and develop. Consequently, as superintendent of Thomasville City Schools, I wish to extend my official thanks and appreciation as well as those of the entire board of education to you for a job well done. We in the entire school community look to you and your family with much pride. Keep up the excellent work!

Superintendent of Schools

Dear Fred and Winnie,

You are a very tremendous example and a very powerful witness of God's exceptional gifts in the life of one of his children! You not only are truly blessed, but you are a great blessing to all of us who have had the privilege to know you. Thank you!

Anne K.

Dear Mr. Allen,

Possessing little talent in the area of acting or singing, Troupe gives me a few hours a year to stand in the spotlight . . . not as a solo performer or even as a single person, but as a Troupe member, which I am so proud to be. [. . .] Even though I stand on the ramps surrounded by a great many other people, I still very often feel as if every eye in the auditorium is on me. It's a great feeling and I thank you from the bottom of my heart for letting me be a part of this truly wonderful group and for giving me the chance to have a small taste of "stardom."

A grateful Troupe member

Dear Mr. Allen,

Never in a million years, when my friend talked to me about auditioning, did I ever imagine the impact you and Troupe would have in my life. [. . .] For all of us who have grown and been changed by your love, dedication, and knowledge, thanks is not enough. And while I am not the proper authority to say this, I will anyways. [. . .] You have made a difference in this world!

Charity M.

Dear Mr. Allen,

It has taken me almost twenty years to put it in writing, but I do want you to know how much I appreciate your patience, your kindness, your enthusiasm and all of the time and effort that you put into making me believe in myself and my abilities. It wasn't "all for [naught]." I use my voice whenever possible. I am a soloist at my church, and I sing at weddings and banquets and other community activities. I have had many people comment on my "talent" or "ability" and that always brings you to mind. I thank God then and there that he sent you and your wonderful family to Thomasville and that he led me to you. I shudder to think where I could've ended up.[ . . .] Young people need you and your guidance still.

Teresa S.

Dear Mr. Allen,

Besides the pride and joy that has come from being part of [. . .] Troupe, you also instilled in me that I could do anything I put my heart and mind to. You put the exclamation point on my love of music and encouraged me to further expand on the basic knowledge and ability that I had. To this day I am grateful for your gifts that you shared so selflessly with us unruly teenagers. Because you pushed us, literally into the spotlight, I have the confidence to tackle situations that I otherwise would have never thought could be tackled—and keep a calm head in the process.

Kathy H.

Dear Mr. and Mrs. Allen,

I am leaving to go to college in one week and I'm starting to really think about what I'm leaving behind. I can't believe I won't be in Troupe next year. It has been such an amazing part of my life. [. . .] I don't think Thomasville will ever truly understand how extremely fortunate and blessed they are to have you, Mr. Allen. [. . .] I have gained so much from Troupe and your advice and guidance. I know it will stick with me throughout my college and life career. You both have been so encouraging, tolerant, and supportive of all the things I did. Thank you both for allowing me to have the freedom and opportunity to truly grow.

Bryan W.

Dear Winnie,

I've written Fred to say thank you for all he's done for our daughter as she moves on to the next phase of her life. However, I owe you a personal thank you for enhancing all that he does for our children. You are the woman beside the great man (not the woman behind the great man).

We are so fortunate to have you involved with our children. I feel that you two (and Allison [. . .] make that three) deserve the highest honor in our community.

Sheila C.

Dear Mr. Allen,

In 1986, singing "in just no time at all" as a senior during the finale, I had no idea how those lyrics would spring to life as I set out for the future at age 17. [. . .] The lessons learned from the unique experience of Troupe transcend the stage and apply to everyday lives of Troupe alumni, wherever they are and whatever their vocations may be. I can still vividly remember coming to the Sunday matinee on the occasion of your 10th anniversary show and sensing the fervor and star quality of that performance. For some unexplainable reason, I recall Mike Slaughter singing "Piano Man" at that show. Well, he was ahead of me in choir and I thought that was really cool. I don't think I'll ever forget the early days of children's chorus, Charades, and The Charlie Brown Gang with Mary Powers as Lucy! During intermission, I asked Mom if I could try out [. . .] and her reply was, "Of course, if it doesn't interfere with swim team practice." Well, not long after that, Sandy convinced me that I could and would make room for both. I am glad I did. Today she and I still enjoy a special friendship forged in the ranks of Troupe, the one-act plays, and the literary meets of 1983–1986. As I write this, I am chuckling about Tracy Anderson's awesome performance with a 5-inch splinter in her foot from the original risers, and Kathy Fletcher's possum attack and ensuing rabies shots during rehearsals for Barnum. When I have the opportunity to visit NYC today, I still think back to my first visit there [with Troupe]. I will never forget the Edison Hotel, *Cats*, *La Cage aux Folles*, or that bus ride! That trip was my first glimpse of a truly international city, one that dwarfs Atlanta in so many ways. Well, I could reminisce ad infinitum. I thank you for those enriching opportunities to create enduring memories.

Brett R.

Winnie and Fred,

You would be amazed at the number of parents of Troupe alum who [. . .] believe that a large portion of their children's confidence and poise is directly attributed to his/her experience with you two. Count me in that camp! What you do goes way beyond the surface, and I am forever indebted to you. [. . .] You are Very, Very special people, and I consider my family extremely fortunate to have been touched in such a positive way by you. A simple "thank you" just does not seem sufficient but will nonetheless have to do. I wish you both nothing but the best—with lots of "stars" (with normal-size egos) and no "stage parents." May God bless you both, for he has blessed us by giving you to us.

Steffi B.

Dear Fred,

It is so hard to be able to express in words how much admiration I have for you. I marvel at what you do and give to every child on that stage. Your influence with my son has meant the world to me and to him. I don't think you ever quite realize the impact you have on these children. You have given them gifts that they will carry with them the rest of their lives. Their knowledge of music, discipline, commitment, and working as a team [. . .] I could go on and on. I am so very grateful to you and Winnie for all that you do.

Debbie W.

Dear Fred,

When [my daughter] joined Troupe her ninth-grade year, she was so very shy in front of large groups of people and sometimes scared to try out for things. I had to beg her to try out for Troupe because she didn't think she would make it. What a difference two years have made in her! What you have given her will last her whole life even if she never sings again.

Cynthia G.

Mr. A,

I wish there had been time to go into more detail about the countless ways you molded the lives of Boomers and Millennials. [. . .] What a difference you made in our lives; a positive difference that keeps getting deeper ingrained in who we are, day by day. I see Graham occasionally and we always talk nostalgically about you. You were his hero at a time when all the adults and coaches wished that they could be it [. . .] the one person who was and still is the most influential man in my life. I just had to write this note since I couldn't navigate the crowds to see you after the show. Thank you for the positive difference you made in my life!

Laura C.

Fred,

How do you keep doing it?

The Christmas show was super—so energetic and full of the spirit of the season! It really brings back great memories of my Troupe years and reminds me how fortunate I was to have been a part of something so special. I was also delighted with the success of the one-act play again this year. Year after year, you keep putting that polish on a group of kids that wouldn't believe they could do what you push them to achieve. I remember well all the hours of staging, rehearsals, and direction that we put in—never really stopping to think how many more hours you were putting in behind the scenes. These past several weeks have brought home to me how much the lives of so many have been touched by you and your family. I know I'm a better person for my involvement in the troupe and the one-act plays back so many years ago. Thank you seems like so little to say, but for what it's worth—Thank you!

Rick I.

Dear Winnie and Fred,

Once again it's "time to take time" to thank you for everything you've done, and continue to do, for our family. This year's concert was so fantastic! The numbers, the choreography, the timing, the pace, the solos, just everything was spectacular and professional! I don't see how you do it year after year, and keep getting better! When our granddaughters joined us [. . .] to watch the [. . .] show, I saw the pride and accomplishment shining on their young faces. I felt their increased confidence and self-esteem. Later I saw that same wonderful look reflected on our children's faces as they started to sing the Troupe theme song. I cried with gratitude for the gift you have bestowed on us all.

Sally H.

Dear Mr. Allen,

It seems that I cannot put into words how much I appreciated you for being my teacher, my counselor, my mentor, but most of all my friend. There is no way I could ever begin to express my gratitude to you through this letter. So maybe one day when I give you a wink from the stage to thank you, it can begin to be expressed. I am very positive that the makeup of who I have become and who I am striving to be is much credited to you for showing me how to explore my own thoughts. I thank you for taking a chance and believing in me. I'll miss you so much.

Mary M.

Dear Mr. Allen,

I did not want the summer to go by without telling you how much I appreciated your influence on my child this past year. This was my daughter's first year in Troupe, and she loved it! [. . .] There are so many negatives in the world today; it is very heartwarming to know that someone so accomplished as yourself cares enough to share and be a positive example for the young people of our community. Please convey my appreciation also to Mrs. Allen, Allison, and all of the others that so lovingly give of themselves for these young people. You are making a difference.

Patsy A.

Dear Fred,

You and Winnie have touched our lives for so many years through your music and love for the young people in Thomasville. [. . .] It's obvious the students have been exposed to something far greater and lasting than anything out of a textbook. Thank you so very much for the opportunities both of our children have received this past year. It has added a special spark, a fire to their lives. We especially thank you both for all the planning that went into the New York trip. Our daughter will always be totally devoted to her real coach, "Fred."

Cathy M.

Fred,

I tried to send a recording I recently made, but it is too big to send [in] an email. I am therefore resorting to a note to tell you that I hope you can hear some maturity that I have developed in my voice. It's all because I do the exercises and practice the way you taught me to do. I sometimes want to speak with you so badly I can't stand it and I wish I could plug-in again, but life goes on! You will never know what it meant to have you as my mentor and to call you my friend. I can never say to Dad that he is the second most brilliant man I ever knew—somehow, I think he knows. [. . .] Besides being a phenomenal intellectual, you topped it off by not ever showing us you thought you were—never a braggart about being a teacher superior to us kids. I think about all the good things you stood for, and how you made all of us "toe the mark." [. . .] You were in the process of building the character of future adults. One thing is for sure—you did your best to see we all would be happy and successful. [. . .] You knew we needed the carrot instead of the whip a lot of the time. So much I owe to you, friend. Again, all that I am today I attribute it to the time I had with you. So many are the ways you were, and are still, my role model. I can appreciate that you told me in a very stern way that I needed to strive to be better when I thought I was already the greatest. I pouted then, but inside this gave me a confidence that you believed in what I could become. Your life lessons are a part of my morning reflections like studying the scripture. I feel sure there are many of us that having now grown older and experienced more of life, realize how you were the consummate teacher. [. . .] We realize how much you sacrificed to be there for us week after week. I think we didn't know how to express it, but we knew back then how much you cared about us as human beings, if not super talents. Well, all of this came spilling out of my heart today, and I was ready to let you hear me sing. I will get the songs to you. Meanwhile, I can think of no better ending than to say I love you!

Hunter M.

# *Notes*

## Chapter 2

1. Civilla D. Martin, "His Eye Is on the Sparrow," 1905 (public domain).

## Chapter 7

1. "There Is a Time," Rodney Dillard and Mitch Jayne. Lansdowne Music and Winston Music Publishers (ASCAP). Worldwide rights reserved.

## Chapter 8

1. "I Believe," lyrics and music by Ervin Drake, Irvin Graham, Jimmy Shirl, and Al Stillman. TRO- © 1952 (renewed), 1953 (renewed) Hampshire House Publishing Corp., New York, NY, Larry Spier Music, LLC, New York, NY, Lindabet Music Corp., c/o The Songwriter's Guild, Nashville, TN. TRO-Hampshire House Publishing Corp. controls all rights for the world outside the United States. All rights reserved, including right of performance.

## Chapter 9

1. "Summertime" (from *Porgy and Bess*), music and lyrics by George Gershwin, DuBose and Dorothy Heyward, and Ira Gershwin. © 1935 (renewed) Ira Gershwin Music, DuBose and Dorothy Heyward Memorial Fund and George Gershwin Music. All rights for Ira Gershwin Music administered by WB Music Corp. All rights reserved. Used by permission of Afred Music. "Summertime" from *Porgy and*

*Bess*, words and music by George Gershwin, DuBose and Heyward, and Ira Gershwin. © 1935 (renewed) Nokawi Music (ASCAP) / Frankie G. Songs (ASCAP) / Ira Gershwin Music (ASCAP) / DuBose and Dorothy Heyward Memorial Fund (ASCAP). Nokawi Music administered in the United States by Steve Peter Music (ASCAP). Frankie G. Songs and the DuBose and Dorothy Heyward Memorial Fund administered by Songs of SMP. Ira Gershwin Music administered by WB Music Corp. Used by permission. International copyright secured. All rights reserved.

## Chapter 10

1. "Lucky in Love," words and music by B. G. DeSylva, Lew Brown, and Ray Henderson. © 1927 (renewed) Chappell & Co., Inc., Ray Henderson Music Company, and Stephen Ballentine Music. All rights reserved. Used by permission of Alfred Music.

## Chapter 11

1. "Summertime" (from *Porgy and Bess*), music and lyrics by George Gershwin, DuBose and Dorothy Heyward, and Ira Gershwin. © 1935 (renewed) Ira Gershwin Music, DuBose and Dorothy Heyward Memorial Fund and George Gershwin Music. All rights for Ira Gershwin Music administered by WB Music Corp. All rights reserved. Used by permission of Alfred Music. "Summertime" from *Porgy and Bess*, words and music by George Gershwin, DuBose and Heyward, and Ira Gershwin. © 1935 (renewed) Nokawi Music (ASCAP) / Frankie G. Songs (ASCAP) / Ira Gershwin Music (ASCAP) / DuBose and Dorothy Heyward Memorial Fund (ASCAP). Nokawi Music administered in the United States by Steve Peter Music (ASCAP). Frankie G. Songs and the DuBose and Dorothy Heyward Memorial Fund administered by Songs of SMP. Ira Gershwin Music administered by WB Music Corp. Used by permission. International copyright secured. All rights reserved.

## Chapter 17

1. Giuseppe Verdi, "*La Forza del Destino*," 1862 (public domain).

## Chapter 19

1. "Have Yourself a Merry Little Christmas," Hugh Martin and Ralph Blane. © 1943 EMI Feist Catalog Inc. All rights administered by Sony/ATV Music Publishing LLC, 424 Church Street, Suite 1200, Nashville, TN 37219. All rights reserved. Used by permission. "Have Yourself a Merry Little Christmas," words and music by Hugh Martin and Ralph Blane. © 1943 (renewed) Metro-Goldwyn-Mayer Inc. © 1944 (renewed) EMI Feist Catalog Inc. All rights controlled and administered by EMI Feist Catalog Inc. (publishing) and Alfred Music (print). All rights reserved. Used by permission of Alfred Music.

## Chapter 22

1. "Happy Days Are Here Again," words by Jack Yellen, music by Milton Ager. © 1929 (renewed) WB Music Corp. All rights reserved. Used by permission of Alfred Music.

## Chapter 27

1. "Once Upon a Time," music by Charles Strouse, lyric by Lee Adams. © 1962 (renewed) Strada Music Co. All rights administered by WB Music Corp. All Rights Reserved. Used by permission of Alfred Publishing, LLC.
2. "As Long as He Needs Me," from the musical production of Lionel Bart's *Oliver!*, lyrics and music by Lionel Bart. © 1960 (renewed) Lakeview Music Co., Ltd., London, England. TRO- Hollis Music, Inc., New York, controls all publication rights for the USA and Canada.

## Chapter 33

1. "Magic to Do," Stephen Schwartz. © 1972 EMI BMPC Corp. and Jobete Music Co., Inc. All rights administered by Sony/ATV Music Publishing LLC, 424 Church Street, Suite 1200, Nashville, TN 37219. All rights reserved. Used by permission.

## Chapter 34

1. "That's All" (from *Tootsie*), words and music by Bob Haymes and Alan Brandt. © 1953 (renewed) Warner-Tamerlane Publishing Corp. and

Mixed Bag Music, Inc. All rights administered by Warner-Tamerlane Publishing Corp. All rights reserved. Used by permission of Alfred Music.

## Chapter 36

1. "The Girl" (from *The Fantasticks*), lyrics by Harvey Schmidt, music by Tom Jones. © 1963 (renewed) by Tom Jones and Harvey Schmidt. Publication and allied rights assigned to Chappell & Co. All rights reserved. Used by permission of Alfred Music.

## Chapter 37

1. "Corner of the Sky," Stephen Schwartz. © 1972 EMI BMPC Corp. and Jobete Music Co., Inc. All rights administered by Sony/ATV Music Publishing LLC, 424 Church Street, Suite 1200, Nashville, TN 37219. All rights reserved. Used by permission.

## Chapter 39

1. "Magic to Do," Stephen Schwartz. © 1972 EMI BMPC Corp. and Jobete Music Co., Inc. All rights administered by Sony/ATV Music Publishing LLC, 424 Church Street, Suite 1200, Nashville, TN 37219. All rights reserved. Used by permission.
2. "Magic to Do," Stephen Schwartz.
3. "No Time at All" (from *Pippin*), music and lyrics by Stephen Schwartz. © 1972 (renewed) Stephen Schwartz. All rights administered by EMI BMPC Corp. (ASCAP) and Jobete Music Co., Inc. All rights for Jobete Music Co., Inc. controlled and administered by EMI April Music Inc. (ASCAP). Print rights for EMI BMPC Corp. controlled and administered by Alfred Publishing Co., Inc. All rights reserved. Used by permission of Alfred Music.

## Chapter 40

1. "Nature Boy," written by Eden Abbez, published by Golden World Enterprise. © 1947 (renewed). All rights reserved. Used by permission.

## Epilogue

1. "Corner of the Sky," Stephen Schwartz. © 1972 EMI BMPC Corp. and Jobete Music Co., Inc. All rights administered by Sony/ATV Music Publishing LLC, 424 Church Street, Suite 1200, Nashville, TN 37219. All rights reserved. Used by permission.

## A Note from Fred Allen

1. Max Erhmann, "Desiderata," in *The Poems of Max Ehrmann*, ed. Bertha K. Ehrmann (Boston: Bruce Humphries, 1948), 165.

# *About the Author*

**Allen Cheney** is a partner and cofounder at Mountview Creative, where he oversees day-to-day operations and project development. His team at Mountview produces a wide range of content, from music videos and commercials to documentaries and feature films.

A native of Thomasville, Georgia, Cheney moved to Nashville, Tennessee, in 2009, after graduating from LaGrange College with a double major in music and business. He began his career in Nashville, writing and producing music; however, he quickly became immersed in television and film production.

In 2012, Cheney was recognized for his contributions to Robin Williams's last feature film, *Boulevard*. Three years later in 2015, Allen coproduced the feature film *Some Freaks*, winner of numerous domestic and international film festivals, and he became executive producer of the international feature film *Heartbeats* in 2016. Allen's work has been highlighted by *Forbes*, which also announced his development of the Fred Allen Project.

**Julie Cantrell** is a *New York Times* and *USA Today* bestselling author, editor, and TEDx speaker. Her work has received numerous awards and special recognition across both faith-based and general audiences.